JESUS IN YOUR BACKPACK

JESUS IN YOUR BACKPACK

A TEEN'S GUIDE TO SPIRITUAL WISDOM

PASTOR WILLIAM R. GRIMBOL

Illustrations by Bridget Halberstadt

Ulysses Press

Published by:
Ulysses Press
P.O. Box 3440
Berkeley, CA 94703
www.ulyssespress.com

ISBN10: 1-56975-608-2
ISBN13: 978-1-56975-608-9
Library of Congress Control Number: 2006938950

Printed in Canada by Transcontinental Printing

10 9 8 7 6 5 4 3 2 1

Managing Editor: Claire Chun
Editor: Mark Woodworth
Production: Lisa Kester, Susan Pinkerton
Interior Design: Leslie Henriques and Sarah Levin
Cover image: © clipart.com

Quotations by Bill Clarke, Kathy Galloway, Madeleine L'Engle, and
Henri Nouwen (from *Resources for Preaching and Worship*,
compiled and edited by Hannah Ward and Jennifer Wild) and by
Michael L. Lindvall (from *The Christian Life: A Geography of God*)
are reprinted with the permission of Westminster John Knox Press.

Distributed by Publishers Group West

To Carl Brandl . . . for being there.

You will make a huge difference in many young lives!

CONTENTS

acknowledgments

I wish to thank the wonderful youth of Shelter Island, who have informed and inspired so much of this book. You are a gift to my life. Many of you will be lifelong friends. You have kept me young, and exhausted.

I also want to thank Nick Denton-Brown for the opportunity of writing this book, as well as for shepherding me through the process. Mark Woodworth's editing has been a true godsend. He has managed to tighten and focus, clean and sharpen, and make the manuscript feel fresh and alive. My debt to him is obvious. In addition, he has been a personal pleasure in every aspect of our work together.

I have valued this chance to work with Ulysses Press. I believe they are doing some important and fascinating work, even breaking important new ground for those who wish to create or enhance their own faith and spirituality.

bible versions

Most Bible passages quoted in this book are drawn from the
New Revised Standard Version (NRSV). Other versions used
are identified as follows:

CEV	Contemporary English Version
GNB	Good News Bible
KJV	King James Version
NIV	New International Version
NJB	New Jerusalem Bible
REB	Revised English Bible

"Probably no word better summarizes the
suffering of our times than the word 'homeless.'
It reveals one of our deepest and most painful
conditions, the condition of not having a sense
of belonging, of not having a place where we can
feel safe, cared for, protected, and loved."

HENRI J. M. NOUWEN

"There lives more faith in honest doubt,
Believe me, than in half the creeds."

ALFRED, LORD TENNYSON

"God asks us in Jesus
to share his anger
when in his name
people's dignity is diminished,
or love is abused,
or the poor are exploited
or when he himself is neglected.
This is true religion:
to act justly,
love tenderly
and walk humbly with our God."

DONAL NEARY, S.J., *COMMUNION REFLECTIONS
FOR SUNDAYS AND HOLY DAYS*, YEAR B

INTRODUCTION: COMING HOME TO YOUR SELF AND YOUR LIFE

"You grow up the day you have your first real
laugh—at yourself."

ETHEL BARRYMORE

"Maturity is reached the day we don't need to be
lied to about anything."

FRANK YERBY

"Maturity begins when we're content to feel
we're right about something without feeling the
necessity to prove someone else wrong."

SYDNEY J. HARRIS

I am a Presbyterian pastor. I've been in the ministry for 30 years. For three full decades I have run a youth group. I am good at it. Stretching the modesty norm, I am *really* good at it. I am often asked why my youth ministry efforts are so successful. My answer is succinct and honest: "Because I truly enjoy adolescents." It may not sound like much of an accomplishment, but it is. It is absolutely all-important.

I often teach other youth ministers about strategies for doing their job effectively. I have conducted a good many workshops on the topic of developing a successful youth ministry or program. Yet I am stunned by how many would-be youth leaders do not like adolescents. They might enjoy working with adolescents who act like children and are receptive and docile. They might enjoy adolescents who act like adults and are sophisticated and worldly. Many, however, just plain do not care for adolescents who act like adolescents.

You are a teenager. An adolescent. You are in the midst of your adolescence. Some will tell you these are the best years of your life. I will tell you they will be some of the most difficult. The time of adolescence is turbulent. It is also thrilling—an adventure, a journey. It is never boring. It can be brutal, but it can also be miraculous.

What makes these years so volatile, so dynamic, such a roller-coaster ride? Change! Everything in you and about you is changing. Your body is growing. Sex has shown up on the landscape, and threatens to become the sole landowner. Your heart is exploding. Falling in and out of love. Moving from one crisis to the next on a daily basis. Your soul is exploring. Asking big questions without answers. Raising doubts about every subject known to humanity. Wondering, wishing, feeling awe. Adolescence is a period of rapid-fire change. A time of almost total transformation. It is as if a revolution is taking place inside you. There is usually some bloodshed.

To love an adolescent means enjoying the sight of blood. It means screaming with you on the roller coaster. It means knowing that members of my youth group will love me on Monday, ignore me on Tuesday, critique me on Wednesday, be sarcastic with me on Thursday, be indifferent on Friday, be enthusiastic on Saturday—all about what's going to happen on Sunday. They'll either have a blast at youth group on Sunday, or refer to it as the sequel to Hiroshima. This is what it means to love adolescents. And I do love them.

As a youth minister, I have many roles. One that is all-important is to help you navigate your way to adulthood. I firmly believe that maturity and spirituality are one and the same. Just as a bird knows when to fly south for the winter, your soul knows when it must move and grow. How it must change, face a crisis, overcome an obstacle. Forgive a grudge. Let go of a loss. So, if you are consciously moving toward becoming an adult, you are simultaneously becoming a much more spiritual person.

It is also part of my job to enable adolescents to develop some kind of relationship with a Higher Power. I am adamantly opposed to *indoctrination*, and strive instead to be a source of *inspiration*. I do not seek to convert anyone to my belief system. In spite of the title of this book, I will apply that perspective to my entire text. I feel no need to ram my beliefs down your throat. I refuse to enter some crazy religious sweepstakes, with Heaven being offered as the grand prize. Instead, I feel called to share my faith with you. Its convictions. Its questions and doubts. Shared without any agenda. Shared simply because it is a huge part of me. Shared as part of my call to write this book.

> "Doubts are the ants in the pants of faith. They keep it awake and moving." —FREDERICK BUECHNER, *WISHFUL THINKING*

As a Presbyterian, there is no denying that I am a Christian. I feel no need to hide my faith in Jesus Christ. I am proud of my belief. My faith in Jesus is a response to myriad factors. My experiences in church and Sunday School. My encounter with Jesus during the 1960s, when many of our national moral leaders were men and women of Christian faith. My own personal exploration of scripture. My spiritual and theological study of the man called Jesus. My own spiritual growth and development. I have had a few epiphanies, the occasional revelation, a pretty bountiful assortment of events that have exposed me to the Grace of God.

I plan on sharing with you the Jesus I know. I also plan to share with you many of the questions that still haunt my faith. The serious doubts I continue to have to this day. I don't believe that faith is a matter of certainty. There are no guarantees or warranties. That is why we call it "faith." It isn't about knowing. It is about taking a leap of faith. A leap across a chasm of doubt. A leap over a questioning obstacle. These leaps don't remove the chasms or the obstacles. They simply give us the courage to keep leaping. I am a decent leaper.

I am comfortable sharing my understandings of Jesus and insights about Him. I love to talk about His ministry and message. I believe He has so much to say to us. Especially to you, who are coping with the wild ride called adolescence. Since you are in the midst of shaping your core values, and constructing your own personal lifestyle, now is a perfect time to carefully explore the impact of this man named Jesus. I am convinced Jesus can help make your adolescence healthier, more hope-filled, and, yes, even happier.

Sharing Jesus in today's world is not easy. So much of what you hear about Jesus comes out of a fundamentalist and evangelical perspective. You are not being asked to get to know Jesus. You are being asked to choose Him. To choose Him over Buddha. Or Confucius. Or as being the newer, nicer version of the Old Testament God. I see no reason for making such a choice. While I believe in Jesus, I find much to believe in other religions as well. I believe God is much too big to fit inside one religion. Since diversity is the hallmark of Creation, would this not also be the case when it comes to faith? I love and celebrate the many paths to be found to God.

Forrest Church, a wonderful friend, pastor, and author, whom I highly recommend to you, told me a lovely story one day. He said there once was a cathedral that had extraordinary stained-glass windows. Each of the windows represented a different religion. Over the years, debates arose over whose window was most beautiful. The arguments grew fierce. The competition between windows grew heated. Some backers of one window would actually throw stones at another window. Acts of vandalism occurred. Windows were spray painted with graffiti. Windows were covered with curse words. It got just plain awful. There was talk of having to cover the windows with bars on the outside.

On a warm, sunny afternoon one autumn, an old woman entered the magnificent cathedral. She could barely walk. The cathedral was packed with pockets of believers. Arguments were raging over whose window was truly the most beautiful, the grandest and most glorious. The words grew angrier and the shouting actually hurt the old lady's ears. She screamed, "Stop! How silly and foolish you are being. Turning this wondrous place of worship into a debating hall. And, you have missed the point. The beauty of these windows—each one of them—comes from the light outside. Without the light, there is no beauty at all!"

> "It is not for anybody to judge the authenticity of the Born Again's spiritual rebirth or anybody else's, but my guess is that by the style and substance of their witnessing to it, the souls they turn on to Christ are apt to be fewer in number than the ones they turn off."
> —FREDERICK BUECHNER, *WHISTLING IN THE DARK*

The silence was deafening. The window worshipers began to saunter outside. The old woman seated herself in a pew. In the holy hush that now overwhelmed the cathedral, she was finally free to pray. She prayed to the Light, as she understood it.

Jesus has been a beacon for me. Lighting the path, making my way easier in this life. I do not believe in Him as the only source of light, nor as the sole path. I know this might be controversial for some Christians, but that debate cannot possibly be waged in this small book. So I will simply declare this to be both my personal and my professional conviction. This is how I approach my faith in Jesus Christ. I look forward to sharing my faith with you, my decisions, my choices. It is my sole hope to inspire you to explore your own beliefs. To become a deeper and fuller spiritual being. To develop a relationship with your Higher Power that is rich and full and intimate. Yes, I want you to get to know Jesus, but on your own terms.

a few faith disclaimers

I am uncomfortable with how Jesus is being presented in America today. The conservative Christian right wing has done a remarkable job of creating Jesus in its own image. The Jesus we hear being preached by most American evangelists is depicted as white, American, southern, Republican, male (of course), and a pro-rich pro-capitalist.

To be a Christian today is thought to be synonymous with being a patriot, and being a patriot requires giving full backing to any and all decisions made by a conservative administration. In sum, we have an All-American Jesus, and worship resembles a pep rally.

The Jesus of my faith, however, does not resemble the above depiction. For me, Jesus is a dark-skinned Jew. He is pro-poor. He is pro-compassion. He is pro-woman. He is about lifting up those who are suffering. He is about celebrating equality. He is the champion of justice for all. He revels in diversity. He is on the side of the outcast. He embraces those the world discards. He is of a revolutionary spirit. His life is viewed as radical and offensive. He binds broken hearts. He picks up crosses. He was the event of Grace. He loves each one of us the same. He forgives us all, all the time. His heart is pure mercy.

I find nothing in this All-American Jesus that remotely resembles the Jesus of scripture. Rather, I find this fanatically American Jesus to be frightening. In truth, this is the conversion of Christianity into a friendly form of fascism—which is becoming increasingly less and less friendly, more and more mean-spirited. It requires that we all believe the same way. We must all speak in religious bumper-sticker slogans. We must all see ourselves as born-again, saved from lives of wanton sin. Our sole goal is Heaven—Heaven being a place populated only by those who believe Jesus Christ to be their Lord and Savior.

I don't share these beliefs. This is not my perspective of Jesus Christ. I cannot comprehend the smoke and ashes arising from the ovens of Dachau or Auschwitz or Buchenwald, only to float down to Earth to bore their way to hell—hell being their destination, owing to a lack of faith in Jesus as Lord and Savior. After 9/11 and the collapse of the Twin Towers, did only the Christians killed there go to Heaven? I find such belief offensive, even ridiculous. The Ku Klux Klan claims Jesus to be their Lord and Savior. I have my doubts that Jesus is thrilled with their selection. Who goes to Heaven is 100 percent up to God. This is not my choice, it is God's. I spend no time worrying about Heaven, other than harboring a deep desire to help build it here on Earth. "You did not choose me, but I chose you" (John 15:16). Leaving this choice to God has freed me to live my faith fully in the moment, the present, the now. In the here and now.

> "Faith is like radar that sees through the fog—the reality of things at a distance that the human eye cannot see."
> —CORRIE TEN BOOM, *TRAMP FOR THE LORD*

I must admit to a belief that everyone returns home to God. I think of Heaven as the eternal residence for us all. Jesus Christ is, to me, the event of Grace. This Grace is so pure and full and overwhelming that every soul will be transformed. Some before death, some after death. The stains of sin will be wiped away, the bigotry uprooted, the fear evaporated. I simply believe in universal salvation. The Jesus Christ

I have come to know would never choose to turn anyone away. We are His beloved children. No matter how we have acquired a flawed understanding of Him or distorted His image, I am confident that God will find the way to bring us home to wholeness.

I have never experienced an angry or door-slamming Jesus. I have never known a Jesus who judges or rejects. I know nothing of a Jesus whose mantra might be, "Come on, make up your mind." The Jesus I know is soaked in Grace. His door remains wide open. He will spend eternity bringing His children back into His loving arms:

One of the Bible's writers says, "I am convinced that neither death nor life, neither angels nor demons, neither the present nor the future, nor any powers, neither height nor depth, nor anything in all creation, will be able to separate us from the love of God that is in Christ Jesus our Lord" (Romans 8:38–39).

The same writer says, "Love is patient, love is kind. It does not envy, it does not boast, it is not proud. It is not rude, it is not self-seeking, it is not easily angered, it keeps no records of wrongs. Love does not delight in evil, but rejoices in the truth. It always protects, always hopes, always perseveres. Love never fails" (I Corinthians 13:4–8).

Jesus cannot give up on us. We are His. Always and forever. His love will never fail us. That is at the center of my faith and my understanding of Jesus Christ.

the essential jesus: home

Picture this. E. T. gets stranded in Los Angeles. Dorothy is forever marooned in Oz. The Prodigal Son is lost till the end of time in the Big City. All three are forced to adjust to life in an alien world. They never feel as if they belong. They never feel relaxed or comfortable. They barely know the language, the customs, the history of the place. The ground always sways beneath their feet. They spend a good chunk of every day pining to go home. Their memories of home begin to fade. Their longing for home only grows.

If Steven Spielberg had written a screenplay in which E. T. never got home, his movie instantly becomes a tragedy. The whole hope of his brilliant film *E. T. the Extra-Terrestrial* is rooted in E. T.'s desire and capacity to go home. In *The Wizard of Oz*, the moral of the story is "there is no place like home." Dorothy would spiritually die if she had to stay put

> "Where we love is home—home that our feet may leave, but not our hearts." —OLIVER WENDELL HOLMES, SR.

in Oz. Kansas may be black-and-white, not the Technicolor vision of Oz, but it is the sacred ground upon which Dorothy finds her soul. Again, a Dorothy caught in the spiritual quicksand of Oz would turn this "make-us-believe" fairy tale into a tragedy of epic proportions. Had the message of the parable of the Prodigal Son been that those who leave God's side may never return, we would all be doomed to life as spiritual aliens.

The concept of *home* is amazingly powerful. I live and work on a small island off the coast of Long Island, in New York State. Scads of tourists come here each season looking for a strong sense of home, which Shelter Island offers its residents. Home-grown vegetables and flowers. Bake sales of homemade pies and cakes and cookies. A true hometown newspaper. Even our miniature town hall and justice hall appear to be from the film set of an old-fashioned hometown. Shelter Island could indeed be the set for a production of *Our Town*. All summer long, and on most weekends, you see folks whose faces speak of a yearning—the yearning for home, the longing to be safe and secure, to belong.

Home is more than a place. It is a spirit. It is a mind-set. A perspective, an attitude, a way of being and doing. Home is where we feel fully free. Free to be human, free to claim all that we feel, free to make mistakes. Free to flop. Free to change and grow and mature. Free to question and doubt. Free to believe and claim convictions. When we are at

> "My home is here. I feel just as at home overseas, but I think my roots are here and my language is here and my rage is here and my hope is here. You know where your home is because you've been there long enough. You know all the peculiarities of the people around you, because you are one of them. And naturally, memories are the most important. Your home is where your favorite memories are."
> —PETER-DIRK UYS

home we feel at ease. Relaxed. Peaceful inside and out. We know where we are. Where we are going. Why we are going there. We venture out, knowing we can return to the safety and security of home. In *my* faith, I experience Jesus as *home*. It is with Jesus that I am most truly my Self. It is within this relationship that I risk sharing the all of me. The whole picture, the big picture. I find in Jesus the freedom to be fully human, fully alive. Jesus provides for me a perspective that eases my anxiety and fear. In Christ I find rest. I find peace of mind. I feel centered, focused, strong and stable. Safe and secure. This, to me, is the essence of Jesus Christ—the spirit of *home*.

I want you to think about home for you. Your real Self. Your actual home and hometown. Are you at home with your friends, or must you be someone else around them? Where is your spiritual home? What does the word mean to you? What are the images your mind holds of home? The emotions? What beliefs do you hold about what home needs to be? It is my hope that we will flesh out this concept together. Give it some meat and muscle. I want the word "home" to speak volumes to you. I know that Jesus has much to say about home. As a place, as a spirit, and as a way of life.

what's in this book?

A lot. A lot of me is in this book. A lot of my faith. A lot that I hope will ignite or inspire your own faith.

A lot about the Bible. About who wrote it, why, when, and where. A lot about what the Bible reveals and teaches. The function of the Bible. What it says. What it does not say. What it hints about. What it points toward. The mysteries it creates, and those it resolves. The history of faith. The history of the people of faith. The history of the human spirit in relationship to the Holy Spirit. It is impossible to know much of anything about Jesus or Christianity without reference to the Bible. It records scarcely a few lines of actual history about Jesus, and even fewer about Jesus as the Christ. The Bible is simply indispensable to our getting to know Jesus, or the faith that was built up around Him.

A lot about Jesus the man. Jesus the very real human being. The man who claims all His feelings. When He loses His friend Lazarus, He weeps. When He runs into scam artists at the Temple, He gets so ticked off that He overturns their selling tables. When He feels doubt, He expresses it boldly: "Father, why hast thou forsaken me?" When He has faith, He declares it with conviction: "Father, forgive them, for they know not what they do." Jesus is at home with being human. He is comfortable in His own flesh. He loves His friends. I am sure He fell in love at some point. He intimately knows the struggles of family. He knows the betrayal of those closest to Him. He even knows their denial of having known Him at all.

A lot about Jesus the minister. About His message of mercy. His ministry of hope. The little stories called parables, and their big meanings. Events we call miracles. The transformation offered by faith. The building of the first churches. The role of the disciples. The disciplined roles advocated for His followers. How Jesus served as the champion of the poor. The binder of broken hearts. The peacemaker. The foot washer. The one who could lift up the low. The one who could lead the lost home.

A lot about the Christ. The one they called the Messiah. The myth. The human attempt to put into words that which defies the limitations of language. Myth, not as falsehood, but as the passionate effort to express the gospel truth. Jesus Christ. The bread of life, the living waters, the vine. A light to brighten the darkness. The presence of Grace. A touch of healing, a balm of mercy. The one who offers new life. A new way of doing. A new way of being. A new attitude. Hope before and beyond the grave. The resurrected one. The one who can both be an intimate friend and yet remain so mysterious that He can leave us dumbstruck.

> "Goodness is the only investment that never fails." —HENRY DAVID THOREAU

A lot about the church. Its role, function, and purpose. Why it exists. How it creates community. How community serves as a fertile context for faith. What constitutes a healthy or unhealthy community of faith. Why we worship. Why we pray. Why we study Scripture. Why we serve or sacrifice. Why we celebrate or commune. Why we get organized.

Why the church's structure. Why its polity or protocol. Why its priests and ministers, elders and deacons. Why its ministry in His name.

A lot about you, the adolescent. About your struggles in adolescence. The crisis of finding your identity. The desire you have to be intimate with someone. The lust to make love. The longing to leave home, and the fear of leaving it. The declaring of independence. The search for spirituality. The locating of your own spiritual truth. Living your faith.

A lot about your overwhelming need to feel at home. To be at ease in your own skin. To feel comfortable with your heart's desires. To know how to nurture and care for your soul. How to be a home for a friend. To find home in (of all places) *home*. To risk departing from home to find another home, this one even stronger and deeper than the one before. Each of your next homes being informed by an everwiser heart. Each home expanding in size, until you are at home in the world. The universe. And beyond. Faith that leads to shrinking away from others is not faith. It is religious indoctrination. The wages of shame. The hiding of guilt.

> "It's not true that nice guys finish last. Nice guys are winners before the game even starts."
> —ADDISON WALKER

A lot about the good life. The genuine good life. About being a good person. A good neighbor. Doing good deeds, having good thoughts and conversations. About having good friends. A good family. How to choose each day to create goodness. How to be good to yourself, to others, to God.

A lot about a living faith, a faith in action. How to walk the walk. How to claim your vision and your voice. How to celebrate a diversity of belief. How to create community. How to create lives and lifestyles that witness to your faith. How to be an individual of integrity, maturity, and dignity. How to be a maker of peace. How to build a saner and safer world. How to make healthy choices. How to forgive and forget. How to stop. How to wave the white flag. How to let go and leave it to God. How to follow and receive. How to love with reckless abandon. How to find home, build home, make home happen.

This is a small book, yet it is loaded. Full of information about Jesus. Full of insights into how Jesus might help you sort out the challenging journey of adolescence. Packed to the brim with ways Jesus can enable you to find your way home to adulthood. Back home to life. Back to your true Self. Back to the basics of being the person you were meant to be.

your spiritual home—not mine

It is my hope that you will learn to feel at home on your own spiritual path. Knowing the terrain, recognizing favorite overlooks. Unafraid of the detours or roadblocks. Excited about the destinations. Faith should not be an alienating experience. Nor should it be an encounter with a world that makes you feel like a foreigner. Faith needs to be a spiritual home. A place where ordinary folks learn how to enjoy extraordinary lives.

This book follows in the footsteps of *Buddha in Your Backpack: Everyday Buddhism for Teens*, by Franz Metcalf, issued in 2003 by the publisher of this book. *Buddha in Your Backpack* is a truly fine book. It is beautifully written, easily accessible to an adolescent reader, and packed with helpful information about Buddha and Buddhism. It is insightful in its application of Buddhist thought to daily adolescent life. In structure and form I am heavily indebted to that book. Not only that, I genuinely loved reading it, and have added it to my confirmation class reading list.

However, there is one huge difference between that book and this. Buddhism is not evangelical. Buddhists make no effort at all to win converts to their faith. They simply share that faith whenever they present Buddhism's story, ideas, and beliefs. Christianity, by contrast, is presently soaked in evangelical language that is demanding of choice, admonishing allegiance, asserting truth claims as universal. For many of you, just hearing the word "Jesus" smacks of being called to be born again, to be saved, or to figure out how on Earth to gain entrance to Heaven. I have had to contend with this evangelical expectation as I wrote this book.

Therefore, I have taken a good deal of time to introduce this book. I want it clearly understood as not being an evangelical treatise. I will make no effort to convert anyone. I have no desire to win followers for Jesus. My only hope is to offer a fair and informative portrait of a man called Jesus. A man the church would come to call "the Christ." It will be up to you to wrestle with the information shared. To form your own views, to examine and reflect, to develop your own spiritual perspective. And finally, to lay claim to your own faith.

I appreciate your indulging me in this—in my need to both claim my faith as well as make it clear where I am at odds with the conservative Christian right, evangelical and fundamentalist Christianity, and even some orthodox Christian doctrine and dogma. I believe it is necessary and vital to the honesty of the book. I hope you agree.

 ## it is both/and, not either/or

Ultimately, spirituality is linked to maturation. As you mature as an adolescent, you become deeper and fuller in spirit. Your heart will become more tender. Your vision wider. Your voice clearer and fuller. Your longings sharper. Some of your dreams will get actualized. Some of your hopes will be declared. You will most likely begin to lay claim to a faith, which may have nothing to do with an organized religion. It could be a belief system that may be very much at home within a particular faith community.

A mature spirituality understands that faith is never black-and-white. Faith is the color gray. Myriad shades of gray. A mature spirituality does not see faith in either/or terms. In terms of either you believe, or you don't. Either you take the Bible as literal truth, or you don't. Either you think Jesus is the Christ, or you don't. Either Jesus is the Truth, or He isn't. A mature spirituality leaves much more room for questions, doubts, mysteries, and the many faces of faith. Mature faith is not about certainty. This is why they call it faith! If we are certain, then we know. Faith is not the same as knowing. Faith must fly on the wings of doubt. Faith simply chooses to trust.

A true adult has no trouble meeting a person of a completely different faith. No need to prove that person wrong. No need to judge, evaluate, or critique. There may be questions asked and dialogue shared. But all is conducted within a framework of acceptance. An adult faith is a tolerant faith. An adult faith works from a perspective of both/and, not either/or. We can have both faith and doubt. We can be both child and adult. We can be both in love and out of love with the same person over time. Life is both/and. I believe Jesus advocates a both/and way of living. A both/and faith is rooted in tolerance. A both/and lifestyle is centered in mercy.

This book is devoted to assisting you as you develop a mature spirituality and faith. It will be my focus to help you both enjoy your adolescence as well as seize it as an opportune time to find your way back home to God—however you may understand Him or Her. I want this book to help make your life easier, fuller, finer, and making more of a difference. I believe that having Jesus in your backpack will help you find your way back home. Back home from your adolescent spiritual travels. Back home to an adult attitude and perspective. Back home to living a life that matters. A life of value. A life that helps make the world a better place. A life that brings out the best in others. A life that pleases God.

PART ONE

JESUS AS
THE WAY HOME

I want to take a risk here. Not
a big risk, not life threatening
or altering. Much more slight—
a little risk. I want to capture
Jesus' spirit. I want to put His
message into a few words.

I want to sum up His ministry. Make it neat and tidy.
I want to find the one story from His many, many stories that
somehow grasps his essence. I don't think it can be done, but
I will do it anyway. Maybe that is the risk, the risk of being the
fool. Foolish enough to try anyway. Fool—a role with which
I am completely comfortable. A part I have often played on
Life's stage.

So I will take the leap, and choose one parable to find for you the key to Jesus' heart.

"Just then a lawyer stood up to test Jesus. 'Teacher,' he said, 'what must I do to inherit eternal life?' He said to him, 'What is written in the law? What do you read there?' He answered, 'You shall love the Lord your God with all your heart, and with all your soul, and with all your strength, and with all your mind; and your neighbor as yourself.' And he said to him, 'You have given the right answer; do this, and you will live.'

"But wanting to justify himself, he asked Jesus, 'and who is my neighbor?' Jesus replied, 'A man was going down from Jerusalem to Jericho, and fell into the hands of robbers, who stripped him, beat him, and went away, leaving him half dead. Now by chance a priest was going down that road; and when he saw him, he passed by on the other side. So likewise a Levite, when he came to the place and saw him, passed by on the other side. But a Samaritan while traveling came near him; and when he saw him, he was moved with pity. He went to him and bandaged his wounds, having poured oil and wine on them. Then he put him on his own animal, brought him to an inn, and took care of him. The next day he took out two denarii, gave them to the innkeeper, and said, "Take care of him; and when I come back, I will repay you whatever more you spend." Which of

these three do you think was a neighbor to the man
who fell into the hands of the robbers?' He said,'The
one who showed him mercy.' Jesus said to him,'Go
and do likewise.'"

LUKE 10:25–37

There is a road that leads to Jericho. My understanding is that it still exists in the Holy Land. It is a trade route.
On both sides it is lined with walls of rock. It became a
haven for bandits. Since there was no escape route, travelers
were fair game to be robbed on that road. They were, often
and repeatedly. If you went that way, you were pretty much
considered brave or stupid, or both. It was sort of a travel-at-
your-own-risk policy.

At the side of that road lies a man, beaten and bloodied,
naked and stripped of all his belongings. He is moaning
and groaning, crying out feebly for help. A Jewish priest is
coming down the road. He hears the man's moans. He is
much too busy and afraid to stop. He goes to the other side
of the road, and scoots on by. Then a Levite, an assistant at
Temple, walks down the road. He, too, hears the badly
wounded man, but he has duties at Temple. His job is
important. He is late as it is. He also passes on by.

A few hours later, a Samaritan is headed down the road. Now, Samaritans were despised by the Jews. They were thought to be racially and religiously impure. This Samaritan stops. He crouches down and places the beaten man's head in his lap. He dresses his wounds. He picks him up and actually carries him to an inn further down the road. He pays the bill in full. He tells the owner to keep a tab. If there are even more expenses, he will pay that bill on the way back from Jericho. The Samaritan departs without ceremony.

This is, in sum, the parable of the Good Samaritan. It is a famous parable. I think it is the one parable that captures the full spirit of Jesus. That reveals His gracious and generous nature. Exposes His theology and belief system in the raw. It is one parable, and yet it speaks of Jesus' entire ministry and message.

First and foremost, this is a story of Grace. I believe Jesus is the event of Grace. To experience Jesus Christ is to know the face of Grace. This is a parable about human kindness and mercy. It is a call to radical compassion, to extravagant love. It is asking us not only to help, but to literally take over. To take on another man's burdens. Not only is a bandage applied, a bill is paid. In this story Jesus gives a

wide framework for the work of ministry. It is human touch.
It is lifting up. It is carrying the burden (one's cross). It is
meeting all of one's needs. For the entire time.

This is also a story about religious folks choosing to
walk on by. Religious folks who are too arrogant or busy or
frightened to have faith. Religious folks who do nothing at
all. They not only fail themselves, but they also hopelessly
disappoint God. They choose a path of indifference. They
fail to get involved. Yes, they may talk a good line at Temple.
They may know the rules and the rituals. But their hearts are
withered. They display no mercy. They live no justice. As far
as love and Grace go, they are a dry riverbed. Nothing flows
out of them.

This is a miraculous story of seeing goodness—pure
goodness!—in someone from whom the world would never
expect it. A Samaritan. Whose blood is believed to be tainted
by intermarriage. Whose faith is supposedly contaminated
by exposure to other religions and beliefs. It is the Samaritan
who, stunningly, offers an act of total service and sacrifice.
It is the Samaritan who lives his faith.

It is to the Samaritan that Jesus points as an example.
Be like him, He said. Not like the religious establishment.

Be of the spirit of the one who knelt and cared for the man at the side of the road.

The Good Samaritan became "home" for the robbed and beaten man. He became his comfort and care. He became his nurturer and provider. What the Samaritan offered was a place of rest to a stranger. His lap, his pocketbook, his mercy. If Jesus is a call to come home, if Jesus wants only to lead us back home, if Jesus desires for us to be home to those lost and alone in our world, then the Good Samaritan is the perfect story to reveal that spirit.

Together, we will now take a longer and fuller look at Jesus. The man and minister we have come to know by scripture, as well as by other faithful storytellers. The message He lived and preached. How and what He taught. How He sought to transform folks. Create new life. Jesus, the man, who would become the Christ. The Christ who created a library of myths and mysteries. And the church that took shape around and within these stories. We turn, now, to getting to know more about a man called Jesus. An ordinary man with an extraordinary story to tell. A good story. Unforgettable, really. One that will etch its words on your heart.

1

JESUS AND THE BIBLE

The Bible is indispensable to the study of the ministry and message of Jesus. It is not only our primary reference but, historically speaking, it is our sole reference. We cannot look to history books or novels or plays to learn about the historical Jesus. Except for a few recorded historical references to a man, a zealot, who led a small rebellion barely noticed by Rome, we have zero facts. What we have is the Bible. And it is a horse of a very different color. The color of air, the color of light, the color of faith. Have you ever tried to paint a rainbow? It is impossible to capture. Even when you come close, in your heart you know something is missing. So it is with the Bible. We know it has much to say. We also know that much is missing from the story.

You don't need to become a biblical scholar. I am not a big believer in memorizing a large number of verses from scripture. I think it is smart to be familiar with the Bible, even as a resource for history or for most of literature. If you are serious about getting to know Jesus, familiarity with it is a must.

You will need to have some basic understanding. Be aware of the context out of which scripture emanates. You will want to know something about the authors, as well as their background. Their cultural and social conditioning. Something about their writing style and tone. Most important, you should become acquainted with the main themes of both the Hebrew scripture (the Old Testament) and Christian scripture (the New Testament).

"In short, one way to describe the Bible, written by many different men over a period of three thousand years and more, would be to say that it is a disorderly collection of sixty-odd books which are often tedious, barbaric, obscure, and teem with contradictions and inconsistencies. It is a swarming compost of a book, an Irish stew of poetry and propaganda, law and legalism, myth and murk, history and hysteria." —FREDERICK BUECHNER, *WISHFUL THINKING*

I would encourage you to approach this as if you were putting together a family history. Your family tree is critical, but the real story is to be found in your family stories. The tales told at holiday tables. The cards and letters kept in scrapbooks. The newspaper clippings that highlight key events: marriages, funerals, baptisms, tragedies, accomplishments, and celebrations. Even the jokes repeated over time. The humiliations you laugh over, and some that still move your family to tears. The moments of great courage or conviction. The causes fought for, and the beliefs lifted up. The faith found and lost. The God present and absent. The legacy, true and false. Jesus' family history is the Bible. Believe it or not, the Bible contains all those elements listed above.

The Bible is a family scrapbook. Only, within its pages the family is the human family, and its scraps are mostly morsels of faith. In every bit of scripture we see the reaching out of the human spirit for the divine spirit. We hear the pleas for God to listen. We note the miracles experienced. The mysteries embraced. We share in the quest for Truth. The adventure of being human. The efforts of human beings to bring Heaven down to Earth. It is a magnificent story, and a mediocre one as well. It shimmers. It is as dull as dirt. It is a book like no other, and yet it is like every other family saga. Bottom line: It is worth reading. And some studying. Some investigation. Take the time to see for yourself. You will be glad you did.

the bible: what is it?

The Bible. What is it? It is a book, a most unusual book. It is a collection of stories and myths and legends. Of poetry and prose. Of history and memoir. It contains letters and parables and sermons. It contains fact and fiction. The fiction is tethered at all four corners to real lives. It contains myths, seen as the highest attempt of a human being to express the Truth. There is much that resembles fairy tale. Magical stories that are intended to *make us believe*. Most of all, there is faith. Faith sometimes expressed with historical accuracy, but often with no regard to history at all.

The Bible is testimony. The human offering of evidence as to why one believes. At times the author of a certain Bible book works hard to enable the reader to empathize. At other times, and with other authors, it is assumed that you are in full agreement. If you read the Bible from cover to cover, both the Christian and the Hebrew scriptures, you will be frustrated. It is not only a daunting task, it will frequently make no sense. You will feel not only lost but abandoned. Where is this going? Why is it going here? How did we jump to this point? It is better to read the Bible in bits. The Psalms. The Proverbs. One of the prophets. A gospel. A letter from Paul. If you plan to take on Revelation, be sure you have a good grasp of what is meant by apocalyptic writing.

Yes, the Bible is history. But it is sacred history. That means it is a record of faith. The attempt by the faithful to document the activity of God. The writers of scripture strove to understand—not simply to know. They were seeking to understand why we live and die at the very same time. Why we are made to grapple with such a potentially paralyzing mystery. Why we can comprehend God, but never explain or prove God's existence. Why we can comprehend Truth, but never claim to own it. Why we need to take leaps of faith to grasp the meaning of life, and death. To say the least, the Bible is a book like no other. It will read like nothing else. It is a spiritual history. It is also spiritual history that makes a point. The authors have something to "sell": their spiritual vantage point, their personal faith perspective. Like it or not, they want us to share their point of view, to see it their way.

Have you ever attended a funeral? Usually the service will contain an opportunity for several folks to share their memories of the person who has died. The stories are rich and varied. Some will make you laugh, others will leave you weeping. At times you wonder if people are speaking of the same person. Attention is paid to fact and history, but what is truly being expressed is impact. How the person made a difference. Their

> "And yet just because it is a book about both the sublime and the unspeakable, it is a book about life the way it really is. It is a book about people who at one and the same time can be both believing and unbelieving, innocent and guilty, crusaders and crooks, full of hope and full of despair. In other words it is a book about us." FREDERICK BUECHNER, *WISHFUL THINKING*

spirit, their legacy, how they made you feel in their presence. Those who eulogize, want you to know and feel what they experienced. They endeavor to bring the person back to life. They lift up their memory so the congregation can recall the significant impact that soul had made on those gathered.

The Bible is written in much the same spirit. It is a magnificent effort to share the impact of God. To offer up to the reader what has moved the authors' souls. This is no easy task—to speak about the presence of God, try to capture a glimpse of Grace, explain being transformed by the Spirit. Are there words for such things? Can they really be captured in human language? Can we truly make sense out of testimonies that emanate from the heart? We want our witnesses to offer only facts. The witnesses in the Bible offered not merely the facts, but also their belief as to why the facts mattered. How they created new life, or healed a broken heart. When you seek to write down a miracle, you have laid claim to an almost impossible task. It is like trying to chew your own teeth. But thank God they tried.

The Bible is a miracle itself. Much of its writing is thought to be inspired. (I cannot imagine that this includes Leviticus, which is a real snore-fest!) It is amazing how the message still resonates. It is almost unbelievable how powerful it remains in human lives. It is crucial, though, not to worship the Bible. It is, after all, a book. It is written by human beings. Even in the case of the life of Jesus, we are offered four remarkably different versions. Every story and line can be interpreted in a thousand different ways. Nobody has a lock on its truth. It may be written in black-and-white, but the gospel truth it contains is all a shimmering gray.

Let me give you an example: the Christmas story. You know the one, the wonderful tale from the Gospel of Luke. Mary and Joseph coming to Bethlehem to be enrolled for the census. The lack of a room at the inn. Having to give birth in a stable. Laying a new babe in scratchy old hay. The bright star overhead. The wise men traveling to see the baby Jesus. This story is never even mentioned in the Gospels of John or

Mark. It is barely alluded to in the Gospel of Matthew. How can this be? How could the three other gospel authors not have heard of this wondrous account of the birth of Jesus? I have no idea. Not a clue.

What I do know is this: The Bible is an expression of human faith. Very human faith. Very human writers. Whether they were inspired or not, their humanity permeates all they have to say. Am I concluding that the birth account is not historical fact? No, I am saying it was Luke's faith. It was his version. Like a story told at the Thanksgiving table, a story that each year is embellished and altered, yet remains blessedly recognizable, real. This is what Luke heard. Experienced, recalled, imagined. Felt inspired to share. It is Luke's story of the birth of Jesus. What is crucial is how true it was for Luke. So true that he was able to tell the tale and put us right there. Was he actually at the birth? A reporter for "The Bethlehem Gazette"? Of course not. This is his sharing of an event he knew only by faith. The birth of an outcast child. A poor, lonely birth in a barn. A birth most of the world would ignore. A birth that brought wise men to their knees. A birth he *faithfully* recorded.

The gospel truth—this is what the Bible seeks to share. Not a defense or an explanation. Not a proof. The heart explodes upon the page. The spirit speaks. The mind and the heart and the joyous imagination have their say. Ultimately, the Bible is written in the spirit of poetry. If I told you the waves beat against the shore like a thousand mad fists, you would not run down to the ocean to look for floating hands.

Instead, you would know what I was trying to share—the experience, the pounding of waves gone wild, the roar of an angry ocean. The fear we experience when standing before the immense power of the sea.

Poetry seeks to put into words that which is true. Beyond what eyes can see, or ears hear. That which speaks to the heart alone. Which moves us to tears. Makes our jaws drop. Leaves us speechless yet, ironically, longing to express our feelings. The Bible is the very human attempt to put into words the love of God. The love of God experienced. The love of God known. The desire to know God. To gain intimacy with God. To be at one. The desire of God to know us. The decision by God to come to us, to live among us, to take on flesh. Or so it is for those who believe Jesus to be God's own Son.

Remember this: The Bible remains pure mystery. We will never fully grasp its meaning. We will never completely know the why of its writing. We are foolish if we claim to know all it says, or how it came to be. If we find in it nothing but answers, we become dangerous. Fanatic. Self-righteous. No questions left, no doubts remaining. The Bible is encased in ice. Enshrouded by milky fog. We can capture a sliver of its meaning. We can get a hint of its truth. Still, it remains as impossible to grasp as a handful of water. We hold its truths for a moment, and then they are gone. Trying to grasp it all is futile. Just let it flow and be fresh for a few seconds.

One thing is for sure: The Bible was never intended to become a weapon. The vehicle by which people judge others. The source of all kinds of persecution. The means for self-righteous hypocrisy. The catalyst for hideous inquisitions. How tragic those are. The Bible's inspired writing, intended to inspire faith, is now being used instead to indoctrinate and alienate. Pounded on pulpits by those who are certain that they, and only they, know what it has to say. Worst of all, the Bible has become a major force in religious brutality. People battling and warring over mere words. Believing their interpretation to be God-given. I cannot even imagine God's sadness at witnessing the Bible's being a cause of bloodshed.

No one, and I mean *no one*, has the keys to unlock all the mysteries held in scripture. Many religious folks make a tragic mistake. They see the goal of reading scripture as knowing its answers. Over the years, sadly, the church has sought to remove the mystery from faith. A faith without mystery is certainty. Dead certain. It is a faith without life. A faith you cannot live. A faith that will no longer change or grow. We must read scripture to gain insight. To be inspired. To experience the response of faithful people to God's presence or absence. We seek to share their questions. We strive to understand their quest. Then we shove off on our own journey. We look to discover our own personal belief. The Bible must never be used as a means of spiritual cloning. Rather, the Bible should be the means by which we discover our own unique faith.

This is a true story about a colleague of mine, a fellow pastor who struggles every Sunday to give a good children's sermon. Children's sermons are, of course, not just for children. They are how ministers are forced to prove to adults that they are good with kids. My friend Rob was to deliver a children's sermon about stewardship. His theme was saving. He had hidden a puppet in a brown paper bag. The goal of the little sermon was to have the kids guess what was in the bag. The puppet itself would serve as the object lesson on saving.

"OK, kids, what is reddish brown or silvery gray, and furry? It has a big fluffy tail."

The kids sat in silence.

"Now listen up, kids. What is reddish brown or silvery gray, has a big fluffy tail, and can scamper from tree to tree?"

The kids were dead silent. Not even a whimper of a sound.

"C'mon, kids. Let's put on our thinking caps. What is reddish brown or silvery gray, has a big fluffy tail, can scamper from tree to tree, and can even run along a telephone wire?"

Apparently, this was the first meeting of Mutes Anonymous.

"Now, kids. C'mon. Think. What is reddish brown or silvery gray, has a big fluffy tail, can

scamper from tree to tree, can even run along a
telephone wire, and...*hides nuts in the winter?*"

Finally, Brenda in the back blessedly raised her
little hand. Rob quickly called upon her, sighing with
relief.

"Well, it sure sounds like a squirrel, but,
knowing you, it must be Jesus."

Rob and his congregation roared. Yet this
story has a moral. There's no mystery in a puzzle that
always has the same answer. It makes the story dull
and the search boring. Even a little kid knows enough
not to waste her time playing this dumb game.

Have you read the Bible? If your answer is no, you are
in good company. Many who claim to know everything it
has to say have never actually read it. I suspect it might be a
good idea to read it. If you are to understand anything about
Jesus Christ, you have no choice. We have virtually nothing
from recorded history. I would recommend the following
approach:

1. **Read Genesis.** Read it as poetry and myth and as a miraculous story—not as journalistic reporting.

2. **Read Exodus.** It is crucial to understanding the Jewish faith
   and people.

3. **Read Isaiah.** He was a formidable prophet, and the links to
   Jesus will be glaring.

4. Read the Psalms. These will help you understand a people of faith who felt close enough to God to share everything.

5. Read the Gospel of Luke. It is a beautiful gospel, well organized and written. It captures the essential message and ministry of Jesus, who is all about preaching good news to the poor.

6. Read Paul's letter to the church in Rome. It will reveal the struggles of the early church, and why so many of us still struggle mightily with Paul.

These half-dozen books will give you a good, solid base from which to explore the meaning of Jesus. They will provide you with a foundation upon which to build. Most of all, they will help you relate to the Jesus who was a Jew, a devout Jew. They will make you see that the Christian and Jewish faiths are both like strands of DNA—they weave in and out of one another, are inextricably bonded. One without the other is like visiting the home of a widow or widower. There will be both a presence and an absence. Each will make itself known.

who wrote the bible?

The Bible was first oral. It was stories and storytelling. Many of these stories were told around a campfire. They were an evening's entertainment. The accompaniment to a sky swarming with stars. If the story was a good one, it would catch fire and spread. From mouth to mouth, family to family, village to village to village. As the story traveled, it would change. Be worn down in parts, be added to in spots. Each telling dependent on the teller's perspective. But good stories last. They lay down deep roots. They may alter with each blossoming, but each season the blooms are familiar. In the case of some sacred stories, such as those at the heart of the Bible, they appear to be eternal.

Good storytelling is good testimony. Good testimony comes from a good witness. One who was a careful listener. Eyes wide open, attentive to details, noticing everything about the mood and atmosphere. Someone who can bring you inside the story, inside the facts, into the heart of the matter. Inhabiting the same space as the storyteller, or even the characters in the story. A good witness gives accurate testimony. If he or she is believed, the results are a conviction. In the case of faith, the results are also a conviction. Convinced that a belief is true.

"Finally this. If you look at a window, you see fly-specks, dust, the crack where Junior's frisbee hit it. If you look through a window, you see the world beyond. Something like this is the difference between those who see the Bible as a Holy Bore and those who see it as the Word of God which speaks out of the depths of an almost unimaginable past into the depths of ourselves." —FREDERICK BUECHNER, WISHFUL THINKING

The Bible was not sent by fax. It is not an e-mail from eternity. It is the result of efforts made by human beings. Yes, they may have been inspired by God, but the human hand is everywhere in the Bible. The Bible is like a patchwork quilt.

The presence of God is in the stitching. The thread that ties together the stories and sayings and sagas. The pieces that shape and form the quilt are decidedly human. Woven by personal experience. Fringed with faith. Cut from the cloth of a life being lived on Earth. God may have provided the poke or prod to write, but the words came from a pen held by a human hand.

The Bible is composed of two great sections. The Hebrew scripture is the faith history of the Jews. It is not an "old testament" but is quite fresh and new. It is filled with the human search to locate their God. It is riddled with an honest faith. One that questions God's presence and absence. It is unashamed to offer complaint, even criticism. It is a history that climbs to peaks of incredible faith, and falls victim to valleys of idolatry and spiritual neglect. It is a book about human faith. The good, the bad, and, yes, the truly ugly.

The Hebrew scripture is a record of God's intimate involvement with a particular people and faith. It is the riveting story of a people governed wisely by great kings, and held captive as slaves. It is a tale of bondage and an exodus to freedom. It is an account of how religion became consumed in legalistic drivel, and how prophets called people back to a genuine faith. It is about a people who prayed and worshiped and followed. It is about a people who became cold-hearted and callous to the needs of their neighbor. The Jews were a people of great faith. They were spiritually spent, having sold their souls for the pleasures of this world. The Jews were, and are, us.

The Christian scripture, by contrast, is mainly about a man named Jesus. His ministry and message. His miraculous healing. His focus on preaching good news to the poor. His bringing home the outcast. His willingness to confront the religious elite and the politically powerful. His passion and compassion revealed. His legacy of unconditional love. His magnificent commitment to peace and mercy. His call to justice. His celebration of equality.

The Christian scripture is also about the activities of the disciples, and the formation of the first churches. It captures the faith of the followers of Jesus Christ. It tells of why they were persecuted and ridiculed. Why Jesus' ministry of love and mercy led to a brutal hanging on a cross. Why the resurrection became central to Jesus becoming the Christ. Why His followers saw him as the long-sought Messiah. How Paul emerges as the chief protagonist in the development of the church. How his letters reveal a close, yet often confrontational, relationship between Paul and the congregations he helped form. The early church had a rocky beginning. It was filled with scriptural and spiritual squabbles. Rife with human desires for power and an addiction to petty protocol. Come to think of it, things haven't changed all that much.

j, e, p, and d

No, this is not a new rock group. J, E, P, and D are the primary sources for the Pentateuch. The Pentateuch consists of the first five books of the Hebrew scripture. These five books are also known as the Torah. The books are called Genesis, Exodus, Leviticus, Numbers, and Deuteronomy. Five books that capture the core of the Hebrew faith. The writers who put together these sources made good use of oral material, as well as some in written form. The material used was ancient.

"J" was the writer who called God Yahweh, or Jehovah. His use of Jehovah is the reason he was called "J." He wrote during the reigns of King David and Solomon, which would be 1000–992 B.C. "E" used the name "Elohim," which meant divine being, and composed his book during the eighth century A.D. "P" wrote during the time of exile, which was about 577–539 B.C. "P" was preoccupied with the rules, roles, and rituals of the priests. "D" stands for Deuteronomy, and would become the primary source for that book. It was composed around 650 B.C.

 ### the priests

The Hebrew scripture has numerous authors. Authorship being reserved for highly educated men (and they were only men in those days). These were men who also held high positions within Temple and society as a whole. Israel was thought of as a kingdom of priests. The priesthood symbolizing God's union with Israel. The word "priest" occurs more than 700 times in Hebrew scriptures. There were three levels of priests. The *high priest* possessed the same dignity as a king (Joshua was a high priest). When

Israel was ruled by priests, this was called a heirocracy. A high priest was seen as the spiritual equivalent of a Pope.

The second level was the *ordinary priest*. Some 24 priestly families took turns caring for the Temple. Priests were responsible for guarding the sacred vessels of the sanctuary and performing the sacrificial duties of the altar. Priests were highly respected in the community. They helped to administer justice. They were even sought for medical advice. A priest could have no physical defects. He could not be sick or impaired in any way. Priestly perfection was considered the norm. This would set a dangerous precedent that still haunts the church to this day. A priest on a pedestal will someday fall. The higher the pedestal, the harder the fall.

The third level of priests were the *Levites*. They were assistants to the priests, the custodians. They did a good deal of cleaning. Cleanliness was of extreme importance in the life of the priest and the Temple. Again, this set a disturbing precedent. The notion that holiness was without blemish or flaw. No stains allowed. Remember, the pursuit of perfectionism is always demoralizing. The pursuit of excellence is always invigorating. Such perfectionism tended to make the priestly faith harsh, rigid, uptight, and unbending. In a nutshell, it often became void of mercy.

the prophets

Prophets believed they were instruments of God's will. Messengers sent by God to give voice to a powerful, often offensive, message. They spoke with authority. They were convinced they were speaking for God. Prophets offered a challenge to God's people. They called them to obedience, to a return to their faith. Prophets warned of faith's becoming stagnant or spoiled, of having lost its focus. They cautioned their people to get centered in God. Demanded a rigorous honesty about their spiritual state.

"The prophets were drunk on God, and in the presence of their terrible tipsiness no one was ever comfortable. With a total lack of tact they roared out against phoniness and corruption wherever they found them. They were the terror of kings and priests." —FREDERICK BUECHNER, *WISHFUL THINKING*

Prophecy is not fortune telling. It is not about seeing into the future. It is about making spiritual predictions from evidence gathered in the present. Prophets were wide awake. Aware of the spiritual state of their people. Prophets noticed the failings of the chosen people. Their wandering away from their true calling. The Jews were called to be a people of deep faith, who helped the poor, who did not worship wealth. A people whose priorities were straight, and whose lifestyles focused on good deeds. Prophets called out the Jews for being selfish, greedy, and godless.

Prophets were seldom popular. Their message was difficult to hear, and even harder to follow. They did not mince words. They said what they meant, and meant what they said. They offered some fairly dire predictions. The loss of life, power, material possessions, and reputation for individuals.

The loss in battle for the nation. Prophets offended folks. Called their neighbors liars or cheats. Pointed out the idolatries of their time. Spoke of God's disappointment and anger with His people. At times, they forecasted the downfall of the whole nation. Prophets were definitely not running for homecoming king or queen. They wanted spiritual results. Transformed hearts and minds. Changed ways. Bettered lives. A morality lived.

The Hebrew scripture is loaded with the messages of prophets, among whom the most prominent are Amos, Hosea, Isaiah, Micah, Jeremiah, Ezekiel, Elijah, and Elisha. To be honest, we can trace prophecy back to Moses, as well as the ministry of Jesus and the early church. The role of the prophets was to bear witness to the dynamic role God played in the history of the people of faith.

Ask yourself, "Who are our contemporary prophets?" On the list I would put Martin Luther King, Jr., Archbishop Desmond Tutu, and the Dalai Lama. Even Al Gore has taken on a prophetic role by alerting the world to global warming and its potential for staggering changes.

judges and kings

After the death of the high priest Joshua, the Israelite confederacy came to be ruled by judges. The confederacy was a loose collection of tribes. Judges were chosen on the basis of their military prowess, personal charisma, proven wisdom, and steadfast faith. Samuel was the last and greatest judge. It was the beloved Samuel who called his people to select a king. The establishment of a monarchy coincided with Israel's becoming a nation. Saul would be their first king. David would centralize power. He even renamed the capital the City of David. Solomon transformed Israel into a nation of splendor. A grand Temple was built, as well as a magnificent seaport.

David is believed to have written more than 70 of the Psalms. Solomon is credited with a few Psalms, most of the Proverbs, and the book of Ecclesiastes. Take note: Israel's political leaders were also their spiritual guides. Kings writing scripture is an important insight into understanding the Bible.

It is also vital to note that each king fell victim to trying to play God. A king's spirituality was often destined to become bankrupt. The gluttony for power frequently robs a man of his faith.

the four gospel writers—the editors

The Christian scripture is dominated by four gospels (meaning "good news"). The gospels are four versions of the same story, from four unique perspectives. Matthew, Mark, Luke, and John were the editors of the gospels and sought to assemble material in such a way as to take a stand or to make a particular point. These four men each offer a different vantage point to the ministry and message of Jesus.

matthew

In composing his gospel, Matthew was dependent on Mark. He wrote an orderly, but not chronological, account of the life of Jesus. Matthew must have lived in a Greek-speaking community because his gospel was originally written in Greek. Matthew is primarily concerned with communicating the gospel to Jewish people. He records nine events that are not found in the other gospels:

1. The dream of Joseph (1:20–24)

2. The visit of the astrologers (2:1–12)

3. The escape to Egypt (2:13–15)

4. The slaughter of the children (2:16–18)

5. The death of Judas (27:3–10)

6. The dream of Pilate's wife (27:19)

7. The resurrection of others (27:52)

8. The bribery of the guards (28:11–15)

9. The emphasis on baptism in the great commissioning (28:19–20)

Each of these nine special events would help Matthew make his case to the Jews. For example, Jews believed that dreams were a medium of God's will. Thus, the use of such dreams would add weight to his case. Matthew sought to provide compelling evidence that Jesus was indeed the Messiah the Jews had sought.

mark

The Gospel of Mark was written just before the fall of Jerusalem to the Roman army in A.D. 70. It is thought to have been written by John Mark, who accompanied Paul on his first missionary journey (Acts 13:13). Mark's gospel would become the core of Matthew and Luke's version. All but 31 verses of Mark are quoted in these gospels. This trio of books—those of Matthew, Mark, and Luke—are known as the Synoptic gospels. Each of these gospels contains the same synopsis, or what is often called the Marcan outline.

Mark's gospel addresses the role of Jesus in the life of the church. Jesus was to be the subject of preaching, the authority for teaching, and the mediator of worship. In Mark the distinguishing feature of Jesus is that of a servant. I use "servant" here not as in butler, but as one willing to spiritually serve others. When we serve others, we serve God.

luke

The writer of the Gospel of Luke was a doctor. A gentile, or someone who is not Jewish, and also a Greek. He is thought to have been a close friend of Paul's. He is also assumed to be the author of Acts. Luke's gospel is beautifully written and comprehensive. Luke is focused on converting the gentiles. Luke also places a special emphasis on the following:

1. The role of prayer

2. The important and positive role of women

3. The significant role of angels

4. The power of the Holy Spirit to transform

5. Jesus as the champion of the poor

6. Jesus as advocate for of the outcast

7. The central importance of forgiveness

8. God's Grace is available to all

9. No one is rejected by Christ

10. God's love is extravagant, and even includes enemies

Luke is, by far, my favorite gospel. To me, it expresses the heart of Jesus. It is an uplifting gospel. Lifting our spirits by calling upon us to lift up the lives and spirits of others. It is also a remarkably tolerant and open-minded gospel.

john

The Gospel of John is attributed to John the Apostle because the writing appears to have been done in the period A.D. 90 to 100. However, it is more likely that the author was in fact a disciple of John's. This gospel is quite different from the other three. It makes no mention of the famous birth story, Jesus' childhood, the temptation, or the appointment of the disciples. It is written from a unique spiritual perspective, and in a language that is filled with poetry and metaphor. Of the eight miracles of Jesus that are recorded in the gospels, six are found only in John:

1. Turning water into wine (2:1–11)

2. Healing the official's son (4:46–54)

3. Healing the lame man at the pool of Bethesda (5:1–9)

4. Feeding the 5,000 (6:1–14)

5. Walking on water (6:15–21)

6. Restoring the sight of the blind man (9:1–41)

7. Raising Lazarus from the dead (11:1–44)

8. Showing disciples how to catch fish (21:1–14)

John's gospel boldly declares Jesus to be the Son of God. In John, Jesus is not simply a great moral teacher, nor merely a very good man, He is clearly God become man.

paul

At first, Paul was a Pharisee. Pharisees were religious zealots. They sought to adhere to all the laws contained in the Torah. Paul was also a persecutor of the Christians. He considered Jesus to be another false Messiah, and the Christians to be fools. Paul is converted to Christ by a direct encounter with the risen Christ. This event is recorded three times in the Book of Acts (9:3–19, 22:6–16, and 26:9–23). Paul's conversion becomes the cornerstone of the early church. It should be noted here that Paul's conversion was brought about without the aid of Christian scripture. The New Testament was as yet not written. Paul converts solely on the basis of experiencing Christ. He is transformed by the Holy Spirit.

Paul's letters account for 14 of the 27 books of the New Testament. His ministry shapes the early church. His many missionary journeys established and sought to maintain several churches. His letters respond to questions on doctrinal teaching. Offer inspiration for moral and ethical conduct. Provide instruction on how to lead an exemplary Christian life. Pose personal requests of the churches and their people. These letters are not academic, but are highly personal and intimate. They are the efforts of a spiritual leader to guide and protect his flock. They should be read as such. I doubt that Paul ever dreamed that his letters would one day be Scripture.

ghostwriters

Have you ever tried to mimic a writer? To copy someone's style? To see the world through someone else's eyes? I recall my early efforts at creative writing. Some months I played Hemingway. Other months Thomas Wolfe. Fitzgerald was also a personal favorite. Ghostwriters are people who write as if they were someone else. Many of the biblical writers did this. As devoted followers of a spiritual leader, they felt able and compelled to speak in His voice.

They worked tirelessly to capture the thought and faith of the one they followed or admired. They were not merely students. They sought to be clones. To write as if they were, in fact, this spiritual leader.

Scholars have debated for centuries the authorship of many of the books of the Bible. This debate will rage on. However, whether it is a ghostwriter or the actual prophet or disciple, the intention was the same, the message identical. These ghostwriters wrote as spiritual clones of the individual they followed.

The message of this chapter: Spend some time with the Bible. Read it when you can. Gain some comfort with its stories and message. Explore a bit of its history. Know something of the culture that spawned it. See when and where it inspires you. Note how it informs you. But do not let it indoctrinate you. The Bible is only holy in human hands. In hands and in hearts that are searching its pages for Truth. Hands and hearts of good folks who study scripture not to become spiritually superior, but to refuel their soul. To keep themselves full of love and life. Full of mystery and good questions. Full of our best efforts to live our answers.

2

JESUS THE MAN

Today's American high school can be an exciting place. A place filled with endless energy and activity. Halls filled with laughter and romance and ceaseless chatter. Classrooms brimming with imagination and creativity and a desire to learn. A community. Even a family. It can, indeed, be a wondrous place.

Today's American high school can also be an awful place. A place filled with endless competing and comparing. Cliques roaming the halls in search of prey. Classrooms of yawning students waiting for the bell. A foreign country, a place of alienation and isolation, a place where many dread going.

For most of you, it is both. You have your good days and your bad days. Some of you sail through high school like a schooner on a bright blue windy day. Others of you can't even get your boat in the water, or if you do, for some reason it keeps tipping over. Some of you are a natural at school. Good at academics. Good athletes. Good social skills. Popular, confident, successful. Still others of you struggle, suffer, try to make the grade. Try to find your niche. Often feel left out. But again, most of you are both.

There is a secret, unspoken but true. Something you *all* have in common. At the end of the day, you are *all* glad to get back to your room at home. Your space. Your place. Filled with your stuff. Your posters on the walls. Your bed with all the right nooks and crannies carved in it. Your smell. Your memorabilia, music, and mess. Your clothes placed neatly in a closet or scattered about the room. It is yours, and you feel at home there. It is a relief to return to your room. No competing or comparing. No head games. No silent treatment from a so-called friend. No worrying about someone's sarcastic remark or indifferent glare. A place to refuel and collect your thoughts. A place to unwind and breathe easy.

Feeling at home. It is sweet. It means feeling comfortable, at ease, cozy, and content. Home is where you get to be the real you. Your room is a sanctuary. You only let in those people you want in. You feel safe there, secure. You can let your hair down. You can fart and burp and pop a pimple. It is a place of privacy. A place where the world cannot enter, unless you let it. Feeling at home is a relief, an emotional release. A chance to step off stage. To walk away from the rat race and the popularity contests.

I would like to see you develop a faith that lets you feel at home. A faith that is all yours. The real you. The *you* that even you like. A faith that expresses what you believe, not what you think you *should* believe. A spirituality that enables you to be exactly who you were created to be—a soul comfortable in its own skin. It is my hope that you can uncover, discover, and recover a faith that fits. Fits like a favorite baggy old sweater you wear not only to keep warm, but also to feel at home in. A faith that claims your vision, and uses only your voice. A faith that whispers in your ear, "You are my beloved child, and you are already enough." If you possess the wisdom to listen, you will feel at home. At ease with your Self and your life.

> "When we share our inner stories, we allow others to enter our lives and partake of our deepest truths. We discover that we share the same joys and tragedies, the same ambiguities and struggles. In the end we are all one story." —SUE MONK KIDD

I would also like to see you feel at home with Jesus. Have a genuinely relaxed relationship with Him. No awkward tension. No feelings of being ill at ease. Light and loose. I want Jesus to be a subject you can easily talk about. A topic on which you readily share your beliefs and doubts. Your deepest questions. I want you to feel not only familiar with Jesus, but even somewhat intimate. I want you to know His manner, message, and ministry. Something of His teachings. The essence of His preaching. The spirit of His healing. Bottom line, I want you to know His story.

We are our stories. So is Jesus. When I know your story, I can feel at home with you. It is my hope that you can come to feel at home with Jesus by knowing His story.

Home is where we keep our stories, keep them safe, let them become sacred. Like a favorite photo album or scrapbook, we take out our stories to remind us of what truly matters. What we care about passionately. The people who have made our lives worth the living. The events that have shaped and formed us. Those moments when we were touched by greatness. Times we received glimpses of Grace, or were glanced by God's presence. Home is where we tend to find the most amazing stories. Simple stories, secret stories, stories that must be told. Gospel-truth stories. Stories from folks who have led amazing lives, or simply chose to be amazed by life itself. I want you to hear the amazing story of a man named Jesus.

feeling at home with jesus

Much of this chapter comes from my imagination. In a sense, I am sharing with you not only my faith, but also my image of Jesus. How I have heard the story. How His life has resonated with my own. It would be pointless to simply string together verses from scripture as a means of telling the story. Instead, I want to offer you my take on the man. My version of the story. My insights and observations. My thoughts and feelings. Yes, my faith.

First and foremost, Jesus was a man. All man. Not macho, just fully human. His life was as dull and dynamic as our own. As filled with laughter and love. Frequented by tears of sorrow and cries of joy. Lonely and surrounded by friends. I have no desire to embellish Jesus. It would ruin the story. It is an adult story, for adults only. Not another Santa Claus tale. No, I like Jesus plain and simple. Free of all the religious hoopla. Not heavily coated in gooey, religious language. Not floating on a cloud. Not without flaw or blemish. I find myself more attracted to the Jesus who fed the hungry and clothed the naked, than to the one who walked on water. What can I do with a water-walking Jesus? The Jesus of tender mercy is the one I can choose to follow.

I recall the opening of a brilliant film by Martin Scorsese, *The Last Temptation of Christ*. The film was met by a huge uproar. Labeled by many religious circles as scandalous.

We religious folks were encouraged not to go to see it. Of course, I went. What was the scandal? Jesus was sexual. He knew lust. He lusted after Mary Magdalene. The last temptation for Jesus was wondering if He might want to marry and have a family, and live happily ever after into old age. Makes sense to me. Of course Jesus was sexual. Of course he knew lust. He made it clear that He was fully man. Whole. Well, this means He had to reckon with sexuality, just like the rest of us.

> "God, the sublime storyteller, calls us into the passion of telling our tale. But creating personal spiritual stories is an act of soul making that does not happen automatically. It comes only as we risk stepping into the chaos of our lives and naming the angels that inhabit the shadows.... In the crucible of story we become artists of meaning. There we meet God most surely." —SUE MONK KIDD

He also knew doubt and despair. He died laughing. He was moved to tears. He was betrayed and denied. He may have even told a lie or two. Maybe just little white ones. I don't know, but what I do know is that His humanity would never offend me. It is His humanness that enables me to feel intimate with Him. I can relate. I can feel accepted and understood. I can empathize. I can know His compassion for me. Without His humanness, I have the big, thundering God who dwells in the clouds. The God who needs us to be afraid. I prefer the one who tells me I need not be afraid. I have enough fear in my life. I don't need to add God to the lengthy list of fear-provokers.

What I hope to capture in these next few pages is the essence of Jesus the man. What made Him tick. Who He was and why. His innards, His soul, the pulse of His story. The plot is not all that important. It is the moral of the story that matters. I want to share with you the man who created the story. Who wrote His story upon the human heart. I want to offer a portrait painted with broad strokes and brilliant colors. Just a few dabs of color for detail. An impression. One you can see more clearly the farther you move away from it.

jesus the boy

We know so little about the boy Jesus. The literary form of biography did not exist back then. His mother was Mary. His father was Joseph. He had five brothers. He probably had a sister or two. Since women were held in such low esteem at this time, we know little to nothing about any sisters. No records were kept. Joseph was a carpenter, and his son would follow in his footsteps. Jesus' family was middle class. They were devoutly Jewish. Jesus would become fluent in Hebrew, and an excellent student of the Hebrew scriptures. His education would have taken place at the synagogue in Nazareth. Jesus attended His first Passover in Jerusalem at the age of 12. He was recognized as a brilliant young man, having engaged His elders in lengthy discourse (Luke 2:11–50).

I think of Jesus as being a very good boy. Not a Goody Two-shoes. Not perfect, by any means. Simply a good boy from a good family. Well-mannered. Intelligent, industrious, obedient, loyal. Showing His parents the honor called for by scripture. Like us all, Jesus was heavily influenced by His family and home life. We are each of us a family portrait. We reflect the family from which we come. Their values and dreams. Their struggles and hopes. Their suffering and joy.

> "The entire life of Jesus up to the time of his ministry has always been called, in popular piety, the hidden life—and on it the New Testament is quite succinct: 'They went back to Galilee, to their own town of Nazareth,' writes Luke about the family after his birth, 'and Jesus increased in wisdom, in stature, and in favor with God and with people.' And that is the digest of more than thirty years." —DONALD SPOTO, THE HIDDEN JESUS

Jesus came from a family that held compassion and justice in high regard. There must have been a good deal taught to him about helping the downtrodden, or seeking the outcast. I imagine His home to be one frequented by strangers in need. His home must have had an open door, and an extra place setting at the table. Since Jesus is highly political, I think it is safe to say that He was raised to believe strongly in a merciful justice. The politics of this home were those of a bleeding-heart liberal. Tolerant. Extravagant in mercy. Willing to forgive. Rigorously democratic. Celebrating equality and diversity. His home must have also been respectful of women. Revolutionary for those times. Somehow Jesus learned to treat women with respect and honor. Though the men of His time thought of women as mothers, maids, and mistresses, Jesus had learned to regard women as bearing the same image of God as His own.

jesus the teen

About Jesus the teen we know even less. It is all guesswork. We can, however, make some good guesses. Jesus was probably quite industrious. A hard worker. Well disciplined. Physically fit. Since He was such a solid student, I think of Him as being reserved. Not shy, but cautious. He was clearly attracted to spiritual subjects. His desire to dialogue with the ruling elders at Temple displays a mind keen on exploring life's biggest questions. Jesus was an intellectual. He was also sentimental. He makes many references to

His love for family and hometown. He must also have been quite sensitive, insightful, and deep. I think of Him as the kind of young man who privately writes poetry. A young man with not only a big heart, but a heart in touch with the pains and needs of His peers. I would bet that Jesus was a confidant to many.

I suspect Jesus was normal. A normal teenager for His time. Full of grand schemes and a longing for adventure. Rooted to home, but wondering about the world out there. He was, however, for more religious than I was at that age. My family occasionally went to church, but I am certain their biblical knowledge was no more than a few lines of scripture here and there. My primary memory of church as a teen was the Christmas Eve when my father and Uncle Ivan sang a rousing rendition of "Joy to the World," when unfortunately the rest of the congregation was singing "O Come, All Ye Faithful." The look my grandmother gave them could have felled a buffalo at a hundred yards.

I am sure Jesus had crushes on girls. I believe He had sexual fantasies and masturbated. I know this will be offensive to some, but that is because they still think sex is dirty, or you are more holy if you do not have sex. Sex is not dirty. You are not made holier by not having it. It is a complex and beautiful aspect of life. Fun, enjoyable, intimate. There is nothing more satisfying than making love to someone whom you truly love beyond measure. Jesus was a teen. There are certain things that all teens do or feel. Romance and sex head that list.

Jesus was a gentle rebel. He understood how difficult it would be to leave home and become independent. He knew the power of family. Family wants us to play it safe. To be secure and successful. Family wants us to be popular and beloved. Yes, family may want us to stand for good things, but when we stop just standing, and actually walk the walk, family begins to struggle. The struggle is simple and obvious: We don't want to see the ones we love get hurt.

Jesus knew full well that His prophetic political life would lead to persecution. Name a parent who would choose persecution for his or her child. Now imagine a parent encouraging a child to follow a path that leads to crucifixion. It is just not going to happen. Jesus rebelled not out of a lack of respect for His family, but out of an even deeper devotion to His God.

Jesus was a dreamer, a big dreamer. He clearly was comfortable heading to the desert to pray and meditate. He spent hours in reflection. He wondered about the "why" of life. Why are we here? Why should I care about my brother or sister? Why do we suffer and die? He lived His questions. He sought answers. He risked adventure. His life was a spiritual pilgrimage. Sometime during His adolescence, seeds were planted. The seeds of wonder and the quest for Truth. The seeds of compassion and passion. The seeds of wanting a life fully lived. A full life. The seeds of wanting to know God, and to be known by the same. In manhood, these seeds would bud and blossom. Bursting forth in a vast array of spiritual gifts.

jesus the man

What kind of man was Jesus? How do you capture a man's spirit? How can I lift up for you the things that made him who He was? Well, you look to His words. His actions, his deeds, his stories and story. You seek out the character traits that define him. Words that not merely describe him, but flesh out His soul. Nail His essence. Let me try. But I need a gimmick, and I have a good one. An honest one, but still a gimmick. I have decided that the best way for me to tell you about Jesus the man is to pretend to deliver His eulogy. That's right. I will share with you what I would have said if I had been invited to speak at Jesus' funeral. Sound gutsy? Corny? Well, trust me, it is both, but I think it will work. I also happen to believe it is the best way for me to accomplish my task. Sharing with you a man named Jesus.

My eulogy begins this way...

Good afternoon. And yes, it is good. Just as good as what we now call Good Friday. All days are good. Gifts from a gracious and adoring God. Today we have gathered to remember a man. A life. A way of being. A way of doing. A new way. A way worthy of following. Today we gather to remember Jesus of Nazareth. Not the brutal, tragic way He died. That is a story for another day. No, today, we pause to remember a man whom I choose to call the Author of Love.

His eyes. Most of all, I will always remember His eyes. Deep and black. Steady and staring. Always giving you His fullest attention. Aware of everything. He was always on notice. He noticed the sigh of a summer wind, or the sigh of a teenage girl in love. He knew whether your hearts were exploding with joy or with grief. He saw through us. To the best of who we are. His vision was clear, like crystal. He could see forever, and did. His eyes were like pools that you could wade in for comfort. Or they would glare at you with a loving challenge. Or they would mist over with His love for the whole of it—this thing called Life. His eyes spoke of His utter enjoyment of every morsel of Life.

His voice was gentle and firm and full. Rich in resonance. It had a hint of echo. A coating of compassion. His words were well-chosen. He was the only man I knew who always improved on silence. He spoke the Truth, always. Short and sweet and to the point. A little story, a little saying. Even His sermons were stunning in their brevity. All rabbis should take note, as well as priests and ministers. His words were always meant to lift us up. Never a word to drag us down. To do damage to the fragile heart. Words selected to inspire and inform us of the goodness of who we are, and the goodness we could live and be.

His message was simple. But hard as hell to live. In many ways it was ordinary. Prophetic. Calling on us to be focused on the poor. Preaching good news to them. We all know what "good news" means. It means help, a helping hand, a helping heart. Feeding the hungry. Clothing the naked. Offering shelter to those who are homeless. Wrapping our souls around those who are grieving. Praying for all those suffering. Celebrating equality. Making peace. Teaching tolerance. Offering forgiveness. Again and again and again. Locating the lost. Bringing them home. Our homes need to be places of rest and renewal for the stranger. Extravagant loving. A loving that knows no bounds and has no conditions. A love even for

> "Forgiveness is a funny thing. It warms the heart and cools the sting." —
> WILLIAM ARTHUR WARD

the enemy. Even when we ourselves are that enemy. The focus of good news is love.

The reason we are all here today is that we have been touched by that love. Touched to our very core. Transformed. Made brand new. Jesus loved us incessantly. Consistently. Without fail. He loved us in spite of ourselves. Seldom because of ourselves. The real miracle was that He loved us, flaws and all. Maybe the flaws, most of all. The flaws forced us to our knees. The mistakes made us malleable. Like a potter's clay. Willing to be molded in His image. Our defeats were a calling to open ourselves to His grace. He loved every human piece of us. He was never ashamed of us. He offered us no guilt. He trusted us to know in our heart of hearts, deep inside, at the bottom of our being. To know that we are made of holy stuff. Divine material. We shall be as gods. We struggled with this notion. He thought our struggle funny.

His hands. Big, thick, calloused. Never, ever clean. A grip like a vice. A handshake that caused me to wince. His hands were always busy building things. From tables to chairs to kingdoms. He was always reaching out. Placing His hands where no one else would dare to go. On lepered skin. On the heads of those whose demons were legion. On the legs of the crippled. On the wrinkled hides of the sick and aged. On the bluish flesh of infants who fought for breath. On the faces of those whose eyes poured forth tears, those whose mouths cursed the ground beneath their feet. He placed His steady hands on the fists of those infuriated, or ready to go to battle. He embraced those who stunk to high heaven. Those who appeared soaked in some vile, evil stew. Those who ranted at a God they claimed to hate. A God they mocked. A God they believed only existed in the minds of fools. His fiercest embrace was reserved for these fools.

His feet. How strange to remember someone's feet. So inconsequential, so easily forgettable. His feet were laughable, ugly. Calloused and corned and bunioned. Filthy. Not a spot of pink. Toes like big barked fingers. Thick and hairy and curled. These were feet of movement. These feet walked. They walked the walk. They were the mobility of His ministry and His message. He went to the need. To the places of peril and pointlessness. He went to caves where the mentally ill hid and shivered and screamed into the vacant night. He went to the homes of women. Risking ridicule and religious rejection. He went down roads nobody else traveled. He went to where the outcasts and losers of the world huddled in the shadows. He went to the cross. Even there, what I remember is not His bleeding feet, but His silent feet. Only a nail pounded through them could keep His feet from speaking. Talking by walking. Walking into the midst of death—and bringing out life.

His heart. It bled. All the time. I have never known a man of such magnificent mercy. Brimming with compassion. He felt every ounce of our pain. Our tears roll down His cheeks.

His heart shared our joys. He loved to laugh. He was quick with a joke. He even enjoyed being the butt of the joke. He was a man of gooseflesh. He truly was. He knew such awe, such wonder. He was forever being staggered by the raw beauty of this Earth. The infinite goodness of the human heart. His was a heart ready to burst. It did burst. The blood that flowed is known as the Grace of God.

His mind was a miracle. Quick and agile, wise and wondrous. He played no games, saw no need to be clever. He simply focused himself on building the Kingdom. One loving, merciful brick at a time. A kingdom where all His beloved children could live in peace and joy. Where everyone would know they were enough. In fact, they would finally all have enough. To eat, to wear, to keep shelter. To find meaning, to have hope. To locate faith.

Who will ever forget His stories? I admit, I am not sure I want to hear one more parable. His little stories with powerful, big points. Two ideas that run parallel, seemingly never to meet. But they do, they become fused in faith, they intertwine. Forming strong knots of belief. The Prodigal Son (Luke 15:11–32). The Good Samaritan (Luke 10:25–37). The sower and the seeds (Matthew 13:10–23). Such exquisitely simple stories, every one of them. Easy to relate to, easy to understand. But to live them, to inhabit their spirit—this is where the challenge lies. The spiritual test. The cross to be picked up and carried.

His acts of healing. Again, utterly beguiling in their simplicity. He healed by touching the untouchable. By forgiving those who believed they would never warrant such mercy. By offering hope to those wallowing in a tar pit of despair. His love and faith healed us. At times physically. Many times emotionally. Always spiritually. Over and over again He said it: "Your faith has made you well." And so it did. And so I do believe.

I have heard it said that He walked on water. He turned a few fish and loaves into a feast for five thousand, and water into wine at a wedding in Cana. True? I wasn't there. Could it be? Anything is possible. With God—anything. I don't hang my faith hat on these hooks, but I feel no need to explain or disprove them, either. If they are true, they are magnificent. More tales of a love that bursts through the seams of reality. If they are not true, they are still marvelous stories from minds filled with the love of God. Either way, they are the gospel Truth.

"The peace of God, which surpasses all understanding, will guard your hearts and your minds in Christ Jesus."
—PHILIPPIANS 4:7

He died. Poor, naked, brutalized. Mocked and persecuted. Worn to a frazzle. Skin and bones, nails piercing hands and feet. Fighting for breath as His weight sagged on the cross. Horrendous. Absurd. That a life lived in such love and mercy could come to such a frightening fate. But then, maybe this was the only place it could go. This story of extravagant, revolutionary love. A love the world could not stomach. A love the religious elite could not stand. A love without the bonds of dogma or doctrine, or the boundaries of petty cultural politics and societal norms. After all, he was killed for being a traitor. A traitor to a world He wished to transform into a Kingdom. A Kingdom of justice and peace and equal where the last would indeed finally get to be first. A world upside down. A Kingdom whose right side is always up.

His life and spirit live on. His soul exists. He has been resurrected. Resurrection is not endless time, it is the absence of time. It is being at home in the moment. Living fully in the now. It is what He taught us all the time. To notice when and where and with whom we lost track of time. It was then, He told us, that you had entered eternity. The Kingdom. A Kingdom available now, a Kingdom meant to be our home, a place where we become the people that God carefully created us to be. A home where we not only grow to understand the whys and the hows, but, more important, where we find the strength to live out our answers.

Jesus of Nazareth. An ordinary man. An extraordinary ministry. A simple, bittersweet message of stunning Truth. A teacher of few words, a mentor and a friend, a loyal believer in us. Again, the author of love. And all He asked in return? To live and love and learn as if there is no tomorrow. Because all tomorrows are guaranteed. They are more of Heaven destined for Earth. They will be coming—ready or not. He asks us to notice. To stop, look, and listen. To pay attention. He is paying us a visit. Whispering in our ears. Poking us in the ribs. Putting a lash in our eye. When we say we cannot believe He is still here, He will laugh out loud and say, "Where did you think I was going? I have nothing else to do. You are my life. Amen."

Being at home with Jesus is not to go someplace. It is to know you are there. That you are enough. That you matter, are beloved, feel respected and admired. Yes, we know all your flaws. We have heard the litany of your failings. We know better. We know, because God frees us to be better, ourselves. To look for what is right. To find what is good. To uncover all that is beautiful in you. Being at home with Jesus is to be present now. In this moment, in this time, exactly where you are. It is to be fully available. Available to the gift of the present. To see the now as a present, a divine gift. Being at home with Jesus is coming to understand that this is your life, and it is worth everything. To you, and to God. You matter. *You do*. Now live this truth.

3

JESUS THE CHRIST

We have just completed a rather brief review of the life and death of Jesus of Nazareth. Now we turn to Jesus the Christ. This is the man some believe to be Divine. The Son of God. Lord of Lords. The Messiah. God become flesh and blood. The divine, choosing out of great love to come to Earth. For you to feel at home with Jesus as the Christ is a matter of faith. A significant leap across a huge chasm. I am not asking you to make such a leap. I am asking you just to hear about such a leap. How and why people have chosen to believe Jesus is God incarnate. How they came to such a decision. What inspired them. What informed them. What happened—not exactly, but at least an impression of the process.

This will not be easy. You will need to trust what is being said. Don't analyze it. Please do not judge it. Just hear it for what it is—human testimony to having discovered faith in Jesus. Sufficient faith to believe He is the Christ. Simply read these reports. Try to put yourself in their place. To experience what they experienced. To feel what they felt. To share in their human understanding of events they believed involved the Divine.

There are numerous ways someone could come to claim Jesus as the Christ. I feel comfortable documenting only a few:

1. Those who experience a transforming moment

2. Those who often receive epiphanies or revelations

3. Those who have gone through a molasses conversion

Millions of folks have found Jesus. Believe that He is the Christ. They each have a story to tell. Though many, if not most, consider their stories to be private. Too personal to share. The following stories are offered not as proof or evidence. They are not meant to call upon you to convert. They are simply an honest expression of how some folks have been moved to believe. Moved physically, emotionally, and spiritually. Moved, as in experiencing a shift. Maybe not a seismic shift, but a noticeable change. A shift in perspective and attitude. A shift in the way one lives, behaves, and acts. A change of heart and mind and even soul. A new being is born. A different way of doing takes shape.

I recall being with my best friend, Bob Shober, in a theater in Beverley Hills. As we enjoyed a great movie, *Running on Empty*, I saw the rows of seats ahead of us began to roll like waves, up and down. Bob casually turned to me and said, "Little earthquake." I responded sharply,

"'Little,' my ass." I guess it all depends on what you are used to. For me this was a monumental event. Shaking my foundations. For Bob it was just life in Los Angeles.

I have heard many faith stories that seem like little earthquakes to me. No big deal: A revelation here and there, a glimpse of grace, a miracle. A mystery wandering into a life and grabbing for the throat. I know the signs. I know most of the symbols. I have to remind myself that these stories are of great importance to the one experiencing them. I need to care about these stories, open myself to feeling them. I ask you to do the same. If you do, you may gain insight into how someone might come to believe that Jesus was indeed the long-sought Messiah.

transforming moments

Dan and Pete were brothers, both in their early 50s. Highly successful educators. Brilliant intellectuals, pure academicians, they lived in their heads. They made their ample living by the use of their talented brains. They were highly respected by family, friends, and people in the community. They were equally lousy at intimacy. Both considered spirituality to be silly religious stuff. They left such things to their wives.

Then Joseph, their younger brother, came down with pancreatic cancer. Joey was a carpenter. Unmarried. The life of the party, the class clown, adored by everyone. The good guy who would give you the shirt off his back. Joey was a devout Catholic. Attended mass without fail. Prayed frequently. Expected grace to be said at every meal. Joseph was dying, a slow, often agonizing death.

Dan and Pete were distraught. They came to me for guidance. We were good friends as the result of my election to a local school board. They both believed Joey needed something from them, but they did not know what. Did he need to talk about dying? Did he need to cry? What was Joey longing to have happen between them? The Filicetti brothers.

I told them probably all of the above. The talking about death. The crying. But most of all, I stated, I suspected that Joey needed his brothers' help to say goodbye to Life. He needed their help in the dying. Pete and Dan moved anxiously about in their chairs. Sniffled and looked away. They said they did not know how. I assured them they did. I asked them to please try.

In a few weeks, the brothers were forced to try. Joey had lapsed into a semiconscious state and had stopped speaking. Everything was shutting down, but still Joey clung to Life. Dan and Pete knew it was time. They summoned all their strength. They held their brother's hands and knelt by his bed. They told Joey it was OK if he needed to go. They understood. The suffering had been too long, too brutal. It was time to say good-bye.

> "Where there is great love, there are always miracles."
> —WILLA CATHER, *DEATH COMES FOR THE ARCHBISHOP*

His big brothers were ready. They would keep his legacy alive, would take care of their beloved parents.

Then they reminded their little brother of how, when he was much younger, they had often thrown him into the pond near their family's summer home in the Adirondacks. Two big brothers swinging little brother back and forth. Joey laughing and pleading not to be tossed into the frigid water. Big brothers ignoring his appeals, and tossing him far out into the chilly pond. Next they told Joey they were going to toss him again. Only this time, to the other side. To Jesus, as they knew he believed.

Fifteen minutes later, Joseph Filicetti died, at the age of 35. Dan and Pete will tell you the ending was beautiful. Joey's breathing gradually slowed. He looked at peace. He had grasped his brothers' hands. He had smiled. Dan and Pete were mutually glad they had seen him smile. Maybe it was more of a smirk, Dan suggested. He simply melted away. "Melted" was the word they used. Then Pete told me that he had felt the presence of Christ, as had Dan. Both brothers told of sensing Christ's being there to catch Joey. Both brothers documented a powerful awareness of Christ's being on the other side. Waiting with open arms, embracing their little brother, welcoming him home.

I will not belabor the point here, but Pete and Dan were transformed. Trust me. Trust their wives, who speak of it often. These two men now live from their hearts. They speak their love out loud. They laugh often and cry hard.

They express a love for life, and keep the memory of Joey alive every chance they get. Two brilliant, successful big brothers are now known in the Filicetti family as the comedy team. The two who keep everyone happy, and say grace before every festive family meal.

epiphanies and revelations

One Sunday, after I had finished preaching to my congregation, I realized that I was feeling lousy. Good sermon, I thought, but no real response. Had anyone heard anything I said? Or did they just not care? I left the church and sped for Poppin' Fresh Pies, a favorite restaurant of mine. Being a compulsive overeater, I sought solace in a burger, fries, and french silk pie.

I was inhaling my food when a small family entered. A well-dressed dad, handsome and about 50. A teenage son, a Goth vision in black and metal. And Grandma. She looked just like a feeding baby bird—all eyes, an angular beak, and a gaping mouth. Grandma was in a wheelchair, and swaddled in several lap blankets. It was August, and outside it was sweltering.

I sat there bolting my food, and contemplating this dilemma. My faith in Jesus was deepening. Even as my ability to communicate to my congregation was lessening. The gospel message is revolutionary, offensive, radical. Today my sermon had been about religious hypocrites. How they were clean and shiny on the outside, but on the inside full of

dead bones. My sermon addressed the need to be a peacemaker. A justice keeper. A diversity celebrator. Remember, I
was young, and expected the
throng to be spiritually moved.
They were not. They were only
anxious to get out the door.

As I scarfed my food down
and pondered, I was eavesdropping
on the conversation at the next
table. Dad and the son were trying
to convince Grandma to have
something other than a Brewer
Plumper special. This consisted of a
hotdog, like those served at the
Milwaukee Brewers ballpark, french
fries, and apple pie with Wisconsin
cheddar cheese. The more menu items Dad mentioned, the
louder came Grandma's refrain of wanting the Brewer Plumper
special. This debate was interspersed with incessant inquiry
as to whether she was warm enough. Yes, she was warm
enough. And she wanted the Brewer Plumper special. Most
of the people at the restaurant now knew this information.

> "Once Jesus was asked
> by the Pharisees when
> the Kingdom of God
> was coming, and he
> answered, 'The kingdom
> of God is not coming
> with things that can be
> observed, nor will they
> say, "Look, here it is!"
> or "There it is!" For, in
> fact, the kingdom of
> God is among you'."
> —LUKE 17:20–21

These three lost souls were a good visual aid for my
day. Three people who loved one another, but could not
communicate. A family with ties hopelessly knotted. Just like
my congregation and me. Closeness without intimacy, a
church family without the capacity to disagree. I got up to
go, feeling smug and sour and childishly self-satisfied.

Grandma reached out her hand to me. She said, "Father!" I figured—what the heck. "Isn't this a wonderful day?" she said. "I am out with my son and handsome grandson. I am having a wonderful lunch—the Brewer Plumper special. I had a wonderful drive here. I live in Santa Monica Nursing Home, and we drove all along the lakefront to get here. Have you seen the lake today? It is aquamarine corduroy. Don't miss it. Bless you!" And she squeezed my hand as I thanked her and moved away.

I drove down to the lakefront. I stood looking out at a lake I had gazed upon a million times before. I was seeing it as if for the first time. It was dazzling. A huge band of aquamarine corduroy. I thought of how Jesus had said the Kingdom was in our midst. And here it was.

The gift of the sea. A pure blessing. Magical, mysterious, miraculous. As far as the eyes could see. A vision of sheer loveliness.

As I drove away, I also thought of Grandma. How she had been Christ for me that day. Reminding me not to miss the beauty of the day. How would I preach to Grandma, or people like her? I asked myself this question in earnest. My answer was simple: I would let her know how much she is loved, and worthy of it. Then the second revelation came my way: This is what my congregation needed, each and every Sunday: To let them know, somehow and someway, that they are loved beyond measure. That they may be hypocrites, just like me, but they are beloved hypocrites. I smiled. I wished I could let Grandma know she saved my day, and may have dramatically altered my ministry.

Revelations. The curtain goes up and you can at last see the play. See what all the fuss is about. Epiphanies. A window opening in the sky. You see beyond, way beyond. To a realm called eternity. Glimpses of Grace. Times when wisdom is received. Your knowledge is transformed into understanding. It all makes momentary sense. The puzzle pieces fit together. The shroud of mystery lifts. The Truth is witnessed shimmering. We are dumbstruck, awed.

Faith is inspired by these times of radical clarity, by visionary seconds. For me it was faith in Jesus Christ. Maybe because of my upbringing, or my studies, or my ministry. Maybe because faith is the name I choose to give to an encounter with God. Whatever the reason, it created faith for me in a risen Lord—Jesus the Christ. Could it have been Buddha? An angel? A coincidence?

Could be. But my experience felt as if I had gained access to the heart of Jesus Himself. Had been touched by His hand. A hand that felt like a withered old woman's. A Grandma's fist I still see merrily clutching a huge hotdog.

molasses conversions

At times, faith is an acquired taste. At times if we act as though, if we only can believe long enough, we will actually come full circle and find ourselves truly believing.

Slowly but surely we turn. Like poured molasses, seeming to take forever, we change. We are altered, in a reverse erosion. Adding layers of faith, as each wave of belief pounds the shore of our souls. A molasses (or slow) conversion is formed by faith, deliberately, over time. It is like being a stamp collector, putting together a fine collection over many years. Its takes time and searching and a good bit of luck. So it is with faith formation. Like Grandma's recipes. A little of this and a little of that. Somehow it comes together into a tasty meal, or, in this case, a living faith.

A slow conversion is a process. A building up, a wearing down. It is a spiral. It is knowledge and wisdom, it is reason and revelation, it is science and religion. It is a great many questions, plus a few answers. It is a path, and an uncharted course. It is a way of being and doing. It is learning in Sunday School, and in the midst of your daily life. It is the worship that takes place in a sanctuary, or in the cathedral of a forest. It is diving into the midst of the deepest ocean, as well as plunging deep into Life's biggest mysteries. It is maturing. Becoming more childlike. It is aging. It is the acquisition of

"Science cannot answer the deepest questions. As soon as you ask why there is something instead of nothing, you have gone beyond science. I find it quite improbable that such order came out of chaos. There has to be an organizing principle. God is to me the explanation for the miracle of existence—why there is something instead of nothing." —COSMOLOGIST ALLAN B. SANDAGE

years, and the loss of innocence. It is knowing one's heart as well as one's mind. It is becoming whole.

My faith in Jesus Christ has been such a process. A search through and scrutiny of scripture. Listening and looking, reflecting, remembering. Recalling Christians I have met. Ministers I have heard. Experiences I have had, or heard tell of. Wisdom gained, knowledge lost. Most of all, it has been the story coming to life in my own life. The story being witnessed on the pages of my present book of life. Suddenly, Jesus Christ is observed on a daily basis. He is my daily spiritual bread. I merely need to invite Him in. Open myself to His presence. It will be there. Not like clockwork. No, it still requires some hard looking and listening. But each day, I experience something that shouts, "I am here!"

There is no way to give you, my reader, a faith in Jesus Christ. Nothing is worse than having a faith rammed down your throat by somebody else. Faith is something you discover, or that discovers you. It is something that grasps you and shakes you, and empties you of your doubts. Then fills you back up again with questions and doubts galore. There are places to look for Jesus Christ. People who claim Him. Churches or gatherings of believers. The Bible, devotional books, scholarly books. There is no guarantee, though, that you will find Him in all the places that advertise His presence. In fact, sometimes these are the last places on Earth you might find Him.

This is why you need to look, most of all, to your life. See if He is in your midst. Look inside and out. Through a spiritual microscope and even a telescope. Live the questions, live your longings. Ask Him to be present. Invite him in, be available, notice. Pay attention. Listen to your life.

Look deep inside it. Be aware of your experience. Be conscious of your day. Create your life. I suspect you may find Him there. In the most mundane stuff. The silliest, most ordinary moments.

I am confident you can find Him in your loving. When you work at it, practice it, and make loving into an art form. Look there.

Still, you may never call Him "Lord." You may never understand Him to be God. I will offend many by saying this, but I believe this is fine. It is the quest that matters. The search and study.

The desire to know God. The passion to understand the whys of our lives. Jesus will be more than satisfied to simply be a part of your life. His divinity is something He will not seek to prove. He feels no need to make you believe. He cherishes your freedom, above all else. He has never demanded that anyone believe. He simply opens doors and windows. In the sky, and in our souls.

It is up to us whether we choose to walk through or peer inside. If He remains Jesus of Nazareth to you, so be it. Seeing Jesus as the Christ is a matter of faith and freedom. It cannot be coerced. It can only be chosen.

It is my hope that this chapter helped you feel at home with the concept of Jesus as the Christ. The faith choice remains yours, and yours alone. I simply wanted you to feel at ease with the notion of why some call Him "the Messiah." Comfortable with how folks came to call Him "Lord." Even if you emphatically disagree, I hope you are now aware that some of us experience Jesus as God. Not just a good man. Not merely a man of high morals, or an ethical hero. For some of us, Jesus helps us know the heart of God. In Him we believe we know God's mind and will.

4

JESUS THE MESSAGE

Jesus has a message. It is a focused directive. With surprisingly few words, not only does He makes it clear what He thinks, feels, and believes, but also He is able to issue forth with a clear pronouncement of how He hopes we might lead our lives. I am not sure that anyone has ever said more with less. We have His Sermon on the Mount. Several of His parables. A few miracle stories. A healing here and there. A couple of faith statements. And a smattering of spiritual wisdom. Jesus was indeed a man of few words. He was also a man of enormous wisdom. His words carried punch and purpose.

I preach from Jesus' message about 50 times a year. I have done so for 30 years. That is approximately 1,500 sermons. Now, I am original. I have never preached the same sermon twice. Honest. Still, I have themes to my sermons. Core teachings that continue to crop up. A message I may have shared in a hundred different ways, but with one central point. Such as forgiveness or mercy, or a call to justice or peace, or a warning about the idolatry of material possessions and money. I suspect Jesus did the same. Scripture does not offer us everything that Jesus said. Not even close. We never hear His whole message. Surely we are missing a good many of the lessons He taught. What we have instead are the larger themes. The broad-stoke arguments that He put forward in His three brief years of ministry.

I would describe the five primary thrusts of Jesus' message as follows:

1. Good news for the poor and the outcast

2. Religion can be dangerous

3. Love must be unconditional

4. Build God's kingdom

5. Grace is all that matters

Jesus spoke to varied situations and audiences. Debating the religious elite. Speaking intimately to His disciples. Most often He simply taught followers who, like Him, were just folks. Folks with no religious training, no spiritual calling. Just people who felt compelled to listen. Clearly, His words were magnetic. Audiences listened, and grew. Those who came to love Him and His message. Those who came to despise the same. It was a combustible context. No middle ground. People were attracted or repulsed. Not much in between.

Let's turn now to examining more closely these five major themes of Jesus' message.

good news for the poor and the outcast

In the world of Jesus' time, the poor were invisible. (Not much has changed!) They had no power, no rank or privilege, no education or social status. They could not study religious Law, so they held no positions of importance at Temple. They were viewed in mass. A blob of humanity with one face and one soul. They did not matter. They were of no consequence. Religious folks thought of poverty as a curse from God. The poor were somehow believed to be failures, not only in Life, but in God's sight as well. The poor were thought to be responsible for their own poverty. They needed to pick themselves up by the bootstraps, not depend on others to give them good fortune or restore them to it.

Jesus' message stands in direct opposition. As much as the world preached bad news to the poor, Jesus singled out the poor for good news. The poor mattered to God. Jesus saw them as individuals. Each having gifts and talents, each being a beloved child of God. God was color blind. God was not interested in religious laws. God loved His children. Jesus proclaimed that the poor were rich in the eyes of God. Rich in mercy and kindness. Rich in justice and peace. Rich in the righteousness of a faith lived.

> "Behold, some that are last shall be first, and some that are first shall be last."
>
> LUKE 13:30

"He has brought down the mighty from their
seats, and exalted them of low estate. He has
filled the hungry with good things, and the rich
he has sent away empty."

LUKE 1:52–53

"Hearken, my beloved [brothers and sisters]:*
has not God chosen the poor of this world to be
rich in faith, heirs of the kingdom which he has
promised to those who love him."

JAMES 2:5

* Brackets indicate my use of more-inclusive language than
  in the original.

Jesus' message calls for turning the world's values
upside down. What the world thinks makes for happiness
and success, is clearly not what Jesus believed to be the case.
The world is obsessed with how things look. The externals.
Money and material things, power and prestige.

Name recognition, being a somebody, being notewor-
thy. Jesus is interested, instead, in the innards of our lives.
Our hearts and minds. Our souls. He reminds us that we
will never be measured by the fatness of our pocketbooks, or
the speed of our cars, or the extent of our fortunes. We will
only and always be remembered solely for the depth of our
loving, and the breadth of our mercy. In these arenas, the
poor excel.

What made Jesus' message truly powerful and radical
was that He called for preaching good news to the poor, but

also called for the rich to know a good share of bad news. This reversal of fortune was highly offensive to the religious elite, who were also the wealthy folks of their time. Jesus used wealth as an acid test for faith. He questioned the integrity of the religious elite. He thought their faith shallow and lacking in true compassion. By asking those of financial substance to give what they had to the poor, He was quickly proven correct. Those who claimed to be devoted to God had a far deeper allegiance to money.

Jesus did not encourage poverty. Rather, He was an advocate for the poor. He wanted them to become visible. He wanted others to treat them with respect as individuals. He wanted the poor to have an opportunity for a full life. He expected the rich to lift them up, to help the poor get on their feet. He expected the rich to create a culture of financial equality. Remember, Jesus was not a capitalist. He did not believe in private property. He would have been appalled at the amassing of fortunes by a few, and the impoverishment of many. He would have loathed a system of justice that favored the rich. He would have been deeply offended by a religion that offered authority and power to only those who could afford to buy it.

"Sell what you have, and give to the poor; provide yourselves purses which grow not old, a treasure in the heavens that fails not, where no thief approaches, neither moth corrupts. For where your treasure is there will your heart be also." —LUKE 12:33–34

JESUS THE MESSAGE ✦ 69

Jesus was also the champion of the outcast. Often outcasts were also poor. Outcasts in Jesus' time were shunned. They were totally cut off from society, ostracized. Who were they? The leper. The epileptic. The mentally ill. The depressed or despairing. Those who were physically disfigured, retarded, or mentally slow. I cannot imagine how a child with Down syndrome would have been treated in Christ's time. If you had a flaw that could be seen, you were thought to be cursed. Possessed of Satan. You were forced out by the same religious folks who espoused great love. A religion that is dominated by fear shows love only when and where it is safe and easy. Loving those folks who are different or diseased was out of the question for the religious establishment of the time. Being rooted in cleanliness rituals and the pursuit of perfection, they felt an overwhelming fear of touching or being touched by sick or disabled folks.

If I walk into an American high school today and ask to know who the outcasts are, I will be met with an awkward silence. The awkwardness is the result of the knowing. You know who are the "losers" in your high school. Who gets mocked and teased and left out of everything. Who has probably not been invited to a party for years. Who has become the butt of jokes, the subject of scorn and ridicule. Everyone knows, including most teachers and parents and administrators. In this way, everyone is part of the shunning.

Why? Why are they left out? Maybe for their looks. Maybe their lack of athletic ability. Maybe their inability to wear the "right" clothes. Maybe they made a single embarrassing mistake. Mainly just from being different. Having an odd or unusual interest. Expressing themselves in unique ways. Choosing not to conform to the cloning standards of today's high school. It doesn't take much to be branded. Often it is simply the result of some popular kid choosing to go after an unpopular one. Putting someone down as sport. The further down the youth is put, the less he or she is able to fight back. Having become an outcast, they begin to think, feel, and act like one. They isolate themselves. They hide. They desperately seek out the company of those like them. Is it any wonder, then, that some of these outcasts explode in fits of rage? Are we not all responsible for creating an atmosphere in which outcasts may find violence to be the only means they can use to respond to the torture or bullying they endure daily?

> "The Spirit of the Lord... has anointed me to preach the gospel to the poor; he has sent me to heal the brokenhearted, to preach deliverance to the captives, and recovering of sight to the blind, to set at liberty those who are oppressed."
> —LUKE 4:18

Jesus wanted outcasts brought home. He wanted them to be included in the larger family. He wanted them embraced with acceptance. He did not ask for tolerance. He asked for love. Love without conditions, love coated in respect, love that celebrates difference. Love that enjoys debate. Love that feels no need to exclude anyone, no need to judge, no need to put down. Love that feels a deep desire to lift others up.

Jesus' involvement with outcasts may have cost Him His life. He touched lepers. He sought out the mentally ill, who often lived in caves outside of town. He spoke with those who claimed a different faith, calling them by name. He displayed acceptance and affection. He showed no fear of difference. He offered no religious shame. He met people with Grace. Unconditional love. Love that is powerful enough to forgive and forget. Even Jesus' close involvement with women was seen as scandalous for His time. Women in those days were treated as being of less value than cattle. They were made outcasts by their gender. But Jesus chose to talk to the woman at the well. He befriended Martha and Mary. He most likely had female disciples, or at least women with powerful roles among His followers. Jesus welcomed women home to lives of full equality and respect.

religion can be dangerous

Jesus was a Jew. He was deeply religious, a passionate reader of scripture. He knew the religious Law inside and out. He came from a religious family. He was accustomed to prayer and worship and devout celebration of the high holy days. His heroes were religious. His morals were carved out of religious beliefs. He was a man whose life and ministry and message were rooted in His religious

> "Judge not, that you may not be judged. For with the judgement you make you shall be judged, and the measure you give shall be the measure your receive." —MATTHEW 7:1–2

upbringing. Religion was at the core of Jesus' life. It was essential to His thoughts, words, and deeds.

Jesus was human. He was young, he was passionate. He also had religious questions and doubts, as well as the confidence to air them. He challenged those beliefs that made no sense to Him. He questioned the religious establishment on how they demonstrated their faith. Over time, Jesus came to see a glaring weakness in religion. A potential trouble spot. He thought there was danger in becoming self-righteous, becoming highly judgmental. Thinking that one is not just a believer in God—but acting in God's place. Acting superior. Believing that one has attained perfection, or at least more perfection than others.

A rigid and harsh religion can become dangerous. Jesus saw how shame and guilt were used by the religious elite to shun good folks, and to treat the poor with disdain. He was witness to religious folks persecuting those who did not believe as they did. He saw the spiritual scorn heaped upon those who had made moral mistakes. Jesus came to reject the whole notion of blessings and curses. He did not believe that God rewarded some while rejecting others. He did not see poverty or disease as a sign of a lack of faith, or of God's revenge.

Jesus rejected religion built upon fear. Fear expects the worst. Religion based upon fear is always looking for the flaw or the mistake. It is consumed in a perfectionism. It becomes riddled with evaluating and critiquing others. Fear- or shame-based religion is obsessed with sin. Naming sins, ranking them, creating a hierarchy of sin and sinners. The religious elite claiming little sins of their own, inconsequential sins, hardly noticeable sins. While pointing out the "whoppers" of others. Fear- and shame-based religion is focused on judgment. It is as if you are put on permanent jury duty. The goal of life being to prove that you have committed fewer sins than others, and are therefore somehow a better person.

Jesus takes the ladder of sin and sinner, and knocks out all the rungs. He announces that Grace is available to all. It is not won or bought or earned. It is never deserved. It is simply the result of God's choosing to love us. God comes down the ladder to us. God comes down as Jesus. A human being who can embrace us. Know us, accept us, enjoy us. And yes, respect us. This is the faith Jesus offered the religious establishment, and, as we know, it was bitterly and widely rejected.

> "Why do you judge your [brother or sister]? Or why do you look down on your [brother or sister]? For we shall all stand before the judgment seat of Christ…. So let us not judge one another any more, but rather resolve that no [man or woman] put a stumbling block or hindrance in [the way of his brother or sister]."
> —ROMANS 14:10, 13

If there was one primary reason why Jesus was crucified, I suspect it was His open love for the poor, and His willingness to be inclusive of those the world despised. This was threatening to those possessing religious or political power. It was a message that could—and did—turn the world upside down. It was a message that challenged the status quo. Created a new world order. Built the foundation of the Kingdom of God.

love must be unconditional

This is the toughest part of Jesus' message for a young person. Adolescent love is notoriously conditional and unforgiving. Adolescent relationships are usually governed by a one-strike-and-you're-out philosophy. Adolescents are not prone to loving those who are tough to love. The risks are too high. The risk of loss of popularity or a place in the clique. The potential for ridicule. The possibility of being lumped with the "losers." Adolescents find no logic in loving an enemy. Are you nuts? Why would I want to do that? Life at high school is tough enough, without engaging the peers you can't stand, or who can't stand you.

Adolescent love is often conditional. The conditions can be a mile long. Do we like the same music or movies? Do we like the same peers? Do we play the same sports? Do we get the same grades? Do we have similar SAT scores? Do we wear the same style of clothes? Do we live in certain neighborhoods? Do we own specific pieces of technology? Do we drive a car? What kind of car? Do we get to go to certain concerts? Do we drink? Do we use drugs? Are we sexually active? Are we not sexually active? Are we of the same religion? Are we of the same political persuasion? As you can see, the list could go on and on.

Am I saying that all adolescent love is grossly superficial? No, I am not. It's true that a good bit of it is determined by appearances. That is a fact of adolescent life. I have experienced both conditional and unconditional adolescent relationships. I have seen some teens develop remarkable relationships. Loyal, honest, intimate, and open. Enduring. I have also watched adolescents dump so-called friends for something as slight as not liking a particular rock band. The range is wide.

Jesus does not mince words when it come to loving. His expectations are sky-high. He sees loving as our calling in life. All of us. As the central task of a Christian life. There is no following Him without loving. There is no claim to faith in Him, without love's being at the center. The love He calls us to live is unconditional. Without any "if's" or "if only's." I would love her if she would just stop being so needy. I would love him if only he was more talkative. Unconditional love comes without the "maybe"

> "Behold, a certain lawyer stood up, and tested him, saying, 'Master, what shall I do to inherit eternal life?' Jesus said to him, 'What is written in the law? What do you read there?' And he answering said, 'You shall love the Lord your God with all your heart, and with all your soul, and with all your strength, and with all your mind, and your neighbor as yourself.' And he said to him, 'You have answered right; do this and you shall live.'"
> —LUKE 10:25–28

clause. It does not leave the door open for a quick exit. Not even a crack. Unconditional love is divinely inspired. It is modeled after what we have come to know in Jesus. Jesus, the event of Grace. The one who reveals the heart of God.

> "As you wish that [men and women] should do to you, do so to them. For if you love those who love you, what credit is that to you? For sinners also love those that love them. And if you do good to those who do good to you, what credit is that to you? For sinners also do the same. And if you lend to them of whom you hope to receive, what credit is that to you? For sinners also lend to sinners, to receive as much back again. But love your enemies, and do good; and lend, hoping for nothing in return, and your reward shall be great, and you shall be the children of the Highest, for he is kind to the unthankful and to the evil. Be therefore merciful, as your Father also is merciful."
>
> LUKE 6:31–36

Jesus asks us to be extravagant in our loving. To work at it. To practice and practice until we become artists at it. Loving is hard work. It requires daily discipline. It demands us to be patient and persevering. Tolerant and adaptable. It asks us to be good listeners. To be available and present. Aware and accepting. Willing to forgive. Capable of forgetting. Our love must be without the need to judge. The need to transform someone into our own image. The love called for by Jesus shows a person true respect.

Jesus asks us to display this love not only to those we find easy to like, but to those we dislike, as well. The people who get on our nerves. Those who are obnoxious, or drive us crazy with their arrogance or ignorance, or both. We are asked to love those who differ from us. Who believe and think and feel differently than we do. We are even asked to love our enemies. For most folks, the thought of loving an enemy is repugnant. How about you? Can you think about it, honestly? What would it take for you to love an enemy? What if you are your own worst enemy? This is really tough love. This is love that requires all our best. The very best of who we are. Jesus never expects anything less of us. Not because He is demanding. But because He has such respect for us. He expects us to do and be even greater than He.

build god's kingdom

Somehow the concept of Kingdom has been lost. If not lost, at least misinterpreted. Or, maybe better put—misrepresented. The Kingdom of God is not Heaven. It is not where we go after we die. It is not a place reserved only for certain qualified folks. It is not the bastion of those who chose to believe correctly. The Kingdom of God is Heaven come to Earth. It is a new way of life, a new perspective, a new attitude. It is the building of a society that is just, celebrates equality and diversity, is merciful and full of compassion, and lives in peace. The key is on Earth. Here and now. In the present.

"Thy Kingdom come, thy will be done, on earth as it is in heaven." These words, taken from the Lord's Prayer, speak of a kingdom not of this world. A kingdom that comes down from above. It is a spirit. A spiritual perspective. It is not a physical structure, not a style of governance, not an economic structure. It is a spiritual vision. It is about a change of heart. It is about God's vision being built on this good Earth. Built with unconditional love and forgiveness.

At times I hear TV preachers speak of the Kingdom as if it were just like Disney World. A place of fantasy and grandeur. Castles and princes and princesses. Magic mountains and lush, treasured islands. Such talk makes me sick. Speaking of God's kingdom as if it were some kind of gated community, a heavenly Club Med exclusively for Christian folks. What has been lost in such a warped vision of the Kingdom is Christ. We lose His love of Creation. His passion for ordinary life and ordinary folks. We lose sight of His desire to see the world at peace. A world where all are fed. No homeless, nobody left out in the cold. Nobody refused treatment for illness because they cannot afford the insurance. Nobody being oppressed

> "The kingdom we are given is unshakeable; let us therefore give thanks to God for it, and so worship God as he would be worshiped, with reverence and awe." —MATTHEW 12:28, REB

because of the color of their skin. No sexism, no homophobia, no discrimination on the basis of age or ability. Equality is the basement of the Kingdom. The foundation upon which it is built.

I understand why folks like the images of Heaven complete with waterfalls and magnificent gardens, golden highways, and palaces everywhere. I think they call it Las Vegas. I understand that image, because it is easier to "sell" than the highly political and economic and social conception offered by Jesus Christ. If the truth be known, none of us are all that fond of equality. It is hard to believe in. Even harder to live as a value. Almost impossible to sustain on a daily basis. How Jesus did it remains His greatest miracle of all.

> "God's kingdom isn't about eating and drinking. It is about pleasing God, about living in peace, and about true happiness. All this comes from the Holy Spirit." —ROMANS 14:7, CEV

If you watch any TV today, you have to be aware that we love shows with losers. Big-time losers. Losers who get humiliated, thrown off, shown the door. Told they are the weakest link. People we get rid of because they did not eat enough maggots, or they failed to lose enough weight, or they were not pretty enough, or did not have the prerequisite business savvy. We like to hear the words, "You're fired!" *American Idol*, the most popular of the breed, is a show built as much on ridiculing the losers as it is on looking for a winner. Any show that simply showcased young talent, without the competitive aspect, would never make it today.

Without the losers, the winning or the talent just doesn't cut it. Human nature likes a winner *and* a loser. Divine nature, though, enjoys equality.

Well, back to the Kingdom. Jesus asks us to build it. To build it now, here on Earth. In our lives, our homes, our hometowns. In our states and our nation. We are confronted with a vision and a voice. A vision of a Kingdom built out of faith, hope, and love. A voice calling us to lifestyles of justice and peace. It is a Kingdom we have seen. In bits and pieces. Moments and minutes. It is not a place, it is a people—God's people living as God created them to live. Nothing more, nothing less. The Kingdom is the spirit of home. It is when the globe becomes home to humanity.

grace is all that matters

In a presidential election in the 1990s, the campaign manager for Bill Clinton, James Carville, put up a sign in the campaign headquarters. It read, IT'S THE ECONOMY, STUPID! This slogan was meant to remind the campaign staff not to lose focus on what truly mattered to the American public in the election. Carville was correct. Clinton won on the basis of keeping his campaign focused on an economy that needed to get out of debt and required a new direction. If Jesus

> "From his fulness we have all received, grace upon grace. The law indeed was given through Moses; grace and truth came through Jesus Christ." —JOHN 1:16–17

had put up a poster in the upper room for all his disciples to
see, it would have read, IT'S ABOUT GRACE, STUPID! The whole
point of His ministry and message. The nature of His being.
The essence of the event of His life,
is Grace.

Jesus Christ is all about
Grace. Grace is the unconditional
love of God. It is the guarantee of
forgiveness. It is God coming to
Earth to free us from shame and
guilt. Freeing us to be human.
Enabling us to love as He first
loved us. Granting us the opportu-
nity to be about only that which matters. Living our truest
longings. Fulfilling our deepest wishes, our heart's desire. It is
Grace that frees us to find faith. Faith that creates the capacity to love. Love that ignites and inspires all hope. Grace is
home. The experience of a peace of mind. An emotional
ease. A physical comfort level. A settling in. Grace is coming
home to your own life. On God's terms, not your own.

> "God was kind! He made me what I am, and his wonderful kindness wasn't wasted. I worked much harder than any of the other apostles, although it was really God's kindness at work and not me."
> —I CORINTHIANS 15:10

The message of Grace is hard for you adolescents to
swallow. You live in a viciously competitive world. A world
of endless comparisons. Rankings, winning and losing,
proving your Self. Making a name for your Self. Trying to
climb the ladder of success. Winning the rat race. Being
measured by what you own and who you know. A world in
love with stuff. A world desperate to make you believe you
need what you know you do not need. Grace pulls the plug

on the nonsense. It puts a stop to all the effort to prove your worth. Trying to defend your Self. Instead, Grace offers you a chance to relax and breathe. To be your truest Self. To know you are enough. Worthy of being loved and respected.

Why would this be hard to swallow? Because it is free. No conditions, no expectations, no points to win, no proof to offer. Nothing to do except be. This is one pill, however, that, if you manage to swallow it, will let you feel healthier and happier than you ever have before.

5

JESUS THE MINISTRY

Jesus conducted a ministry. For three full years, He served as a rabbi, priest, and pastor. He was often called "rabbi." His ministry was small and simple. It was politically liberal and economically akin to socialism. He advocated a new world order. He called for the building of a Kingdom. This Kingdom would have no kings, no princes or princesses. No political or religious elite. No social castes. It was to be pure democracy. Spiritually pure. Governed by the Holy Spirit. Created by the mind of faith. Governed by justice. Devoted to peace and peacemaking. And unconditional in its loving.

Jesus' ministry called upon Him to play many differing roles. These roles defined his ministry, gave it its character and flavor, created its tone and texture. These primary roles are as follows:

1. Jesus the preacher

2. Jesus the teacher

3. Jesus the pastor

4. Jesus the prophet

5. Jesus the friend

It is in fulfilling these roles that we see Jesus come to life. His ministry is His life. They are inextricably linked. Jesus becomes His message, lives His truth, follows His bliss. He walks the walk. It is the walking that is the ministry. Ministry is never merely words. It is faith in action. It is an act of creation—creating community, creating life, creating the spirit of God.

jesus the preacher

I am a preacher. Just as Jesus was a preacher. It is an odd job. Preaching goes beyond teaching. It is an effort to transform the listener. At times the preacher will poke, prod, or push his or her listeners. At other times he or she will strive to comfort or console. At certain moments a preacher wants to move a gathering to tears. At other moments a preacher wants to get folks off their rear ends and into action. A preacher needs to be serious. Can be funny. Knows how to make a point and then leave it. How to say a lot in less than 30 minutes. How to be a regular person, or even a learned rabbi. A preacher must know how to inform without inundating. Inspire, not indoctrinate. Illuminate, not blind.

Good preaching does require a good voice. Good delivery, some dramatics. Nothing is worse than a monotone in the pulpit. A good preacher is a good storyteller. Good storytelling is knowing how to take the listener on a journey, uphill and downhill, thinking you are hopelessly lost but always finding your way. A pilgrimage that expresses a deep desire to return home. To come back to Life, Self, God.

I suspect Jesus delivered many sermons. The gospels were written 80 to 100 years after He actually preached. For purposes of scripture, these sermons were condensed into one major sermon. It is best known as the Sermon on the Mount. Its contents are a true patchwork quilt of spiritual material, and it offers strong evidence that this is several sermons rolled into one. This sermon is another example of how Jesus calls upon His followers to take a road less traveled. Not to follow the ways of the world.

The sermon begins with what are now referred to as the *Beatitudes*. This is a series of admonitions. It is a reminder of what God considers blessed. How God understands happiness. Jesus defines blessings and happiness as belonging to those who are poor in spirit, who mourn, the meek, the merciful, the pure in heart, and especially those who are persecuted. Again, Jesus' message turns the world's values upside down. Mourning, meek, and merciful? Those are the folks who are blessed? A tough way to start a sermon and a ministry.

Jesus challenges his followers to turn the other cheek. He calls upon them to love their enemies. This is a major break with worldly values. It goes directly against the religious establishment, which believed in an eye for an eye, a tooth for a tooth. That was the ethical norm of Jesus' time. God is portrayed as angry, revengeful. Retribution is seen as the rightful claim of the religious. Jesus offers a whole new way of thinking and behaving. This requires a new attitude, a whole new faith. No longer is the goal to get even, but to be an expression of Grace. The difference is infinite.

He goes on to warn His followers about religious hypocrisy. Having a show-off faith. Jesus despises those who feel the need to pray out loud in public, or to give offerings for all to see. He wants a quiet witness. A faith that speaks in acts of kindness. A gentle faith that does not call attention to itself. A simple faith that feels no need to boast. Bottom line: Don't wear your religion on your sleeve. Quit talking about it, and just live it.

The sermon then makes a strong stand on money. Jesus warns of money's addictive power. He confronts His followers with a basic spiritual truth—that you cannot worship God and money at the same time. Money is seen as so powerful that it can even challenge God.

He also addresses the issue of anxiety and worry. His message is again direct and pointed. What do you gain by worrying? Do you think you are in control? Here He challenges His followers to trust in God. To believe their needs will be met. As God's beloved children, they will receive excellent care.

The Sermon on the Mount also takes a strong stand against being judgmental. Followers are told to take the log out of their own eye, before pointing out the speck in their neighbor's. Can't be more graphic than that. A log or a speck? I guess that says it all.

In many respects, this single sermon delivers the whole message outlined in Chapter 4. The Beatitudes offer good news to the poor and outcast. That sermon questions the hypocrisy of the religious establishment. Only an unconditional love could turn the other cheek, or find it in its heart to love the enemy. The Kingdom will be built by those who are neither addicted to money nor bloated with anxiety. Grace lies at the center of this sermon, as it lies in the call to not judge others.

The actual Sermon on the Mount is contained in Matthew, Chapters 5, 6, and 7.

jesus the teacher

Jesus was a most effective teacher. His teaching device was the use of parables. Think of parallel lines—two lines that shadow one another, two lines that will never meet, always remaining an equal distance apart. In the case of a parable, there are two story lines—one that takes place in reality, the other occurring on a spiritual plane. One that is common and ordinary, the other uncommon and extraordinary. One stating the facts, the other stating the gospel truth.

They remain apart until a moment of revelation. These parallel story lines, at one point, converge. They momentarily intertwine miraculously. They knot briefly. Coming together in an epiphany, a synchronicity, a serendipity. The two become one—a marriage of metaphors.

This teaching method enabled Jesus to speak to a wide range of folks. Parables were accessible to those with no education, as well as those who considered themselves scholars. Parables were open and available to all. An equal opportunity teaching strategy. The stories were spoken in the daily language of regular folks. Using themes common to an agrarian culture. Examples of a sower and his seeds.

A mustard seed. Workers in a vineyard. Sheep and shepherds. The metaphors Jesus used were rooted in the world in which He lived and ministered. These were not stories of kings and queens and palaces. They were stories crafted from the daily events of those trying to carve out a living from the land.

Why parables? I believe Jesus knew that people remembered stories. People can easily forget an idea or a concept. They do not forget a good story. A story also allows a listener a point of entrance. A listener actually becomes a part of the

> "A parable is a small story with a large point. Most of the ones Jesus told have a kind of sad fun about them. The parables of the Crooked Judge (Luke 18:1–8), the Sleepy Friend (Luke 11:5–8), and the Distraught Father (Luke 11:11–13) are really jokes in their way. With parables and jokes both, if you've got to have it explained, don't bother."
> —FREDERICK BUECHNER, *WISHFUL THINKING*

story. It is as if we are there. Inside the tale, a member of the cast of characters. A good story also gets us out of our heads and into our hearts. This is exactly where Jesus wanted His followers to be. Living in your head leads to being judgmental. Living in your heart frees you to locate the Grace within you.

A good story always heads home, brings the listener back in touch with their soul. Reminds them of what truly matters in Life. Enables them to feel and think and believe deeply. Confronts them with a gospel truth. Too good not to be true. Home. Where God runs to meet you halfway down the road. Where God and humans converge in a miraculous embrace of unconditional love. Just like an epiphany created in the telling of an exquisite story.

jesus the pastor

A major portion of one's ministry involves addressing the needs of those who are suffering—physically, emotionally, or spiritually, or sometimes all three. Ministry pays attention to human need. Ministry notes those who are hurting. Those who are disappointed, depressed, despairing, or brokenhearted. Ministry offers comfort to those who are troubled in body or spirit. Ministry lifts a helping hand to those who have been beaten up, or beaten down. Ministry keeps an eye out for those who have lost their way, or their hope, or even their minds. Ministry is allowing another person's tears to roll down your own cheeks.

Jesus was a good pastor. Available. Attentive. Affectionate. A very real healing presence. He offered a helping hand. He touched those in pain. Physically they were held or embraced, or simply made to know that He was present. He reached out to the suffering. He did not avoid that which was repulsive to the eye or stomach. He emotion-ally offered empathy, genuine concern, real care. A helping of compassion. He would also offer prayer and a passing of the peace. His ministry was one of presence. His was a healing presence. He was in touch with those in need. He literally touched them. He also reached in and tugged at their heartstrings, and grabbed hold of their souls.

> "Rejoice with them that do rejoice, and weep with them that weep."
> —ROMANS 12:15

A key to Jesus' pastorate was forgiveness. He knew that the role of forgiveness was pivotal. That guilt and shame were an enormous source of human suffering and pain. That illness, whether mental or physical, can be relieved by receiv-ing Grace. It was Grace that Jesus offered. It was Grace that restored ease. When the heart and mind and spirit are at ease, then "dis-ease" sometimes disappears. Jesus offered forgiveness freely and fully.

Another critical aspect of being a pastor is to celebrate. Celebrating those events in life that are significant. Celebrating accomplishments, or little things, or moments of great gratitude. Often we become consumed in the busyness of life. The frenzied pace carries us away to a world of worry. We forget to pause and rejoice over the good things. The special times and moments that matter so much. Jesus remembered to celebrate. A wedding at Cana. A friendship with Martha and Mary. A chance to rest and enjoy a fine meal. We too need to be there for our neighbors, in good times and in bad. To share in their times of sorrow and joy.

jesus the prophet

The role of the prophet is the toughest role in the ministry. It means to issue a fierce challenge to your followers. It means to lead with courage. Calling upon people to make changes, to choose a different path. Confronting them for living a lie, or failing to follow their faith. It is making folks aware when they have wandered far away from God. When they are missing the mark. When they are lost, and do not know it. When they are addicted. When they are worshiping false gods—such as money and material things. When they have become indifferent to the needs of others. When they have grown selfish and lazy.

It was the prophetic role that cost Jesus His life. It is always a risky role. Nobody wants to hear they are wrong. Nobody wants to be called to repent or to change. Most of us prefer to deny that we are living lives displeasing to God. The impact of the ministry of a prophet is like being punched in the gut. It takes your breath away. The hope is that you will fill back up with a new and healthier spirit. The prophet is the one sent by God to knock us off our pedestals.

Many of us have a long way to fall. The fall can hurt. The fall frequently enrages, and the one on the ground may scream in anger for having been pushed. The prophet offers the shove. A spiritual push in a whole new direction. But first, we must have our feet squarely on the ground. Prophets smash all pedestals to smithereens.

> "Then came Peter to him, and said, 'Lord, if my brother sins against me, how many times should I forgive him? As many as seven times?' Jesus said to him, 'I say to you, not seven times, but seventy times seven.'"
> —MATTHEW 18:21–22

Prophets zeroed in on *the message*. They wanted it heard again. They wanted it spoken with fresh vigor, with the urgency restored. They wanted their audience to experience the message as if it were being heard for the very first time. They wanted their followers to return to the business of preaching good news to the poor, and building the Kingdom as the dwelling place for the outcast. They wanted their followers to love extravagantly, recklessly, without fear or conditions. They wanted their people to be the presence of Grace for a world in pain, a world in which most had hopelessly lost their way.

Jesus was that kind of prophet. In my experience, He is *The Prophet*. It was his message that was, and is, spoken by all prophets before and after him. Jesus' message turned the world's values upside down. Jesus' ministry turned us upside down. He shakes us awake. He gives us the proverbial kick in the behind. Tells us to start living the faith we claim. Jesus demands that we get back on track. Following a way that leads home. A path of discipleship. A road that requires those who travel it to pick up their own crosses and bear them along the way. It is a journey that requires maturity. It may be for adults only. Maybe you need to find that out.

jesus the friend

How can Jesus be thought of as a friend? After all, He is not here. He is not with us. He can't take a spin with me in the car. We can't just go for a walk. How can I be close to something that is in my mind? Isn't that like calling Santa Claus a friend? Or, worse yet, like having an imaginary friend? I haven't had an imaginary friend since I was 6.

We are all living, and we are all dying. We are doing both at the same time. At all times we are spirit. We were spirit before we were born. Our spirit saturates our lives. Our spirit goes on beyond the grave. This spirit is a presence. It is real. It creates a feeling, many feelings. It touches us. It is how we touch others. It is the presence of our soul. Our message, our ministry, our calling, our gifts. It is the reality of being known inside and out. Fully understood. So much so,

> "The prophets were drunk on God, and in the presence of their terrible tipsiness no one was ever comfortable. With a total lack of tact they roared out against phoniness and corruption wherever they found it. They were the terror of kings and priests."
> —FREDERICK BUECHNER, *WISHFUL THINKING*

that one has become one with another soul. Soul mates. We all will have those friends who are forever. It was Jesus' hope that He himself could be such a friend to us.

Jesus tells us that He will remain with us long after He has physically left Earth. He tells us He is leaving us with a wonderful presence, a counselor, a force of wisdom, a compassionate friend of great insight—and that is the Holy Spirit. The Spirit will be our advocate. Reminding us that we are God's chosen ones. God's precious and adored children. A divine creation. The Spirit, if we choose to look, will show us the way. The Spirit, if we choose to listen, will tell us where we must go, and why. The Spirit, though, will not hold our hand. It has respect for our maturity and integrity. The Spirit will guide us, point the way, offer instruction. It will remain up to us to follow.

Jesus can be as present as we allow Him to be. He can be as spiritually alive as we free Him to be. If we choose to converse with Him, share our lives, ask for His help, seek His guidance, then the Holy Spirit takes on greater and greater power. The friendship deepens. We know more of what God wants. We feel in tune with God's will. We feel we know His hopes for us, His wants and wishes. We feel ready and willing to follow and deliver. Jesus can be our friend when we allow Him to be a very real spiritual presence in our lives. Such a presence can indeed become more real than the voice you reach on a cell phone.

"Let me shift metaphors and imagine the power that is implicit in the Spirit in another way. In the summer I sail on Lake Michigan, a body of water that is seldom calm in July and August, at least not along the lee shore between Big and Little Points Sable. But on those rare flat days, the big lake can be like a mirror eighty miles wide. And every once and again on such a summer day, a series of great waves will appear out of nowhere, a huge V-cut in the water slicing across the lake. They are, of course, the wake of some good sized ship. Our little boat rocks, the halyards slap against the mast, the sails flap and everyone grabs the coaming to steady themselves. The odd thing is this: Very often the ship that made the wake is nowhere to be seen. Perhaps it is already around Big Point Sable or lost in the summer haze. You never actually saw it with your eyes, but you know it passed by. There is really no other explanation. You also know—even though you never saw it—that it had to have been a vessel of immense power to trail such a wake.

"We mortals never 'see' God in the literal sense of that verb, but again and again we sense the passing presence of God in the movement that God's unseen Spirit quickens in the world."

MICHAEL L. LINDVALL,
THE CHRISTIAN LIFE

6

JESUS THE MYSTERY

I recall a summer vacation when I was 7 years old. My father had named me copilot for a trip to Watkins Glen, New York. I had all kinds of maps in the back seat with me, and I desperately wanted to help my dad navigate his way to New York. At one point on the trip I mentioned to him that I had just seen a sign with Mayor Daley welcoming us to Chicago—again. This was the third time. When Mayor Daley welcomed us for the seventh time, my mother blew a gasket. Huffing and puffing, my grumbling father reluctantly pulled into a gas station to ask for directions. My mother berated him for not being willing to admit he was lost. Not asking for assistance. I simply wondered why it is always so hard for adults to admit they don't know something.

There are major portions of Jesus' ministry that I cannot explain. That I cannot prove. They make no logical sense. They can only be appreciated by a mind of faith. Even then, there is always a shadow of a doubt upon it. There are

His miracle healings. When Jesus helps folks regain their sight or hearing, or enables them to walk again, or frees a mind infested with demons. Then there are what I call nature miracles. Jesus walks on water. Jesus calms the storm. Jesus feeds five thousand with just a few fish and loaves of bread. And finally there is the resurrection. The biggest miraculous claim of all: life beyond the grave, life eternal. In all these cases, I don't have much to say. They remain mysteries for me. At times I believe. And at times I don't.

I see all of Life as a miracle. If I stop to think about Life as a whole, it is amazing, hard not to believe. I mean, really, to call all of this coincidence or chance seems patently absurd. Still, by the methods of science, I can't explain away the mysteries or the miracles. I can't offer you proof positive that the resurrection occurred. I wasn't there with the disciples to see Him rise and chat and leave them all hopelessly dumbstruck. But then again, I can't explain how and why my brain works the way it does, or how my heart manages to pump its way throughout my life. I can't give an answer to the why of dawn or dusk or death. Oh, yeah, there are some scientific theories I can toss around, but they offer me nothing in terms of understanding. Science is good at the knowing part. The understanding part remains the province of faith.

Have you ever woken up on a morning and looked outside, and everything is coated in ice? The sun is out and the whole world shimmers. It is gleaming. If you watch closely, you will see several folks running around with cameras trying to capture the image of this visual feast. It is awesome. The landscape is transformed. Even houses that sagged and suffered from neglect are now radiant in a coating of ice. Trees look like sparklers. Bushes like lace the color of light. Within a few hours it is gone, melted away.

Miracles are like an ice storm. They are mysteriously present, and then gone. Yes, they are beautiful. They can also be both dangerous and damaging. It is wise not to move in an ice storm. Smart to stay still and watch, look hard and deep. A branch can snap at any moment. An electric wire might descend in sparks to the ground. It is as if the Earth has announced, "Stop! Look! Listen!" As if God was whispering in your ear, "You don't want to miss this!" These metaphoric moments speak a language all their own. It is the language of faith. At times we speak this foreign tongue. At times, though, we can't remember how to speak a word.

Jesus is mysterious. His ministry is repeatedly mysterious. His message is seldom so. The mystery is a power, a transforming power. An ability to offer a blast of Grace, a blast that can level a demon, can create hope where there was none. A fullness of love that can open a blind eye. At times Jesus' miracle is a swarming forgiveness. The removal of the grime of guilt can let a lame person walk. The chipping away at a coating of grief can bind a broken heart. Though I cannot account for the why or how of a miracle, I can still offer up some insights. I can at least attempt to point out some of the Truth—as I see it. It will be like pointing out

fireflies on a summer night. "Look there! There's one!" It is
the best I can do.

healing miracles

The Bible reports many miracles of healing. I
will choose only one. Let me try to unpack its meaning as
best I can. Some of you will take this miracle as a literal
truth. Some will take it as a metaphor—a poetic image, a
symbolic tale. Some will hear it as a bit of both. For me, it is
a mystery, nothing more, nothing less. I believe it happened. I
doubt we know exactly how. We have only the story. The
story is a weaving of fact and fiction. Like all good stories, it
is anchored deep in an abiding truth. I call this truth the
gospel truth.

The miracle I will analyze is found in the Gospel of
Mark 5:1–20. It is the healing of a man who was believed to
be possessed with demons. The man described these demons
as being a legion. A "legion" is a military term coming out of
the Roman army. A Roman legion was three to six thousand
men. Suffice it to say, this man felt possessed by a great many
evil spirits. As I share this fascinating story, I will strive to
point out how and why a miracle may happen. Again, I
cannot do so in any definitive way, but I will at least strive to
share some of the spiritual experiences and events involved
in the healing of a soul. Ultimately, all miracles are about the
healing of a soul.

This man is mentally ill. He feels infected, possessed. "Demons" are a good name for the experience some people have of certain kinds of mental illness. The anxiety, the raw fear, the voices that can be heard, the head ready to explode, the stomach churning, the cat clawing at the back of your neck. Demons—little angry critters crawling around your insides. This man was emotionally and spiritually sick. Extremely so. He had lost his mind. His mind was now owned and operated by the demons of his disease.

This man was frightening. To himself, to others, even to the religious establishment. He was a walking sign of another power. They saw him as Satan's poster child. Sadly, this led to the man's being ostracized. He was forced to live in a cave, well outside the city limits. His lonely existence only added to his terror. He was alone, cold, hungry. Living in a world of rodents and wild animals, he was prone to scream all night. He was naked in every way—physically, emotionally, spiritually. He was in the raw. Without the comfort of covering. Without warmth, without touch.

> "A cancer inexplicably cured. A voice in a dream. A statue that weeps. A miracle is an event that strengthens faith. It is possible to look at most miracles and find a rational explanation in terms of cause and effect. It is possible to look at Rembrandt's Supper at Emmaus and find a rational explanation in terms of paint and canvas. "Faith in God is less apt to proceed from miracles than miracles from faith in God." —FREDERICK BUECHNER, *WISHFUL THINKING*

Miracle #1: Jesus seeks him out. Jesus goes out of His way to go out to him. He approaches him without fear. In a clear voice He calls the man by name. In so doing He communicates that this man matters. He is not just a body in a cave. He is not just a bunch of demons. He is a very real person. He is not Satan's child. He still belongs to God. Jesus brings him greetings of Grace. He touches the man. I imagine Him embracing the man fully. The touch must have startled him. A human touch—it had been so long since he had felt that. The warmth of Jesus' hand melts some of his terror. The mentally ill man wilts in relief. He can breathe. He can feel the air going in and out of his lungs. His chest fills with fresh air. Still, anxiety remains.

Miracle #2: Jesus has a revelation. He sees a herd of pigs nearby. He demands the demons to come out of the man and to go into the pigs. In psychiatric terms, this is called transference. It is the same philosophy behind beating on a pillow. If you need to get something out, at times it needs somewhere to go. In this case, into the pigs. Jesus shouts His demand. The shouting scares the pigs. The pigs scamper like lemmings, and plunge over the cliff and into the sea. Not a great day for the pigs, but independence day for the mentally ill man.

Miracle #3: The man is now rid of his guilt, his grief. The terrible anxiety that had plagued his mind, haunted his being, irritated his every move, destroyed his life. Left him a genuine nervous wreck. The demons are gone—over the cliff, drowned. Remember, pigs were known for being filthy animals. To the religious establishment, they were thought of as unclean, and therefore could not be eaten. It is into these filthy animals that Jesus wisely transfers the filth of this man's life. His dirty secrets.

The miracles of Jesus are all rooted in the same Grace exhibited here. A Grace that is fearless. A Grace that reaches out to the outcast. A Grace that touches and transforms. Bringing wounded and weary folks back to life. Cleaning up hearts and minds. Restoring a right spirit. Offering renewed purpose, a new hope. Allowing those who could not see any light at the end of the tunnel to finally see a glimmer there. A Grace that opens us up—our eyes and ears, our hearts and minds, our spirits and lives. Opens us to the reality that we are loved beyond measure. Cherished. Yes, even adored. Just like a babe in Bethlehem.

the calming of the storm

This is a physical miracle. A mystery of Jesus showing power over nature. It could be a literal truth, or a metaphor, or some of both. Again, I have no way of explaining its meaning, except to say what it means to me. This story is found in the Gospel of Matthew 8:23–27.

Jesus is with his disciples on a ship, crossing a lake. Jesus is dead tired, bone weary. He sleeps. The disciples are chattering. The air is limp. Puffy, greenish clouds lurk on the horizon. An occasional flash of lightning pierces the clouds. The distant rumble of thunder is heard. In minutes everything changes. The winds whip up, lashing the boat. The waves build, higher and higher. Now the boat is running through huge troughs. The disciples can no longer see land, or even the horizon. All they can see are terrifying walls of water. It is pouring rain, raining so hard that the sheets of rain are almost coming at them horizontally. The disciples are wet and cold and frightened. Meanwhile, Jesus is sleeping. The disciples decide it is time to wake him.

Jesus awakens to a monster storm. He shocks the disciples by showing no fear at all. He prays out loud. He rebukes the storm. As quickly as it came up, the storm departs. The water calms. The ship returns to sailing on a gentle breeze. The sky is a pastel palette. The air smells fresh and fragrant. The seagulls dive for fish. The disciples marvel at the power of this man Jesus to even calm a storm. They are dumbstruck, astonished. They can't believe their eyes. The wind and rain have vanished.

"Ever since the time of Jesus, healing has been part of the Christian tradition. In this century [the 20th century] it has usually been associated with religious quackery or the lunatic fringe, but as the psychosomatic dimension of disease has come to be taken more and more seriously by medical science it has regained some of its former respectability. How nice for God to have this support at last."
—FREDERICK BUECHNER, *WISHFUL THINKING*

If we are to take the story literally, then nature is under God's control. That being said, it would raise a good many questions about tornados and hurricanes, or tsunamis and earthquakes. Why does God allow such events to take place? Is God comfortable with the loss of innocent lives to these natural disasters? If we choose to see God as being in control of nature, then we have to accept both the calming of the storm as well as the ravages of many other storms in life.

Maybe it was all about timing. Jesus rebukes a summer squall, and it evaporates. Summer squalls often burst on the scene and flee just as quickly. Maybe it was simply Jesus using this occasion to challenge his disciples' lack of faith. He was not afraid. He had great faith that things would be fine. He chose to trust in God. He himself was the calm during the storm, a man full of faith. The disciples chose to see these events as being synchronized, perhaps as revealing God's power to command nature to obey.

Maybe it is a metaphor, after all. An excellent poetic image. Stating how, with God, all things are possible. More important, asking disciples to recognize the power of faith to calm all storms. Those on the inside, as well as those on the sea. A strong faith removes fear. Faith expects the best. Fear expects the worst. Faith, when trusted and lived, triumphs over fear.

None of us was there. We don't know what happened. We never will. We have only the story. We may have the framework of faith to hang the story upon. We have our beliefs, or lack thereof. The fact remains: It is a mystery. Does it matter how we explain it? Is that important? It may be important to you as an individual. It may matter to your faith tradition. What I think matters is that a little story, like the miraculous calming of a storm, still has a good deal to teach us.

I believe in the power of faith to calm things down. I love the image of a Jesus who was so at ease in His life that He slept right through a storm. I love the notion of Jesus not being afraid. Having conquered his fears, and having been in synch with Life as a whole—as the waves roll, Jesus snores.

the resurrection

Many would tell you that the entire Christian belief system rests upon believing in the resurrection of Jesus Christ. The resurrection is the rising of Jesus from the dead. It is His appearances to the disciples and to others as well, after the crucifixion. It is a belief in eternal life. A belief that Jesus declares victory over the grave. That Jesus opens the door to eternity for us all. For many people, this single belief is the one upon which all others hinge. If He is not resurrected, then He is not worthy of being worshiped. If He did not indeed rise from the dead, then He may be worthy of admiration, maybe even devotion—but not worthy to be the recipient of our prayers.

Resurrection means life in the absence of time—not endless time. For Christians, resurrection offers us an eternity of being with Christ. We know little of what this means, other than that it is thought to be a peace that passes all understanding. The ultimate experience of coming home, an experience of belonging, of being rooted, being grounded in

Grace. Feeling total calm. An ease. The absence of worry and anxiety. The presence of comfort and joy. Resurrection is the happening of hope.

I am not sure exactly what I believe. I know I believe in life after death. I believe there is something beyond the grave. I feel God was with me before I was born. He has made Himself known throughout my life. And I am faithfully confident that He will be there in what we call "the beyond." But what will that be like? Who will be there with us? How will we experience God? I haven't a clue. I simply choose to trust this spiritual concept. I take this leap of faith. It is not a notion to which I cling. Yes, I accept the reality of death. To be honest, I would be bored to death with an endless me, an eternal Bill Grimbol. Enough already. I just believe there will be another kind of life awaiting us—one utterly new, totally transforming. A coming home that yields bliss. Still, it is a mystery to me.

> "The idea of the immortality of the soul is based on the experience of man's indomitable spirit. The idea of the resurrection of the body is based on the experience of God's unspeakable love." —FREDERICK BUECHNER, *WISHFUL THINKING*

Jesus never ranks beliefs. He never says you must believe in everything or nothing. He never zeros in on one belief, and makes that the litmus test of faith. I believe the same to be true with resurrection. In fact, He states that if people are unwilling to believe in the message of the prophets, He doubts that they will be able to believe in the resurrection. I do not believe Christ requires us to believe in the resurrection. But I know that a good deal of Christianity requires such belief. I encourage you to consider it for yourself. To embrace this mystery. It cannot shrink your faith. Mysteries *always* expand our faith. Even just the consideration of a mystery widens the scope of our spirit. It is indeed possible to believe in Jesus and still have many questions about resurrection.

I believe in a resurrection. I don't know exactly what this means to me. I am not sure if I hold this belief because I have experienced the presence of Christ, or if it is the result of scripture telling me that the disciples saw him, as did Saint Paul on the road to Damascus. I have certainly heard about the empty tomb. I have never known another one. I have my doubts. At times they are strong. I suspect I believe in resurrection because eternal life is something I understand. I understand eternity when I lose track of time, or when I see something so merciful I get a lump in the throat. I experience eternity every time I am moved to tears. Tears that never lie. Tears that tell me of the presence of God, before, during, and after the resurrection.

Eternity offers me some freedom from denying death. The denial of death is an enormous waste of time and energy and talent. Just like Jesus, I have known my days of fearing death. I will know many more. But, on the whole, I have come to accept death. I embrace the terms under which Life is given. I trust that our spiritual life remains past the grave. I find that to make sense. The ongoing nature of the human spirit is not hard to swallow. Nor is the notion of a human spirit's being swallowed whole by the divine Spirit.

No matter what I say, I must admit there is mystery on the tip of my tongue. I don't know . . . I do believe. Back and forth. The rhythm of faith. The beat of the human heart.

Let me conclude by saying that I deeply appreciate the chasms of doubt created by mystery. I cherish the moment when I believe that I understand. The gap closes. I feel as though I could walk across it. I also appreciate the times of flight, when I put on the wings of faith and choose to believe I can soar. I also value the times when I am so haunted by questions that I refuse any travel to the cliff's edge. I love how faith forces us to mature. To deepen and grow. To make wild and crazy choices. To play it spiritually safe. Mystery is the great fuel of the spiritual life, and I consider myself one of the seekers. I hope you, too, will seek for your answers. Be fearless.

Here are some mysteries to ponder. They will make you stretch. They will strengthen your faith. They will deepen your soul. They will truly make you a better person:

1. Why colors? What is the meaning behind each color?

2. Do you believe in genetic engineering? When? Where? How? Why?

3. Why must we fall in love, rather than walk into it?

4. Why do we dream? Daydreams? Night dreams? Dreams for our futures?

5. What creates evil in a human soul? Is there such a thing as an evil soul?

6. Where is the universe headed? Are we making progress? Toward what?

7. Do you believe in miracles? Why, or why not?

8. What mystery haunts your mind most often?

9. Are there any sins that are unforgivable?

10. What can we learn from stars?

This list can go on and on. Make up some questions of your own. It is a great way for a youth group to function—not having some adult telling you *what* to think, but having someone who *invites* you to think. I, for one, would like to see you do most of the work.

7

JESUS AND THE CHURCH

I recently read a wonderful book, *A Fractured Mind*, by Robert Oxnam. It is the extraordinary story of a man coping with being a multiple personality. Robert was the victim of early childhood abuse, both sexual and physical, and of the various personalities formed to protect his badly damaged soul. I was fascinated to read how Robert's personalities were initially unaware of each other. Functioning as totally separate individuals. Experiencing life in dramatically different ways. It would take Robert years of hard, diligent, therapeutic work, and a most loving and supportive wife, to bring all these personalities together. A few remain. Most have been integrated into the Robert who wrote the book.

I share this with you because, as I read this haunting book, I often thought of the church. Yes, the Christian church. It struck me how Christianity is hopelessly divided. There are Christian churches whose worship feels foreign to me. Some Christians speak of Christ as if He were a best buddy, or someone they owned. Dogma, doctrine, and denominationalism have wreaked havoc on the Christian church as a whole. The faces of the church are myriad. A few churches have had one too many facelifts. They barely resemble Jesus, as I understand him.

It is as if the church is stuck in adolescence. Churches competing and comparing. Ripping one another apart. Putting one belief system down, in order to push their own up. Many churches still ridiculously claiming to be the only true church. The place where the "real Christians" go. An exclusive club. A large cliché. It is a sad and juvenile way for the church to exist. The Christian church needs a huge dose of maturity. To celebrate its wonderful diversity. To learn how to dialogue and compromise. To find common ground. It is happening here and there within the church, but it seems that every step forward is met with a resounding call to take five steps backward. Ironically, this was exactly the same battle that Robert Oxnam waged during his early adulthood.

I would like you to feel comfortable with Christianity. I want you to know something about the Christian church. No, this is not an invitation to join. I would simply like to describe some of what you might find there. I would hope you could feel familiar with some of its rituals. At ease with its spiritual habits and customs. Aware of the theology and belief system. Conscious of the ethical and moral stands it takes. But I can't! There is no one church. There is no single paradigm for being a Christian. The differences are dramatic. Night and day. The range of Christian belief is as wide as the sky. At best, I can familiarize you with the spectrum of Christian belief. Offer you some insight into why differences exist. Explain how Jesus remains the single thread uniting all these churches together.

I want you to feel at home with both Christianity and the church. But I am not sure this is feasible. Christianity has more facets that a five-carat diamond. Christians differ widely in belief and practice. Tying this together would require magic. Since I am no magician, I will simply try to share with you my impressions of the Christian church. Big bold strokes. Major themes. Theological currents that traverse the whole terrain of Christianity. This time, feeling at home will amount to no more than comfort. A certain comfort level. Not ready to move in, but at least knowing the address. Being familiar with the layout. Perhaps having picked out your room.

pyramids and rainbows

The Christian church is human. Because it is human, it is also political. The politics of the church are formally called polity. It means how the church organizes itself—its structure, the way it chooses to function. For many churches, there are ample rules and regulations. Dogmas and doctrines to uphold. We Presbyterians have a manual titled *The Book of Order*. Though it can be a handy tool for conducting church business, it is also a monument to the human need to have things neat and in order. To be in control. The hallmark of the Presbyterian church is definitely the committee.

Each church has a different form of governance. A different take on the Bible. A different vision of how the church should manifest itself on Earth. And, of course, each church has its own unique voice. The accents may be varied. At times it may sound as if we are speaking some strange dialect. Impossible to fully understand, even if occasionally it seems vaguely familiar. At times we may be speaking altogether different languages.

In confirmation class I explain how the Presbyterian church was the model for the government of the United States. It is a system of checks and balances. A system that both demands and celebrates democracy. Shows respect for the individual faith. In Presbyterianism, the pastor is the minister, but not the ministry. Rather, the congregation is the ministry. The congregation selects the pastor. Elects elders and deacons to lead the church family. And is the bottom line for all decisions made regarding church life. The congregation is accountable to the Presbytery, the ruling body of church elders within a district. The Presbytery is accountable to the Synod, a larger regional body. Everyone is accountable to the General Assembly—a yearly gathering of ministers and lay leaders who establish the vision and voice for the church for the year.

I see the Presbyterian system as a rainbow. It has no top or bottom. No real rankings or hierarchies. There are the congregations, each one unique, each respected for its style and substance. Ministers being of no greater value than lay, and understood simply as chosen leaders. Congregations and congregants having no special status. No one whose vote or voice counts more than that of anyone else. A rainbow is an excellent symbol for true democracy. No rungs on the ladder. No hoops to jump through. Simply the rainbow itself—an arc of absolute equality.

I was formerly Lutheran. The Lutheran church is structured more like a pyramid. There is a bishop, who has tremendous control over when and where a minister will work. Though congregations have power, it is clear that the authority lies with the pastor. As a Presbyterian, though, I cannot conduct a wedding or baptism or funeral without an elder present. The elder is there to represent the faithful intent of the people. As a minister in the Lutheran church, I could perform rites of the church without consent or any layperson's being present. Small but quite symbolic differences. Simply put, the Lutheran church gives ministers and bishops far greater power than lay leaders. It has a clearly defined hierarchy.

> "If we cannot now end our differences, at least we can help make the world safe for diversity."
> —JOHN F. KENNEDY

The Catholic church remains the best example of a pyramid structure. We start at the top with the Pope, who is also seen to be infallible, beyond questioning. Then come the cardinals and archbishops, followed by the bishops and priests and nuns. Finally, the congregations and the laypeople themselves. These are very clear rungs of leadership and spiritual authority. A priest receives the confession of a layperson, without the individual's going directly to God. Only a priest can celebrate a mass. Only a priest can perform most rites of the church.

The pyramid structure is also at work in declaring the ethical stance of the church. Take abortion, for example. The Catholic church is not a democracy. Though there are many pro-choice Catholics, the fact remains that the church as a whole is expected to follow the dictates of the Pope. This is not open to debate. The is a done deal, and it is done at the top. In Vatican City, where the religious establishment lives and works. The Vatican itself is a clear indication of the pyramid structure. Only those at the top are allowed access to its innards.

Catholic. Anglican. Episcopalian. Lutheran. Presbyterian. Methodist. Congregational. Baptist. Evangelical. Born-again. Quaker. Unitarian. From the highly hierarchical, Catholic, Anglican, Episcopalian, Lutheran, to the Quakers, who often function without liturgy or clergy, the Christian church finds multiple ways to express its faith in Jesus Christ. Polity being only one of them. Either a pyramid model, with a clear-cut small top, larger middle, and massive bottom. Or a rainbow, where parity of colors is the rule. Many varying structures are used to bring people together. To create community. To enable a gathering to become a congregation. A congregation to become a church family.

literal or liberal

Another major point of division within the Christian church is the matter of the Bible. Is it the literal truth? The ultimate authority, with the final say? No doubt about it. Black-and-white. No wiggle room. No allowance for interpretation. *Or* is it a collection of stories and sagas, poetry and metaphor, fact and fiction, history and myth, legend and fairy tale? Isn't it all open to interpretation? Isn't is all a matter of faith? An issue of personal perspective? Aren't those ministers who claim to know exactly what the Bible says, in point of fact, playing God?!

> "America is a religious nation, but only because it is rigorously tolerant and lets every citizen pray, in his own way."
> —FROM AN EDITORIAL IN *THE NEW YORK TIMES*

In the spirit of David Letterman, here are my top 10 beliefs about the Bible. Read them not as a list of rules, but as a perspective shared:

1. The Bible should not be worshiped.

2. The Bible is not a book of answers.

3. The Bible has the right questions.

4. The Bible was intended to be a means of inspiration, not indoctrination.

5. The Bible requires excellent scholarship if it is to be even minimally understood.

6. Much of the Bible is an expression of faith. Trying to put into words what can never be adequately expressed.

7. The Bible can be terribly confusing, even contradictory. It is riddled with mysteries.

8. The Bible continues to be written by the Holy Spirit. Written in human lives. Each of us is called to write a fifth gospel with our own life.

9. The Bible must never be a means of dividing people. Keeping us from loving one another. Preventing compassion from being experienced. Mercy shared.

10. The Bible is not the whole Word of God. All experiences of the presence of God are the Word. The Bible is, however, an amazingly reliable source of the Word of God.

The power I bestow upon the Bible is in terms of respect and interest. I am devoted to its study. I do not kneel to it, nor do I believe I am required to obey its contents. It does not rule me. But it is a profound source of wisdom for me. Its influence is enormous. It has informed my ethics and morals. I never lose interest in what it has to say to my life, or about Life as a whole. It is the Bible that taught me to look for God's handwriting on Life's pages, for the rest of my life.

My approach to the Bible is liberal. "Liberal" is not a bad word. It means tolerant. Open-minded. Willing to compromise. Building consensus. Being fair and respectful of other viewpoints. Mature enough to be questioned or doubted. Unafraid of inquiry or debate. Welcoming of dialogue. Liberal means not rigid or unyielding. Not legalistic or self-righteous. Not superior or condescending. To be liberal is to be flexible and adaptable. Not flexible as in lacking a backbone, but flexible as in being aware that one must keep on growing and changing and maturing.

the call to be a community

Christianity is shaped by churches. It is a religion built on and by churches. These churches are a gathering of folks around a particular style of worship and polity, centered on hearing a particular minister or choir or both, or established as the result of tradition, ritual, or custom. Scripture tells us that the church is a place of intimacy. It refers to the church as the people of a God. A family or household. A bride of Christ or the body of Christ. Each image is highly personal. The church is to be a place where we feel spiritually at home. It is here that we should feel comfortable enough to confess our sins, or offer our most passionate praise. Here where we will share our sorrow or joy. From a funeral to a baptism, a wedding to Sunday worship, church

> "Life is a gift for which we are grateful. We gather in community to celebrate the glories and mysteries of this great gift." —MARJORIE MONTGOMERY

is where we gather to celebrate the spiritual movements of our lives.

As an institution, the church expresses a belief by its very existence. A belief that we members of it can accomplish more together than we can alone. An admission of just how much we really need one another. A wish to experience the true power of community. The desire to belong to something larger than ourselves. Something that will support and sustain us. Challenge us to be true to our real Selves. Inspire us to be better than we dreamed we could be. A true community can be a furnace of transformation. A context that enables us to bud, blossom, and flourish. In the same spirit as Jesus choosing to surround Himself with a band of disciples, the church expresses the capacity of community to do and to be ministry.

the call to be disciples

Christians are called to be disciples. They are encouraged to follow the way of Jesus. They are challenged to pick up their crosses—to face the problems and issues of their lives. What do we mean by discipleship? In part, we mean carrying on the legacy of the first 12 disciples of Jesus. We look to them as spiritual role models for what to do and be. We also can use them as guides for what not to do or be. The disciples were decidedly human. At times, a real motley crew. So diverse they could barely agree on anything. They doubted. They betrayed. They denied Jesus even existed.

They competed for Jesus' affections and worldly fame. Still, they were good examples of ordinary lives lived with extraordinary faith.

Every church has a different perspective of discipleship. At the core, however, I suspect you will find most disciples sharing many of the following character traits:

1. Patient and kind

2. Willing to serve others

3. Ready to make sacrifices

4. Tender hearted and tolerant

5. Gracious and generous

6. Forgiven and forgiving

7. Courageous

8. Mature

9. Holding deep convictions

10. Being fully alive

11. Awake, alert, and aware

12. Faith full, hope full, joy full

13. Happy

14. Wise

15. Believes in miracles

16. Loves a good mystery

Quite a formidable list. Being a disciple is not easy. It will take practice. It is an art form. Most of all, obviously, it will take discipline. Discipleship requires a person to have life in focus. To know what ultimately matters to them. What their top priorities are. What they are willing to live and die for. A true disciple leads a life that is the genuine good life. It is all about goodness. Being good. Doing good.

Think about it for a moment. Whom do you know who possess the qualities listed above? How do you measure up? What do you think of the list? Did you notice some of the seemingly glaring contradictions? To serve and sacrifice, and to be happy. Is that possible? Only from a spiritual perspective. Only when we see our lives through Jesus' eyes. Only when we conform our heart to Christ's.

Many of us think of discipline (which comes from the root of "disciple") as a negative. A grind. Beating us down. Holding us back. Wearing us out. I believe Jesus saw discipline in a whole new light. He saw discipline

> "The central task of the religious community is to unveil the bonds that bind each to all. There is a connectedness, a relationship discovered amid the particulars of our own lives and the lives of others. Once felt, it inspires us to act for justice.
>
> "It is the church that assures us that we are not struggling for justice on our own, but as members of a larger community. The religious community is essential, for alone our vision is too narrow to see all that must be seen, and our strength too limited to do all that must be done. Together, our vision widens and our strength is renewed."
> —MARK MORRISON-REED

as the way to freedom. He told His followers they were free to obey. Jesus saw discipline as the means to becoming the people we were created to be. Not wasting time or talent on trivial pursuits. Not climbing ladders that lead nowhere, except to a fall. Not being a success in the world's eyes, but failures in God's. Discipline brings out our best. It forces us to conform our will to Christ's. It frees us to be genuine. Good. That is the crux of the matter—we finally get to do and be good without being ashamed.

If you are to feel at home with Christianity and the church, you will need to comprehend the role of the disciple. It is primarily a role of following. Trying to be an instrument of God's Grace. In point of fact, trying to *be Jesus*. To inhabit His Spirit. To be inhabited by His Spirit. To be swallowed whole by His hope. To be at one with Him. Like synchronized swimmers after years of practice. In synch, functioning as a unit. To understand being a Christian is to be aware of the role and the responsibilities of being a disciple. Many are called, but few are chosen. This means that many aspiring disciples talk the talk, but few of them walk the walk. How many true disciples do you know?

> "Self-respect is the fruit of discipline; the sense of dignity grows with the ability to say no to oneself." —ABRAHAM JOSHUA HESCHEL

One last thing. Discipleship demands choice. You cannot worship money and material things, and also claim to worship Jesus Christ. You cannot say you believe in Jesus Christ and still consciously act like a bigot. Discipleship expects a decision. A yes or no. Are you following me, or not? You cannot follow without movement. Without standing up for something. Without walking the way. Without taking the road less traveled. To the beat of a different drummer. These choices are neither

"Discipline is remembering what you want."
—DAVID CAMPBELL

easy or popular. The choices made by true disciples often lead to risk, ridicule, even persecution.

The call of the world is deafening. Make it big. Be a somebody. Be a winner. Grab your piece of the pie. Live as if there is no tomorrow. Do it until you are satisfied. Image is everything. The call of the world makes a lot of noise. An incessant drone, like the background music at a supermarket or on an elevator. It is difficult to choose to follow the path of the disciple. A path that promises pain. A journey that may lead to a personal cross. Being a disciple is not for sissies. It is also not for the immature. One more thing: If following Jesus does lead to popularity and climbing the social ladder, it is an artificial Jesus you are following. Trust me.

church ritual and routine

Have you ever noticed how every home has a particular smell? Unique to that family? Like it or not, it is true. We all have a family scent. We also have family rules, roles, rituals, and routines. Ways we celebrate a birthday or a holiday. How we discipline or negotiate. How we communicate. How we express our dissatisfactions or dreams. How we grieve. What we do with guilt. How we forgive. Most of all, how we love. We are a family, and every family has a style of living. A lifestyle.

So it is with the church. Each church will have a different focus on how its members worship. Some use upbeat contemporary music. Others only sacred and classical. Still others have no music at all. Some churches adhere to a formal liturgy, while others let the Spirit move them as it will. I would say the common ingredients in most Christian worship are as follows:

1. Time for prayer

2. A time to confess sins or wrongdoing

3. The singing of hymns

4. Scripture is read

5. Sermons are preached

6. A financial offering is taken

7. The sacrament of baptism may be performed

8. The sacrament of communion may be shared

9. Time to announce church family activities

10. Time for meditation and reflection

11. Often a choir that sings an anthem or two

12. It is also quite common to have prayer requests made, for folks who have passed or are suffering in some way

Most churches also conduct Sunday School for the benefit of children and youth. Many have youth programs that meet weekly. The minister or deacons, or other designated lay leaders, take care of home or hospital visitation. Committees are formed to administer everything from finances to the church decorations.

Sacraments are designated by scripture as an expectation of a Christian and of the church itself. Baptism is a ceremonial washing that initiates the individual into the faith community. Some churches baptize infants, authorizing the parents and godparents or the larger church family to help raise the child in the ways of Jesus Christ. Other churches believe that baptism is for adults only. Done when a person can make the decision to follow on their own. The role of baptism, together with the beliefs surrounding it, is quite varied. In the Presbyterian church, baptism is an official welcoming of a child into the church family. The child's parents make a promise to include Christ and the church in the child's upbringing. Presbyterians do not see baptism as required for entrance into heaven. I know of no Christian church that does not include baptism within the spiritual life of its congregation. Dunking or dipping. Sprinkling or spattering. There is probably a church somewhere that uses a hose. The symbol is the same—a fresh start afforded by a new relationship to Jesus Christ, washed clean by His blood.

Communion is also a sacrament. The bread and wine represent the body and blood of Jesus. In the Catholic church, the bread and wine is thought to be the *real* body and blood of Jesus. It has been transformed. In most churches, the belief is symbolic. In all cases, the sacrament of communion is believed to be a vital means of creating connectedness to Christ. This sacred meal nourishes the soul. Offers the recipient strength and support. It was at the Last Supper that Jesus ordained the communion meal as a feast of remembrance in His name. As an infusion of the Holy Spirit. As a vital means for drawing close to Him. "Do this in remembrance of me." These are the words Jesus spoke. For the Christian, what we are remembering when we take communion is the length to which Jesus went to show us His love. To being nailed to a cross. To a brutal, drawn-out death. For the Christian, this is a bittersweet meal. A spiritual feast of great substance. A small morsel and drink, which offers big help to the Christian.

> "Love is the spirit of this church, and service its law. This is our great covenant: to dwell together in peace, to seek the truth in love, and to help one another."
> —JAMES VILA BLAKE

Christianity is diverse. The range of churches is equally so. It is important to find a church that you can feel at home in. You will want to ask questions about a church's polity, worship style, and theological perspective. Don't hesitate to be aggressive in finding a church that is a good fit for your spiritual needs. I do not believe in going to church simply to feel less guilt. God does not take attendance. Church needs to meet your spiritual needs. You also need to be invited to participate in the ministry. To offer your gifts, as well. There will never be a perfect fit. There will never be a perfect minister, even if some churches seem hell-bent on finding one. Every congregation will be loaded with human flaws. The key is whether or not you feel yourself growing there. Does the church inspire you? Are you being challenged to mature? Does worship make you think? Invite your deepest feelings? Touch your heart? Tug at your soul? If it does, then you have found a church home. Obviously, all this must be predicated on a belief in Jesus Christ. Otherwise, why be there?

The church continues to preach the message of Jesus. Continues His ministry. It is the church that is called and created to keep Jesus alive and well and in our midst. Preaching good news to the poor. Binding broken hearts. Calling for peacemaking and justice. Encouraging forgiveness and unconditional love. Being a sanctuary, a safe haven. The church is to be a place where your soul is spiritually nourished, given its "marching orders," and sent out into the world to build the Kingdom of God. The church is meant as a place of Grace. A spiritual home, where Jesus still functions as the head of the family. A home where all the voices of the family are shown respect. Where love rules.

PART TWO

B^{EI}NG AT H^OME

My favorite story in Scripture is the parable of the prodigal son. It is found in the Gospel of Luke. The fifteenth chapter, verses 11–32. Let me paraphrase the story for you. Putting

it in contemporary language we can easily understand.

Once upon a time there was a father with two sons. The older son was obedient and good. He did his duties, and made a significant contribution to life on the farm. The younger brother was just as good, but not nearly so obedient. He found life on the farm to be a drag. He was bored to death.

On one of the younger son's worst days, frustrated out of his mind with the routine of farm life, the endless chores, he went to his father and made a rather obscene demand. He basically told his father to drop dead. He asked for his inheritance now. He had places to go and things to see. Shockingly, the father gave it to him. The father was moved to tears as the younger son strode off into the sunset. The older brother smirked smugly and never said good-bye to the younger.

The younger son loved life in the big city. Many nights he partied all night long. He sowed more than a few wild oats. He became a lady's man. He drank barrels of wine. He spent money like it was going out of style. Eventually, he ran out. The money vanished from loose living. There was more bad news. A famine had hit the region. Folks were starving. The young son was forced to flee the big city just to find something to eat.

He wound up chowing down at a pig trough. All of which gave new meaning to the phrase, hitting bottom. On his knees slurping down muddy oats, he came to his senses. He said to himself, "I need to get home. Even my father's workers are treated better than Life is treating me now. At least I will get three good meals a day, a warm bed, and a roof over my head. I don't deserve to be called his son anymore, but maybe my father will take me back as a laborer. It is worth the risk. The humiliation." Wounded in soul and heartbroken, he headed for home. All the way he was wracked by guilt. He was deeply ashamed of his actions. Appalled by his own foolishness. Facing his father would be a nightmare of embarrassment. He could not even imagine seeing his older brother. What could he say? What words would adequately express his remorse? How can you say you are sorry for such gross unloving behavior?

As he dragged himself along the road, he thought he saw something coming toward him. It was foggy and vague, but struck a chord of familiarity. As the vision came nearer, the young son was dumbstruck to see it was his father. Running. A waddling gallop, coming at him with arms opened wide for an embrace. The young man was moved to run. Tears trailed down his cheeks.

Father and son literally crashed into each other. Spinning round and round. Tears and laughter.

A tornado of love.

Though the son was ready to become a farm hand, or at least go to his room and be grounded for life, the father

had other ideas. The father wanted to throw a huge party.
A celebration with all of their family and friends. He wanted
to have the best food, and even make sure his son had a new
suit to wear to the party. It would be the social event of the
year. A huge feast. People came from far and wide. They ate
and drank and danced. They laughed and cried and talked.
The father gave thanks before the meal, and spoke in
wobbly voice of his love for his beloved child. "My boy was
lost, but now he is found." He could say no more. Nothing
else needed to be said. He had said it all. The young son was
home. Now about the older son. He was furious. He pouted
during the whole party, refusing to step foot on the dance
floor. He refused to eat a thing. He told his father it was
unfair. He was the good son. His brother had squandered his
fortune, and was no longer worthy of respect, let alone love.
The young brother was a loser. He would always be a loser.
Just wait and see. The older son spoke with confidence,
certain his young sibling would screw up again. "Then who
will clean up his mess? I may not stick around this time.
Who will pick up the slack? Do all his work for him?" He
spoke with a voice of dripping sarcasm. The older son was
brimming with the arrogance of worldly wisdom.

His father came to see him. Sought to console him.
The father had no real answer for the claim of unfairness.
He knew it was unfair, at least in the eyes of the world. But
to God, it was more than fair. It was right. To God all that
mattered was a beloved child had come back home. He was
once lost, but now was found. The father still had celebration trembling in his voice. The young son danced all night
at his party. He could not believe how good it felt to be
home again.

There was no place like home. No place on earth.

I believe Jesus wants you to feel at home. I believe
Jesus is calling you and me to come home. Coming home is
a daily decision. A process. A matter of baby steps. Inching
our way back to where we can truly be who we were created
to be. No masks or phoniness. No competing or comparing
ourselves with others. No rat race. No climbing silly ladders
of success. No, the Jesus of my faith wants us to give up our
bright lights, big city dreams, and come home to the simple
ordinary good life on the farm. A life that is good enough
because we are good enough. A life where we can feel at
ease. Relaxed and ready to receive. A place where we will be
fully present. Aware and available. Living fully in the now.
Rejoicing in the gift of the moment.

Jesus celebrates your homecoming. He will throw a party for those who see the light. Those who find themselves at the bottom, a pig trough, and are wise enough to come to their senses and come home. Why? Because he wants you to be you. That is all. Nothing more. But it is everything. He wants you to be you, because you are a beloved child of God. You are respected and cherished. Adored. Jesus wants you to know the embrace of Grace. God's passionate love for you. God's belief in you. Yes you! Jesus wants to lift up your chin and stare you in the eyes. To communicate to you how much you matter. How much God cares.

Obviously, I am not talking here about coming home to your hometown or birthplace. I mean coming home to the real you. Adolescence is a prodigal age. A time meant for moving away. Rebelling. Sowing wild oats. Every adolescent spends half of their time complaining they are bored to death. It is only when they come home they begin to realize they are simply bored with themselves. Coming home for an adolescent means coming back to Life. On Life's terms. It means accepting Life and Self, flaws and all. It is being confident you are enough in God's eyes.

It is my profound hope this book helps you to find your way back home. To hear what Jesus has to say about life on the farm. I want you to take a look at the map Jesus offers. It is a map that asks you to follow. Again, I stress, the choice of following this particular map is up to you. I simply hope you will consider what Jesus has to say. Think about it. Reflect upon it. Pray on it. Remain open to it. It will help. I believe that. It will help you locate your spiritual home. A place where you feel centered, grounded, content, satisfied, energized, enthused, dreaming dreams, knowing hope and joy, and loving it all to the hilt.

Every adolescent has big dreams. Most have some pretty outrageous hopes. Expectations which reach for the stars. This is as it should and must be. Think of these wishes as bubbles. Small universes. Floating and flying. Reflecting rainbows on their thin surface. The world, and many adults who populate it, see it as their job to poke these bubbles with sharp pins. "Just wait until you hit the real world!" "Just who do you think you are?" "Don't be ridiculous, what do you think your chances are of accomplishing that?" "You need to leave the fantasy world, and bring it down to reality." These pin pricks work. They also hurt. Many adolescent dreams have been dashed by adult warriors and a wicked world, armed to the teeth with sharp objects of scorn.

Home is a place and a people where these bubbles get to float. High and far. Think of the people who are home for you, as those who chase after these bubbles, and as they lazily head earthward, blow with all their might to keep them afloat. Home is a belief in you. A faith. The people of home will do anything to help you become your dreams. And when a bubble bursts, these are the folks who will remind you that you are already enough, and then help you launch aloft another bubbled dream.

Like the Wizard of Oz, Jesus wants you to know you already possess all you need to have a good life. A beautiful life. A life of sweet satisfaction and abundant fun. Remember, the Wizard was not a bad man, he just wasn't all that hot at being a wizard. He gave people what they already possessed. He really could only point people in the direction of home. He could not take them there. So it is with Jesus. He gives us back our Selves. He points the way home.

Coming home. Coming back. Returning to being the person you were created to be. Not some social image. Coming home to your real Self. Being at home in your body. With your sexuality. In your mind and heart and soul. With your family and friends. At school, or in the world. Being at home is to be true. It is to live that truth. It is claiming in faith your right and responsibility to be your Self.

But remember: There are expectations. Consequences. Imagine the prodigal son, who is now nestled in his own bed at home, waking up to a knock on the door. He answers it, only to find a young pregnant girl, begging for a meal and a bed to sleep. We expect him to throw open the door. To invite her in. To offer her food and lodging. We expect he will be a new person now that he is back home. He will be his godly self. Not lazy or selfish. Gracious and kind. We assume this to be the case. It is the assumption of faith. The trust we show in believing Jesus creates new life.

8

BEING AT HOME
WITH BEING HUMAN

I need to start this chapter with a strange story. Well, maybe not all that strange, but a little gross. I apologize. But it does the trick, makes the point I need to make. Bear with me, and try to follow the story.

I went to St. Olaf College, a great school in Northfield, Minnesota. I miss it to this day. I went to college during the infamous late 1960s. During my junior year, there was a nationwide student strike to protest the war in Vietnam. The strike had been initiated by Princeton University, where organizers called for a moratorium to begin on, I believe, April 15. The cause and the strike spread like wildfire. St. Olaf became part of that strike at a community-wide gathering that voted to join the cause. The community debate and vote were orderly, civil, and passionate, and included a surprise birthday cake for the college president, Sidney Rand.

Hearing the entire campus community singing "Happy Birthday" was pretty moving, considering the circumstances.

I recall the moratorium as being a time rich in intimacy, dialogue, learning—a time when we students were challenged to be involved in our world and our own lives. Socially, politically, economically, ethically, and morally. I had never heard faculty members and students share their thoughts and feelings so openly or candidly. I had such respect for the restraint shown by the administrators, who worked long and hard to cope with a situation they had never faced before. Those administrators gave new meaning to the words "patient" and "kind." They felt responsible for the well-being of all of us. I know this was no small, easy task.

I won't ever forget the debate between Major Thorpe, of the Political Science department, and Howard Hong, of Philosophy. It was an extraordinary event on campus. Held at the Lion's Pause, then a campus snack bar and hangout. The place was mobbed. The debate fierce. The ideas well-spoken on both sides. No answers, just a slew of questions. Except for Major Thorpe calling Howard "Dr. Cong," it was education at its very best.

Early in May, a Community Council was formed. Students, faculty, and administrators were all represented on it. Our mission was to guide the campus through this extraordinary time. How would we be graded? How would seniors handle applying for graduate schools? Would there even be a graduation? What about final exams and papers? There were other issues as well. The unspoken fear of violence. The question of outside intruders or political inter-ference. The unanswered question of just when the moratorium would be over. How would the campus have been affected? How would things have changed? Would it be permanent or temporary? These concerns included the Community Council itself.

A day-long retreat was planned. It was to be held at a rustic camp near campus. Nothing fancy, but away from it all, so participants could get down to the difficult business at hand. The first morning was hard work. Emotions were getting frayed. We were trying to take on too much, too fast. Problems were being set up like dominos, and as each one fell, another fell as well. The complexity of the situation was incredible. We took a break. Thank God. I really had to go to the bathroom. Number 2. I sprinted to the stall, and was quickly seated. Just in time. It was only then that I noticed there were no doors on these stalls. Across from me, doing the same thing, horror of horrors, was President Sidney Rand. I was desperate for an escape route. There were none. Wiping myself in front of him was out of the question. Watching him wipe was even worse. We never spoke. We avoided eye contact like the

> "The truth about a man is, first of all, what it is that he keeps hidden."
> —ANDRE MALRAUX

plague. I kept my head bowed until I heard him buckle up and shuffle off. The relief was enormous. How embarrass-ing. I could not look at the man for the rest of the retreat, or for the remainder of spring semester, for that matter.

Now, here is my point. I am sorry it took a while to get to. We are all human. We all take a dump. We all pretend we don't. Why are we humiliated by something so common? Why is this so horrible? Unspeakable? Well, part of it is that we just don't need to watch. Simple as that. We know it happens, but we have no need to be a spectator, as if it were a sporting event. But it goes beyond that. It goes to our difficulty in seeing ourselves and others as being *just human*. Just human. Why do we say it as if it is something puny or pathetic? Why are we so uncomfortable with the notion of our own humanity?

Coming home begins on the day you can celebrate being a human being. When you can accept that it is the will of God for humans to be human. We spend a lifetime trying to be anything but human. We try to play God. We attempt to be perfect. We strive to be like robots. Efficient and flawless. We are the victims of our own grandiosity. Our artificial arrogance. Home is when and where we can stop pretending to be something we are not. Something God would never hope us to be. A swollen head with a shriveled heart. God wants us to come home to being fully and honestly human. But what does this mean?

being human = dying

It means we die. Every day we are living, we are also dying. It is a fact of life. This is not a dress rehearsal. It is the performance. We hope to make it the performance of our lives. Home is where you know you cannot pretend to be something you are not. This means being immortal. If you are to become a spiritual person, a mature individual, you must accept the conditions of Life, which includes our terminal nature. Jesus makes us face this truth. His own death serves as a vivid reminder that we all must die. His ministry was neither a denial of death nor an attempt to escape it. Jesus chose to face death head on. To claim His fear and move beyond it. Full of faith. He asks us to do the same.

Death is a powerful mentor. I recently took my high school youth group out into the graveyard behind the church. We gathered in a quadrant marked by four large maple trees. I told the group that the folks buried there were more like them than they imagined. Buried there were folks who had wants and wishes, needs and dreams, passions and heartbreaks, successes and failures—just like them. No matter when they died or who they were, it was their humanity that bound us to them, the living to the dead. I next asked what these folks might say if they could come back. I asked my youth to imagine a spiritual presence arriving right now—a ghost, a spirit, however you understand such. I asked my youth to imagine a spiritual visitation from beyond. What would that visitor have to say about Life and how it should be lived? I asked the youth to close their eyes and contemplate for a full five minutes. They later said the five minutes felt like five hours. They reluctantly let themselves reflect upon the spiritual assignment. Here are some of their responses:

1. Don't sweat the small stuff

2. Don't waste your time or talent

3. Live life to the fullest

4. Forgive people, and don't hold a grudge

5. Be true to your Self

6. Don't try to impress others

7. Don't spend a lot of time worrying about what you cannot do much about

8. Listen to your life; listen to your Self

9. Don't ever live a lie

10. Pay attention, especially to the little things

11. Notice the beauty around you

12. Appreciate what you have

13. Count your blessings—often

14. Have a positive attitude

15. Have faith

16. Be generous

17. Be hopeful

18. Look for the best in others

19. Make somebody's day

20. Share a good laugh, share a good cry

That's a pretty formidable list, both poignant and profound. Death has much to teach. We need to let it in, to learn with it and from it. Strange as it may sound, we need to learn how to die. It is a major aspect of both spiritual growth and the human experience.

being human = feelings

Feelings are neither positive or negative. They are simply present. Neutral. Like Switzerland, they exist, but are not meant to take a stand. They are there to inform us. To keep us posted. To offer us insight into what we are experiencing, and how this may be affecting us. I often think of feelings as God's vocabulary. I believe God often expresses Himself or Herself best in the simple language of emotions.

Jesus is an advocate of experiencing our emotions. Naming and claiming them. When He loses His friend Lazarus, He weeps (John 11:35). When He sees people ripping off others at the Temple, by selling doves for three and four times what they were worth, He gets furious; He actually tips over tables to demonstrate His anger (John 2:14–16). Jesus feels compassion for those who suffered (Matthew 14:14). He invites

> "Feelings are everywhere— be gentle." —J. MASAI

people who are weary and depressed to find rest with him (Matthew 11:28–30). When Martha is full of fussing and fretting, He warns her not to sweat the small stuff (Luke 10:41–42). Jesus is not stoic. He is not detached. He is never callous. He is a man of great warmth and sensitivity, and He feels things deeply, humanly.

I find adolescents having a tough time with emotions. Trying to pretend not to feel what they so clearly do feel. How many times have you been jealous, and could not admit it? How many of us go down to the basement to retrieve something, and then race to the top of the steps, still afraid of the boogeyman at age 17, or 57? Why is it so hard to admit that we are afraid? How many of us have cried ourselves to sleep, because we have been badly hurt by a friend? How many of us have fallen in love, only to have the feeling not reciprocated? How many of us worry ourselves sick, while trying to act cool, calm, and collected? How many teen suicides could be prevented by simply encouraging young people to admit when they are depressed?

I may be wrong about this, and I do not mean to offend anyone by my conjecture, but I wonder what might have happened at Columbine High School, had emotions been honestly expressed and bullying behavior addressed. What if the two boys who did the shooting had been able to talk about their sadness, sense of isolation, and the teasing they experienced? What if they had been able tell their parents of their swarming unhappiness? What if there had been a way for them to let others know how it feels to be on the outside looking in? Orbiting the popular crowd. Angry and getting angrier. Stuffing down what you feel. Becoming like a volcano, and then, when you erupt, the damage can be considerable. What if . . . ? What if being a man did not mean shooting a gun, but the honest expression of an emotion?

Jesus wants you to come home to your Self. This includes the spectrum of what you feel. The difficult emotions, the complex ones, the ridiculous ones. From the silliest little fears to the biggest disappointments. The harder we try to deny what we feel, the more energy we apply to holding our feelings in or down. And the unhealthier we become. We lose not only energy and time, we lose contact with our soul. What happens to these emotions? They do not go away. They can fester, be transferred unfairly to somebody else, even become the means for scapegoating others. Feelings are meant to be felt. Noted and expressed. Named and claimed. Dealt with and integrated into our lives. In a nutshell, learned from. They are never meant to be denied.

> "Jesus Christ is easily the most important figure in the history of mankind. It makes no difference how you may regard him, you will have to concede that. This is true whether you choose to call him God or man; and, if man, whether you choose to consider him as the world's greatest Prophet and Teacher, or merely as a well-intentioned fanatic who came to grief, and failure, and ruin, after a short and stormy public career.... [His teachings] have influenced the course of history...more than Alexander, or Caesar, or Charlemagne, or Napoleon, or Washington." — EMMET FOX, *THE SERMON ON THE MOUNT*

The basic message is this: If I do not know what you feel, I do not know you. I do not know your soul, your spirit, your essence. I may be acquainted with your image, but I haven't a clue about who you truly are. Our best friends are those who know our emotions both before and while they are being felt. For me, this is what enables me to call Jesus a friend. I feel known by Jesus Christ. Understood and accepted. Even those feelings for which I feel shame. I know that Jesus not only accepts but affirms me and them. It is just a feeling. Again, neither bad nor good. Simply a bit of spiritual information being passed along by a wise God.

being human = co-creator

Being human is not all about fragility, flaws, and failing. God has also given you dominion over this Earth. Dominion, notice—not domination. What does this mean? It means that God understands you to be a co-creator with Him. You are called upon to create Life. Not just physically. Emotionally and spiritually, as well. This creativity may be expressed in the writing of a poem, the composing of a song, the repairing of an engine, the climbing of a mountain, the building of a solid relationship. Creativity is not being artsy-craftsy. It means having the courage to use your gifts. To know what you are talented in, and to choose to demonstrate those abilities. Creativity is all about making something, making good, making peace, making a living. Most important, making a life.

What are you doing or being when you lose track of time? Whatever that is, it is then that you have gone to Heaven. Heaven is not a time or place. It is not endless time. It is the absence of time. Losing track of time is when Heaven has come to Earth. Are you aware of your gifts? Do you claim your talents? Are you ready and willing to discipline your passions? Creative folks take the risk of failing. They risk flops. They also take the leap of faith. They strive to make the world a bit better by adding a touch of their own talent. Creativity is action. It is choosing to live your longings. It is not procrastinating, not wasting time, not being lazy. It is an investment of time and energy and talent. It is trying to make a difference in the world.

Humans make a difference. We matter. We are capable of great things. Masterpieces. We are also capable of doing little things with great love, which was the spiritual mantra of Mother Teresa. We create things—new ideas, a new life, a new world. We can inspire change. We can ignite transformation. Jesus was one solitary man. Think of what was accomplished by His brief time on Earth. Then think of Jesus' belief that you can do even greater things than He.

 ## being human = forgiven and forgiving

We are human. We are imperfect. We make mistakes. We can be hateful and spiteful. We can be mean and manipulative. We can lie with a straight face, and with a crooked one.

We can claim to love that which we, in fact, hate. We can say we believe in something for which we have only polite contempt. We can dash someone's hopes, and walk away as if it never happened. We may not even be aware that it happened. So we all need to be forgiven. Every day. We need to work at being rigorously honest with ourselves. Seeing ourselves for who we truly are.

There is no greater test of one's maturity than the capacity to forgive, as well as the recognition of our own human need to be forgiven. The individual who can admit to their flaws and failings, who can say out loud when they have acted with malice or conceit, who will repent for a wrong done knowingly, or even without a clue—that is a person of substance. A person in process. A soul striving to improve, to become whole, to be more loving.

Jesus wants you to know you are forgiven. Jesus expects you to forgive. Do you forgive? Can you? How many relationships have you lost in the past year, strictly as a result of your refusal to forgive? How many folks have you blatantly hurt, but as yet cannot admit your actions to? How many lies have you told, to others and yourself? How many times have you faked concern or caring? How many times have you covered your own butt, rather than face up to a mistake you made? I wince in pondering my own answers to these questions.

> "Forgiving and being forgiven are two names for the same thing. The important thing is that a discord has been resolved." —C. S. LEWIS

When we know forgiveness, we know home. We can feel a wondrous sense of ease. A calming of the soul. A settling down of the spirit. The fury vanishes. The waters turn from chop to glass. We feel renewed, refreshed. We get fueled

"He who cannot forgive others destroys the bridge over which he himself must pass."
—GEORGE HERBERT

with energy. The energy is passion. The passion is love. We are ready to live and love and learn again, after we experience forgiveness.

Home. Of all the emotions and spirits it provides, the greatest of these is to be forgiven. To know that our mistakes are not being counted. That our scars are never noticed. To feel that we now have a clean heart. A fresh start, a new hope, a new beginning. This is what home can offer us. This is why I refer to Jesus as the way home, for it is Jesus who grants us the Grace. The Grace that frees us to spiritually experience the unconditional love of God, a love that forgives and forgives and forgives.

9

BEING AT HOME IN YOUR BODY

Time for true confessions. I do not like talking about my body. My first wife, Christine, died suddenly, following complications of surgery. It was completely unexpected. In the two years after her death, I put on 112 pounds. I literally stuffed my grief inside my frame. If you had asked me whether I had gained weight during this period, I would have said, "Oh yes, maybe 20 or 30 pounds." I had no idea I had gone so totally out of control. When I finally stood on a scale, I was speechless. It was then that I knew the depth of my own addiction. I am not only a compulsive overeater, I also have a serious eating disorder. Obesity, like anorexia, leads to a distorted body image. I did not see or feel the weight. I was aware of it only when I saw a video or photograph of myself. Then I was detached enough to really look. Then I saw a man I hardly recognized.

I will share my lowest moment with you. It was the day I knew I needed to seek big-time help. It was the day I lost my penis. No, it wasn't severed. It just disappeared under layers of belly fat. Retreating into the folds, until I needed a searchlight to find it. Yes, it is OK for you to laugh. It is funny. Especially to a teenager. However, for me it was a true wake-up call. Is this who I want to be? How I want to live? Of course not! Nobody wants to be obese. It is embarrassing. The shame I feel is daily and enormous. I am paranoid. I think people can see nothing else but my poundage. It makes me feel like crap. When I feel like crap, I want to eat. I want to eat a lot. Of comfort foods. The vicious cycle begins all over.

> "Your body is the baggage you must carry through life. The more excess baggage, the shorter the trip."
> —ARNOLD H. GLASGOW

Christine has been gone seven years now. I have lost 14 of the pounds I put on. Still, I am presently 345 pounds. I would like to be 200 pounds, my wedding weight, and a fair goal. Getting there will not be easy. It will mean changing a good many behaviors. Getting professional help. Seeing a dietician. Attending Overeaters Anonymous meetings. Working on making healthy choices. Using portion control and exercise. I believe I can do it. I still lack confidence, having failed in many previous efforts. But the key is that I have not given up. I know what I need to do. Addiction is a disease that seeks to convince you that you can't do it.

Whispering in your ear, "You will fail again! Give up. You will just put the weight back on. It is hopeless." I suspect that hopelessness and perhaps all diseases are linked.

I felt acute anxiety about writing this chapter. I feel better now with having told the truth. At times we think that if we lie perfectly still and do nothing, our nausea will go away. Usually, the only way it departs is when we throw up. Now I have thrown up, in front of you. I've let you know that I will be writing about a subject with which I struggle. I do not believe this disqualifies me. I believe it puts some qualifications on what I have to say. The qualification is this: What I have to say, I probably need to hear more than you do. I am fine with that, and I hope you are, as well. Neither of us has much of a choice.

acceptance

Jesus would want you to feel at home in your own body. Relaxed. Content with how you look. Comfortable in your own skin. I believe Jesus would discourage your being obsessed with your appearance, if you are. A fitness addict is still an addict. I can't imagine Jesus being thrilled with seeing us spend a good deal of time gazing in a mirror. I can't imagine Him being an advocate for cosmetic surgery, or becoming a body builder who looks like the Michelin Man.

My experience of Jesus Christ is as a champion of common sense. You'd think that common sense would dictate a healthy perspective on the body. Taking good care of oneself physically. Having a lifestyle that encourages moderation and balance. Allowing ourselves time to rest and relax and play. We need disciplined time to create and work. We need time with friends and family. Intimate time, when we both receive and give loving. We need to eat good foods. Not junk. We need to keep our bodies well exercised and in good shape. In truth, you already know most of this. This is Health Class 101. It is more a matter of making healthy decisions. Daily choices that are right for you and your body.

Most of all, I feel strongly Jesus would want us to *accept* the bodies we have been given. I think He would find our "nip and tuck" culture to be repugnant. Nose jobs and tummy tucks and face-lifts. The fanatic desire to look like a certain celebrity. How sad, how expensive, how absurd. I know people say, "Well, if it will improve your self-esteem, then go for it." But I think Jesus would call our culture on the carpet. A culture that pays way too much attention to appearances. A culture that needs to look beneath the skin for the true beauty of a soul. Think of all the cosmetic surgery performed in America in a single year. Then imagine all the money for those surgeries being donated to the hungry or homeless. You get my drift. Jesus would not buy the shallow reasoning behind our obsessive pursuit of physical beauty.

> "Work consists of whatever a body is obliged to do, and play consists of whatever a body is not obliged to do." —MARK TWAIN, THE ADVENTURES OF TOM SAWYER

I had a young man in my youth group in Milwaukee who was losing his hair. Admittedly, it was early. He was 19. We all encouraged him to spend whatever it took to get hair replacements. It cost a mint. It also looked like he had hair transplants. I saw him recently.

He is bald, handsome, and happy. He told me that he wished one adult had had the courage to say to him, "Just accept who you are, live with it, and enjoy it. You are way more than your hair." I wish I had been that person, but I was afraid of his experiencing any emotional pain whatsoever. Ultimately, the $50,000 he wasted on recovering his hair caused him a great deal more emotional pain than his original hair loss.

Jesus would want us to accept our bodies, our looks, the very process of aging. Unless there was an accident or illness that caused an injury or deformity in obvious need of correction, I cannot see Jesus being thrilled with a people and culture who are endlessly trying to create the perfect look. It is shallow and juvenile. On some spiritual levels, it is just plain sick.

drugs and alcohol

In some ways, I am sooooooooo tired of talking about this topic. It is hard to talk about drugs and alcohol in a culture that celebrates them the way ours does. As you may remember from a previous chapter, I live on Shelter Island. It's a fashionable resort near the infamous Hamptons, on Long Island. The most successful people in the world come out here to relax and play. Much of that play means holding a drink in your hand. The amount of alcohol consumed on our island is staggering. The drug use stunning. We all know it is primarily an adult problem, but we address it only in the adolescent population. The youth see and hear and experience this double standard.

It is also tough to talk about drugs and alcohol, when everyone is certain they are neither an alcoholic nor a drug addict. They claim that they are not now, and never will be, addicted. How do you talk honestly about something that inspires such lying? The young guys in my youth group recently told me they only drink because they like the taste. I told them I like the taste of 7-Up, but I can't remember drinking six bottles in a row. It is hard to admit that we like getting high. It is difficult to assert how attractive it is to go into the "no-feel zone" of chemical use. A place where we can pretend to be on top of the world. At least until the crash. And the crash does come—every time we use.

> "What is dangerous about the tranquilizers is that whatever peace of mind they bring is a packaged peace of mind. Where you buy a pill and buy peace with it, you get conditioned to cheap solutions instead of deep ones." —MAX LERNER, THE UNFINISHED COUNTRY

Would Jesus be opposed to the consumption of alcohol? Well, he did drink wine at weddings. I am sure he got drunk as a young man. I doubt it was often. I can't imagine He used drugs of any kind, though some drugs were used within religious ceremonies. Again, I think the answer would be one of common sense. Can you be honest about your use? Can you really control it? Is it occasional and careful? Do you have a genuine respect for any potential trouble? Do you understand addictions and how they develop, to say nothing about how hard they are to kick? Do you realize that nobody ever starts using, believing that they will become addicted? Do you know your family background in this area? How attractive is it to you? Do you like using a lot? How much time and talent are you wasting? Do you have to try to stop? Remember, people who are not addicted do not have to try.

I suspect Jesus would understand alcohol from a recreational and social standpoint. I can see sharing a drink at a meal or as a means of relaxation. I believe the issue for Jesus would be quantity and purpose. Drinking to get smashed, or wasted, or totaled—these labels speak for themselves. I doubt Jesus could or would see the point. As for drugs. I truly cannot imagine when and where or how Jesus might feel that any use was either healthy or productive. I know Jesus would not see the value of altered states. I cannot imagine Jesus being enthusiastic about seeing you, a young healthy teen, taking up something that has such negative, even deadly, potential. Try it on. I mean, talk out loud to God, as you understand God. What would you ask? What would you hear in return?

I don't believe Jesus would condemn addiction or an addict. I think Jesus would issue warnings. Ask for rigorous honesty. But I am certain He would see addiction as a disease. Not an issue of willpower. A disease that may require professional intervention. Treatment. I am convinced Jesus would challenge folks who have become addicted to drugs and alcohol, urge them to get the help they need. I feel He would also ask His church to be a source of support and advocacy for getting such help. Calling drinking or drugging a sin is of no help. Claiming the true realities of drinking and drugging is an issue of maturity. Jesus would ask you to make mature choices. Healthy and adult decisions.

 ## balance

Zeke Ziolkowski was a bruiser. A real brute. *The* bully at Roosevelt Elementary School. He had an effective means of punishment. A surefire way of letting us know he was in charge. We were weak little boys. Losers, every last one of us. He was the giant with hair, you know, down there. The one who could hit a baseball and throw a football farthest. The one who made every basket, because he towered over us. He blocked our shots and kept rebounding the ball until his went in. The sight of Zeke at recess made you queasy. The appearance of him after school meant you were to be put on the dreaded teeter-totter. Yes, that seesaw on the playground was Zeke's chosen method of punishment.

Zeke would haul one of us poor fools onto the teeter-totter and quickly hoist us up into the air. There we sat as Zeke would harass us unmercifully. Pointing out each of our most noticeable flaws. Mine, of course, was being pudgy. Piggy Billy. Bill the Pig Swill. Grimbol the Grim Bull. I said he was big, not bright. He kept us up there until he was ready to leap off, which would slam the teeter-totter down to the ground. This slam was at the speed of light, and hurt our butts to beat the band. Zeke loved seeing us run off holding our behinds, trying not to cry until we got home.

> "Fortunate, indeed, is the man who takes exactly the right measure of himself and holds a just balance between what he can acquire and what he can use."
> —PETER LATHAM

Being up there was terrifying. Paralyzing. You knew you would be coming down. The only issue was when. That, and how hard. If there was a puddle below, you also got the joy of getting drenched, and having your pants look as if you had just exploded with diarrhea in them. It was the perfect symbol for being out of balance. The balance of power being lopsided. A teeter-totter can be fun when used as a means of trading balance. Zeke used it as an effective means of torture.

At times, we let our lives get totally out of balance. We get overwhelmed or burned out. We get so tightly wound that we feel like we could snap. We can be so paralyzed by stress it gets impossible to rest, much less sleep. Many times we are our own Zeke. Our own worst enemy.

We lose balance because we take lousy care of ourselves. We don't eat right, or we eat too much, or not at all, or we make ourselves throw up. We don't exercise, or we exercise too much. We don't get enough rest. We fail to nourish our bodies with stillness and quiet. Time in solitude, and time together with those we love. Time for being creative, and time to re-create our selves. It is easy to get ourselves hopelessly out of balance. It is hard to restore our balance.

You have had times when you knew you were ready to fall. Come slamming back down to Earth. You may have made the choices that got you there. You also know there is no way down but coming down. It will hurt. It will be embarrassing. But, once down, you can at least restore the balance again. When you are doing too much, expecting too much of yourself and others, trying to be perfect or to keep everyone happy. You are bound to fall off the pedestal. The stress will get the pedestal to sway, and it is only a matter of time until the human you hits the ground—hard.

Jesus was in balance. He knew when to be with His disciples, and when to be in the desert alone. He knew when to preach a message of comfort or prophetic challenge. He could choose to be silent and let His being speak, or He could speak aloud with clarity and authority. He could be tender and merciful. He could be demanding and fierce. He was in touch with the world. He was often fully out of touch—off tending to the needs of the spirit. Good Friday and Easter—the culminating events of Jesus' life. The rhythm of Life itself. Pain and struggle. Joy and celebration. Let the good times roll. Let me get out of this rut. And so it goes.

Our bodies have a built-in system for maintaining balance. It is called *homeostasis*. This is the body's divine instinct to have its systems stay in balance. Our *home tem-*

perature is 98.6 degrees for most people. When it is much higher or lower, our systems are out of balance—we are sick. The body knows when it needs to come home. To return to balance. If we get overheated, we sweat. The sweat cools us off. We feel fine again. Blood sugar, blood pressure, cholesterol, eyesight, our hearing—each system of the human body has a range of what is acceptable. The body wants to be in balance. Illness or pain can be thought of as a warning light. The body has alarms to alert us to being out of balance. Simply put, the human body needs to be at ease with itself. If it is ill at ease, we become prone to dis-ease. Dis-ease means to be out of balance with Life itself.

temporary temples

The Bible encourages us to think of our bodies as a Temple. Mine is reaching the dimensions of the Crystal Cathedral. (Just kidding.) What is meant by this is: Consider your body to be the home of God. Our bodies are sacred, precious, worthy of ultimate respect. Even a bit of adoration, though not of the conceit variety. Our bodies are sanctuaries for our souls. This is the residence of our spirit. God's handiwork can be seen all over and within the human body.

Think of it this way: *You* take over all the functions of your body. Concentrate long and hard. Now, take over. You make the heart and lungs pump. You get the liver and kidneys and pancreas to do their flushing and sorting jobs. You make the blood travel. The stomach empty. You sort out the sugars. Add just the right amount of acid to the mix. You get the brain to send its impulses to the muscles. To move your hands and feet. You get the vocal chords to clang together to give you a voice. You call upon your bowels to empty. Do it all. Let your brain take over all these functions.

Crazy, right? Well, of course. The body is an amazing machine. Its systems are intricate and delicate. The body is a warehouse of mystery. We are not sure why or how things work, we just know they do. We take it for granted. It is an assumption, an accepted blessing. If there is one good example of Life being crammed with the presence of God, it the miraculous human body. Just the thought of having to run all our bodily systems is overwhelming.

Jesus would hope that you treat your body with a good deal of respect. Take good care of it. Rest when it tells you to rest. Nourish it with good foods, natural foods, vegetables and fruits being at the top of the list. Keep it limber and loose. Ready to move. Give it some discipline. Build adequate muscle. Use or lose it, as the adage says. Do not take unnecessary risks. Do not forget: You are human, and so is your body. It can break. It can have a complete breakdown. It can feel ready to snap at the seams. Heed the warning to stop. In fact, maybe most of all, listen to your body. It is incessantly informing you of how it

> "Don't you know that your body is the temple of the Holy Spirit, who lives in you and who was given to you by God? You do not belong to yourselves but to God: he bought you for a price. So use your bodies for God's glory."
> —I CORINTHIANS 6:19–20

is doing, as well as how you are being. It is an excellent witness to your life. It can offer key evidence to your innocence or guilt.

Our bodies are temporary. They are terminal. They will shrink and wrinkle and sag with age. Things will head south for the long winter. Joints will begin to ache. Muscles will start to rip and tear. Our feet will declare their unhappiness. Our hair will recede or thin or vanish. Our teeth will decay and rot. I know, you are just a teen. Still, you need to embrace the reality of aging. How you treat your body now will affect how you will age. If you live as if there is no tomorrow, your future will likely include a good deal of physical suffering. You are building lifelong habits right now. Hard to break. Smoking is a great example of an addictive habit that will get harder and harder to quit as each year passes. My own bad eating habits were sown during adolescence. I always ate late at night while studying. Chips and soda. Pizza. Donuts. My late-night academic companion is now the inner tube around my waist.

I also believe Jesus would ask you to show your body a bit of reverence. Not worship, not kneeling to it as an idol. But certainly giving it its proper due. Our bodies deserve to be treated well. A pinch of adoration might help us make healthier choices. Start each day by acknowledging your body as a gift—a gift of extraordinary value, one we need to honor. Grant it some recognition. Pay attention to it, notice how it is doing, be in dialogue with it. You get the picture. Again, it is just plain common sense. Coming home to your body is keeping your body in good shape. Maintaining it. Sprucing it up. Upkeep. A great word. Keep our bodies upward bound.

sexuality

We are all sexual. Mightily so. I am still surprised to realize how much time sex is on my mind, at my age. When I was an adolescent, it was hard to think about much else. Having sex is a choice. Whom we have sex with is also a choice. Sexuality is not. Sexuality is a matter of natural attraction. Those who try to speak of homosexuality as a choice are clueless. They are defending a position that they know makes no sense. Gay or straight is just who we are. We don't ask for it, create it, or choose it. We are just it. Can you imagine a 13-year-old waking up one day and saying, "Hey, I think I'll be gay"? Of course not.

If someone tries to tell you homosexuality is a choice, then ask them when they chose to be heterosexual. They will look at you with puzzlement. Or comment on the ridiculous nature of the question. The question is only ridiculous because they know they did not choose to be straight. They simply knew they were. They were honest with their attractions.

> "If any thing is sacred, the human body is sacred."
> —WALT WHITMAN, 8, "I SING THE BODY ELECTRIC," *LEAVES OF GRASS* (1855–1881)

They knew whom they wanted to kiss. They knew whose touch turned them on. They knew what made them melt.

We all do. Heterosexuals may have the occasional surprise attraction to someone of the same sex, but it is just not lasting, nor does it meet the deeper emotional and spiritual needs. A homosexual may have a physical relationship with a person of the opposite sex, but again, it is just not something that satisfies over the long term.

I know what the Bible says about homosexuality. I also know the Bible tells women to obey their husbands, and slaves their masters. I know the Bible tells women to stay at the back of the church with their heads covered. The Bible makes it clear to some folks that women should not be ordained. That only men can be ministers. I do not agree with any of it. We have grown. We have deepened spiritually. The Bible must be read with discernment. Discernment means to distinguish what is essential from that which is peripheral. That which may have been true for certain tribes millennia ago, but may no longer be. Something that has lost meaning with the passage of time, or is a matter about which we have garnered new and important information.

Jesus says literally nothing about homosexuality. I see homosexuality as an area we have just started to learn more about. I believe we now know it is not a crime, not a sin, not a perversion of what's "normal." I laugh when I hear people talk of the homosexual agenda. Ask them what is on the agenda. Ask them to name one single person they know who was talked into being homosexual by someone touting the gay agenda. One! There have always been gay and lesbian folks. There always will be. The repression and persecution they have suffered at the hands of the Christian church is a matter of shame. Vile and disgusting. A gay person can serve Jesus. They can follow. They can be like Christ. There is nothing that would make that not so.

Be honest with your sexuality. It is sad for anyone to deny who they are. What they think or feel or believe. What attracts them sexually. If you are gay, there is no reason not to be honest with yourself. Jesus accepts who you are. Your heart knows this to be true. You can now find many churches that will accept and welcome you. The repression of sexuality can lead to depression and suicide. It produces many loveless marriages. It serves nobody, least of all Jesus.

Sexuality unfolds. It is a process of revelation. Attractions. Fantasies. Experimentation. Masturbation. Kissing. Falling in love. Cuddling. Fondling. Foreplay. Making love. It is like the spreading of a fan. It only gets better and more beautiful as it opens. The denial of who you are sexually is the equivalent of keeping a fan folded up tight. Never to be revealed in all its beauty. Never to be used for its purpose, to create a gentle breeze, a life force. That is a crazy way to live. Unnecessary, unhealthy, un-Christian.

The church is finally and slowly and reluctantly coming to terms with homosexuality. Just as it took a long, long time to see a woman in the pulpit, the church is coming to grips with an acceptance of homosexuality. Just as people used the Bible to prove women were never meant to be ordained, so it is used by some today to ostracize gays and lesbians. Eventually, the church will come to its spiritual senses. Love and forgiveness will reign. The church will no longer be comfortable with the role of keeping people away from fully serving Jesus Christ.

Every year we have many gay bashings and murders. They are presently on the increase. If children are taught that gay men and women are sinners, and will be going to hell anyway, or that AIDS is God's chosen punishment for them, then do not be shocked by how they deal with the gay community. Be they gay or straight themselves, the message they may be hearing from the Christian church is hateful, discriminatory, and just plain cruel. When will the church confess to its complicity in this violence toward gay men and women? We are often cited as one of the chief reasons why folks feel free to punish gays. Beat them up. Kill them. Taunt and mock them. Because it is assumed God hates them and their behaviors. Telling someone "I love you, but I hate who you love" is absurd. You cannot cover up hatred or discrimination. The grime will show through.

Let me close this section by quoting briefly from Frederick Buechner, who writes eloquently about homosexuality in his masterpiece, *Whistling in the Dark*: "To say that morally, spiritually, humanly, homosexuality is always bad seems as absurd as to say that in the same term heterosexuality is always good, or the other way around. It is not the object of our sexuality that determines its value but the inner nature of our sexuality" (pp. 62–63).

sexual readiness

A major issue for every teen is whether be sexually active. The decision is not easy. It require a good deal of honesty, plus a relationship with strong communication. The church has long advocated no sex outside the bonds of marriage. I can respect those who choose to follow that religious norm. I can also understand the struggle that many of you have with this perspective. The difficulty is obvious. In biblical times, adolescents often married between the ages of 12 and 13. If you were talking about waiting back then, and you meant until Tuesday, it was no big deal. Most of you do not expect to be married until your mid-20s. This makes the matter a great deal more complex. Will I wait for 10 years? Maybe 15? Is this healthy on any level, from physical to spiritual?

I strongly encourage you to talk this matter over with your parents, or with adults you truly trust. Adults whom you respect. Adults whose own sexual values appear to be worthy of modeling. The topic of readiness for sexual expression needs to consider a great deal:

1. Can I handle the possible consequences of sexual activity?

2. Am I ready to be a parent, should this happen?

3. Am I aware of all potential sexually transmitted diseases, and have I asked all the necessary questions?

4. Can I handle being dumped by someone I am sexually active with?

5. Am I aware of the hurt I might cause if I were to do the dumping?

6. Is there a strong commitment in our relationship?

7. Is there strong communication? Can we talk openly about sex and our values?

8. Is this a joint decision? Have we carefully considered contraception?

9. Why are we choosing to be sexually active? It may seem obvious, but it isn't. It must be a decision that involves our heart, mind, body, and spirit.

10. Can my family handle my decision? Will a decision to be active need to be kept secret? How will this impact my relationships at home?

11. What are my own sexual moral values? How did I determine them? Have I had an honest exchange with God, however I understand God.

12. Is this a decision I may regret? Why?

13. What might be the benefits of waiting?

14. Am I emotionally ready? I may be physically ready. What about spiritually?

15. What role do I want sex to play in my relationship?

I could go on and on. This is not a light decision. There is no such thing as casual sex. All sex communicates something deep and profound. It is the nature of being human. There certainly can be sex without love. There cannot be sex without feelings. That is an impossibility.

I would also encourage you to consider a few other things. Abstinence, which involves everything but intercourse, it pretty much a farce. It is as dumb as President Clinton's saying he "never had sex with that woman," because the sex was only oral. Only oral? What does that mean? Be honest about your sexual involvements. Be clear on what you can and cannot handle. Do not be afraid to say no to activity you are not comfortable with or ready for. Do not, however, equate sexual abstinence with holiness. Not being sexually involved is far from some sign of spiritual purity. It is a moral choice. This is significant, but it is not qualification for sainthood.

We all make sexual mistakes. I can think of no other area in which more mistakes are made. Why? Because sex is powerful. The sex drive, difficult to control. The falling in love, long and hard. We can easily be overwhelmed by feelings. We can have a few drinks and make a pretty stupid decision. We can think sex is a way of keeping someone around. Again, the list of sexual mistakes is endless. Be gentle with yourself. Be good. Treat yourself with respect. Learn from your mistakes. Keep growing sexually. There is a ton to learn. Wisdom will not come swiftly.

What does Jesus expect in this arena? Honesty, most of all. Jesus was sexual. I am sure He had his crushes, and fell in love. I would be quite certain He masturbated, and may have had a sexual relationship. I am shocked that many in the church find that appalling. In a world of rampant violence and hate, crime, abuses of every kind, and war, it is amazing that the church—many churches—can still get the most upset about sex. I do not believe this would be the case for Jesus. I suspect that He would confirm that sex is good and beautiful. Needs to be handled responsibly and respectfully. The more love involved, the better. I believe Jesus asks us to care about one another. To treat each other with gentle and gracious respect. Our sexual choices and decisions should be even more so. Filled with a genuine concern for our partner. A willingness to see sex not as something we do or make, but a beautiful side of who we are. A side we share only with those we trust.

sexual abuse

My late wife, Christine, had been sexually abused. The impact on her was huge. When she died she weighed over 400 pounds. Many women who have been victims of incest find weight to be a security blanket. A way of keeping men away. Why, they ask themselves, would I want to be sexually attractive? This was a question that haunted Chris and me throughout our entire married life. Sexual abuse is often shrouded in secrecy. A conspiracy of silence. The same is often the case in date rape, or rape by a stranger or family member. The shame is so thick, the truth so hard to accept, that it seems easier to deny it. The denial can be deadly.

There is no way around sexual abuse. It must be faced. It must be spoken of, spoken about. It must be claimed by those who are victims. The perpetrators must be named. Honesty is once again called for in every aspect of dealing with this issue.

If you have been the victim of sexual abuse, date rape, or other rape, it is truly not your fault. It is important for you to get the help you need. A person with whom you can talk. A plan for healing. It will take time and tenderness to restore your sexuality. To bring back a sense of freedom and spontaneity. A high level of trust. A capacity to give pleasure and be pleasured. You deserve no less than the full benefits of a good, healthy sexual relationship. Insist on it. Work to find it. Enjoy it.

The beginning of healing is in recognizing that you did nothing to deserve it. Not one damn thing. It has nothing to do with anything, other than a complete abuse of power.

other sexual topics

What about dating? Well, what about it? Not much to say. Most of you don't "date" anymore. You just get involved with someone. You hook up. The relationship grows more out of friendship than formal dating. Dates are events, which spoils them. The big dance. The fancy dinner. Not exactly the context for a relaxed evening of enjoyment. These dates become more of a fashion show, or a means of trying to impress someone. I am not opposed to that. I doubt

Christ cares. I just think it is best to spend time in more relaxed casual settings. Be together as friends. See a movie or a game. Take a walk, or go for a drive. It does not need to be some romantic extravaganza, which seldom lives up to its billing. By the way, spending hundreds of dollars on a prom is nuts. You know it, and I know it. This isn't a date, it's an event. A well-choreographed and staged event. It has little to do with a relationship, and everything to do with performance and showing off.

What about masturbation? What about it? Been there. Done that. Still do. So does almost everyone. It is just a part of life. I guess it can be excessive. You will know that if it happens to you. It is not unhealthy in any way. Not physically, not emotionally, and not spiritually. It is a nonissue. It only becomes an issue when we heap all kinds of unneeded shame on the practice.

What about pornography? This is a toughie. I think most folks have taken at least a peek at some porn. We all agree that porn can be a pretty sleazy business, and there are rampant abuses within the industry. This is especially true for women, and those underage. The prevalence of drugs. The use of youth desperate for money. The use of young drug addicts is well-documented. So, it is hard to say anything supportive of this business. It would be like showing sympathy for a drug cartel.

I believe Jesus would fully understand the pleasure in observing a beautiful body. I do not believe Jesus would be in any way offended by nudity. I do think Jesus would draw the line at seeing another human being used solely for the physical gratification they might offer us. This does smack of a meat-market mentality. An inappropriate fixation on large penises and breasts. An unsettling focus on genitalia. Ironically, the result of pornography is numbing. It just turns something exciting and wondrous into something mechanical and dull.

I have heard many folks defend porn as a great means to improve your sex life, to enhance your fantasies. To be honest, you might think Americans would have this sex stuff down pat by now. After all, sex is used to sell most products. It is the focus of much of our media. We talk about it, look at it, discuss it ad infinitum. When is enough enough? At this point, by the world's standards, we Americans should all have a Ph.D. in sex.

Sex without love is still pretty boring. Porn is porn. It will not kill you. You are not evil for watching it, or looking at it. I just think you need to be honest about it. What is the point? I guess if the point is to be aroused, mission accomplished. But how does this affect you as a person? As a spiritual being? I cannot answer this for you. This one requires some mature soul-searching.

Well, I think I have covered everything about the human body except the heartbreak of psoriasis. It is time to move on.

10

BEING AT HOME IN YOUR MIND

"The mind is a terrible thing to waste." Have you heard that slogan before? It is a slogan still used in promoting the work of United Negro College Fund. I agree with this catchphrase. It is hard to imagine anything worse, and I have witnessed the waste of more than a mind or two—including my own, from time to time. How? you might ask. How can you waste a mind? Here are few ways:

1. By choosing to have a closed mind

2. By thinking you have all the answers

3. By thinking the answers are always written in black-and-white rather than shades of gray

4. By letting someone else do the thinking for you

5. By never taking your thoughts, or those of others, seriously

6. By never challenging your mind to grow and learn

7. Be failing to ponder the great mysteries

8. By settling for simplistic, easy answers to Life's most compelling and complex questions

9. By refusing to read, study, or reflect

10. By being actively anti-intellectual

11. By letting drugs and alcohol wither your mind's muscles

12. By being intellectually lazy

13. By letting yourself be indoctrinated

14. By being a purely passive learner

15. By never asking a question, or risking the sharing of an answer

    I recently got furious when I overheard a few members of my youth group bragging to one another about how miserably they had done on an exam at school. I asked them why they were so proud. They immediately went quiet. Heads bowed, ashamed. I queried them as to why they took so little pride in using their brains. They all pled to being "stupid." I told them they knew this was a barefaced lie. They were not

> "The mind is its own place, and in itself can make a heaven of hell, a hell of heaven." —MILTON, *PARADISE LOST* (1667)

stupid, they were just being wasteful. Wasting good minds, wasting their God-given time and talent.

I believe Jesus would, first and foremost, expect you to see your mind as a gift. Your intelligence, something to treat with respect. Jesus would want you to use your mind in service to others. Make a difference. Make the world a safer, saner, even simpler place in which to live. Big ideas in service only to making big bucks would not impress Jesus in the least. Quite the opposite. They would be highly offensive to Him. Jesus would admire the mind that seeks solutions to some of the world's problems, to human suffering. Jesus would never want to see you waste even a morsel of your mind, no matter what. It is yours and that of God, who created it. It is worthy of honor. Even a simple mind can be a good one that can help create a good and decent life.

> "We should take care not to make the intellect our god; it has, of course, powerful muscles, but no personality."
> —ALBERT EINSTEIN

an open mind

Jesus desires our minds to be open. Our minds need to be a good host. Welcoming new ideas and information. Receiving the arrival of a new question or mystery. Our minds must be a place to which the door always remains open, even if just a crack. A shut mind is a dying mind. A closed mind turns ugly— smug and complacent, bored and boring to experience. A mind that is bolted and locked is a mind in hiding. What is being hidden is the treasure of who you are. You are your thoughts. Your thoughts help make you who you are. They are the engine of your creativity, the seeds of your uniqueness.

Just consider for a moment someone we call a know-it-all. The know-it-all has a closed mind. No more questions. No need to listen to anyone else's input. No need to consider others' opinions or beliefs or ideas. The case is closed, without hearing any evidence. I have the answers, and that's that. Their only real need is to pontificate. To lecture others. To share all their "wisdom" with the world. Is there anything more distasteful? Do you want to share time and space with such a soul? No. It is not only boring as hell, it is also obnoxious. It is like being with a child who is truly a spoiled brat. There is nothing to do but let the tantrum (er, lecture) run its course.

An open mind, by contrast, loves a good question. Enjoys the chance to consider a new idea. An open mind is fearless. Takes risks, explores uncharted waters, loves good debate. Appreciates genuine dialogue. An open mind is flexible, adaptable, capable of change. It is never fixed or rigid. It refuses to see an answer as *the* answer. A mind that is open chooses to be fully awake and aware. Alive to the possibilities of the questions that inhabit the day. When a mind is

> "It is not enough to have a good mind; the main thing is to use it well."
> —DESCARTES, *DISCOURSE ON METHOD* (1639)

"Be not conformed to this world; but be ye transformed by the renewing of your mind, that ye may prove what is that good, and acceptable, and perfect will of God." —ROMANS 12:2 KJV

open, it is free. Free to live and learn. Free to ignite the spirit, to enlarge the soul. Free to be fully present. Fully your Self. The Self that Jesus claims to have created.

The Scribes and the Pharisees, you may recall, did not have open minds. After all, they were the religious elite. It was to them that Jesus unleashed His severest criticism. The Scribes and Pharisees worshipped the Law. They sought to find in the Law a solution to all ethical and moral issues. When Jesus challenged the Law, they were appalled. The Law, they said, was rigid and unbending. It could not be altered in any way. The Scribes and Pharisees believed that their knowledge of the Law made them special. They considered themselves a people apart, a religious clique, a spiritual elite. What was sad about the Scribes and Pharisees is that, in the process of worshiping the Law, they lost their own hearts.

Placing the Law before people drained the Law of the mercy that is the essence of Jesus Christ. Jesus valued the Law. He revered the Torah. He, however, also believed that the Law could grow and mature, could deepen and gain fullness. The Law was always to be in service to the love and Grace of God.

A closed mind talks a good line, but does not walk it. While Pharisees memorized the words of the Law, they failed to live the words' spirit. What's worse, they used the Law to condemn others. Being quick to point out the flaw or failing. Ridiculing those who they believed fell short of their own religious expertise. Jesus told them they were like white-washed tombs—clean and shiny on the outside, but, inside, full of dead men's bones. He warned them to worry less about dietary laws. It is not what they put in their mouths that should concern them, but what comes out of their mouths. Jesus was furious with the Scribes and Pharisees for closing their minds to His ministry and message. He demanded that they stretch and grow. They refused. They chose to see their faith shrink to the size of five books—the limits of the Pentateuch.

 ## empty and full

"God approaches our minds by receding from them.

"We can never fully know Him if we think of Him as an object of capture, to be fenced in by the enclosure of our own ideas.

"We know Him better after our minds have let Him go.

"The Lord travels in all directions at once.

"The Lord arrives from all directions at once.

"Wherever we are, we find that He has just departed.

"Wherever we go, we discover that He has just arrived before us.

"Our rest can be neither in the beginning of this pursuit, nor in the pursuit itself, nor in its apparent end. For the true end, which is Heaven, is an end without end. It is a totally new dimension, in which we come to rest in the secret that He must arrive at the moment of His departure; His arrival is at every moment and His departure us not fixed in time."

THOMAS MERTON, *NO MAN IS AN ISLAND*

Our minds can get cluttered. Overwhelmed with worry, consumed by fear, filled with noise and nonsense. At times, our minds can become a din. A place of pandemonium. A chamber of bedlam. A context suited only to chaos. Here a mind cannot think, cannot create, cannot solve or resolve. Cannot contemplate, reflect, or remember. When the mind is jammed with a discordant jazz of thought, we sometimes want to scream. We need peace of mind. We need some silence, a bit of solitude. We need a setting conducive to thinking.

At these times, we need to literally empty our minds. Let the anxiety drain off. The worries evaporate. Kick out all the *shoulds* and *oughts* and *musts*. Do away with our lists. Choose to take a vacation from trying to figure everything out. Our mind wants what we can never have—control. Maybe it's human nature, but we desire to have our lives in order, even though Life keeps coming in and messing things up. A smart mind gives up the battle. Admits to being powerless. That control is out of reach. That we could just surrender to a Higher Power. (This is borrowed from the brilliant Twelve Steps, a spiritual program used in the treatment of most addictions.) Once empty, the mind can breathe. It is ready to receive. It is ripe for picking up some wisdom.

A good mind is not a mind ready to burst. A good mind is not a mind glutted with excess information. A good mind is not one that knows a little bit about everything. A good mind knows when to empty, and how to fill itself up. Filling up with good stories, good thoughts, great ideas. Pondering the wonders of our world. Reflecting upon its mysteries and madness. Considering the human needs we

> "Make your own the mind of Christ Jesus."
> —PHILIPPIANS 2:5 NJB

must try to meet. How the world might be transformed and renewed. How we can be peacemakers and ignite hope. A good mind creates goodness. A good mind makes good choices. A good mind lives a genuinely good life.

Do you know how to empty your mind? Meditation is an excellent means of doing so. So is prayer. Emptying means letting go. Waving the white flag. Giving up efforts at control. Freeing ourselves of expectations. Just being still, quiet, alone. Letting Life come in, but only in little bits. A glimpse of Grace. A glance from God. A word to the wise. Emptying is listening—listening hard, listening with your heart. Emptying is being struck dumb. No longer in awe of one's own mind. Consumed in thought. No, this is when the mind is rested and at rest. Welcoming and receptive. A good host. Gleaning the good news as it comes through the door of the open mind.

> "I am telling you not to worry about your life and what you are to eat, nor about your body and what you are to wear.... Can any of you, however much you worry, add one single cubit to your span of life? So do not worry, do not say 'What are we to eat? What are we to drink? What are we to wear?' It is the gentiles who set their minds on all these things. Your heavenly father knows you need them all. Set your hearts on his kingdom first, and on God's saving justice, and all these other things will be given to you as well. So do not worry about tomorrow."
>
> MATTHEW 6:25, 27, 31–34 NJB

The Bible contains a wonderful little story that speaks clearly about the cluttered mind versus the receptive one. It is the story of Martha and Mary. Jesus has come to visit the two sisters. Martha is trying to be the perfect host. She has cleaned the house and readied the meal. Now she is trying to set the table. She complains to Jesus that Mary is not helping her one little bit. Mary has been sitting at the feet of Jesus, listening to Him speak. Jesus explains to a frustrated Martha that Mary has made a wise choice. Being a

> "The Lord answered, 'Martha, Martha, you are fretting and fussing about so many things; only one thing is necessary, Mary has chosen what is best; it shall not be taken away from her.'" —LUKE 10:41–42 REB

devoted listener is of far greater value than a perfectly pre-pared and served meal. I can bet Martha was ready to tell Jesus, "Well, then, don't eat it!" But she was wise enough, and faithful enough, to get His point. It was simply a matter of priorities.

Filling the mind with good things should be a top pri-ority. Listening to our hearts, as well as to the hearts of others. Listening to God. Taking the time for quiet prayer and reflection. These are of far greater value than trying to win the rat race. Our frenzied pace often leads nowhere. A quiet mind can get us back on track. In pursuit of priorities that matter. Priorities that last—eternally.

 ## embracing the mystery

If you are smart, and sufficiently mature, you will quickly recognize that the older you get, the less you know. The less you feel certain about. The mystery, on the other hand, grows and grows. Expands and inflates and radiates its paradoxical spirit out into the world. The myster-ies of Life are endless, and endlessly fascinating. Why are there stars above? Who designed DNA? Is there life beyond Life? Why was there a Holocaust? Does prayer make a dif-ference? Who are your heroes? Do miracle cures ever happen? Everywhere you listen, Life is telling you another parable. A little anecdote with a big meaning. A tiny tale that reveals a giant Truth. A never-ending story with never-ending meaning.

I, for one, value technology. I believe it has saved and enhanced many lives. The progress offered by computers, for example, is dazzling. Still, technology has an odd quirk to it. Ultimately, it appears to create as many nightmares as it fulfills dreams. Though I value the impact of e-mail, I desperately miss seeing a message written in colored ink by an expressive human hand. Though I value how technology has transformed the face of medicine, to give another example, I wish I could experience a few more unmasked human faces in the process of having my health cared for. Though I value the immediacy of the cell phone, I don't want to be reached anytime, anywhere. At times I want nothing more than to be hopelessly out of touch. Yes, technology in all its forms can do wondrous things, but it cannot embrace a mystery. Sure, it can supply us with a ton of data, can sort it and collate it. But the mystery itself can only be beheld by the human mind.

Spirituality is about beholding. Lifting up the mysteries. Trying to see the light. The seeking of wisdom, the searching for Truth. Jesus is never impressed by the mind that unravels the mystery, but only by the mind that leaps in faith from the mystery unraveled to the one being woven. Jesus never offers us answers—He offers us a Life. A new perspective. A new way of doing and being. A life that is soaked in mystery. A life that creates more questions each day than the mind can count.

Over the past few years, I have encouraged my high school youth to be Sunday School teachers. There is method to my madness. My youth are great teachers. The younger kids adore them and, of course, want to be just like them. My youth take their position as role models quite seriously. I have found that expecting my youth to be first-rate teachers has led them to be just that. They come prepared, excited and enthused, ready to dialogue with the kids. They love to paint and play and tell them stories. They are naturals.

> "The test of a first-rate intelligence is the ability to hold two opposing ideas in the mind at the same time, and still retain the ability to function."
> —F. SCOTT FITZGERALD, *THE CRACK-UP*

My youthful staff get many things from the children, but one thing stands out: They get back in touch with some childlike curiosity and imagination. They are reminded of the joy to be found in believing that you can figure out all the whys and hows of the world and of Life. This past summer, for instance, we asked our children to create an entire world of their own. They were the designers. They created their own birds, fish, animals, flowers, plants, fruits, vegetables, trees, and bushes. They even created their own people. It was fascinating. I listened in on one class when Nick, a high school senior, was asking why God created fish. The answers were wonderful, and worth a giggle or two. One child said the ocean was God's goldfish bowl, and God liked looking at the fish, but sometimes He forgot to feed them. Another child asked where God flushed His dead goldfish. Another child said God was really grumpy the day He made sharks.

Nick spoke to me after class. We both laughed about the responses. But Nick's statement to me revealed the magic of teaching. "I haven't let myself ask these questions since I was a kid," he admitted. "These are huge questions. Big, whopping mysteries. I loved sharing with the kids. Letting ourselves travel off in our minds, to a place where we'd figure out all the mysteries of the world. I hadn't been there in a long time. It was a blast."

So be a kid once in a while. Let your mind entertain a mystery. Let it roam through a dark and wild forest littered with stars overhead. Let your mind dive to the depths of the vastest ocean. Let it explore the rocky terrain of the human heart. Let yourself go.

wisdom

Ultimately, Jesus desires wisdom. Wisdom is not the accumulation of knowledge. It is the use of our knowledge to come to an understanding. Wisdom is knowing with our hearts. It is having a mind that no longer necessarily conforms to all the values of our culture. It is having a mind transformed. Turned inside out. A mind that seeks to make peace, create hope, inspire love, and forgive. It is a mind that speaks with humility, that reveres simplicity, that celebrates diversity. A mind that enjoys a good mystery. That can grasp a miracle.

Savor the magic of a glimpse of Grace. A mind that is often struck dumb. Yet a mind that, in this stupidity, receives divine knowledge. A mind that knows when to keep its mouth shut, so that the Word of God can be heard. The Word of God, which is the experience of Jesus the Christ.

One of the questions I asked, at a recent dinner/dialogue for high school youth, was who was the wisest person they knew. I loved their answers. Especially because a few said it was me. Then Mia asked who I believed was the wisest person in my life. I was stunned. Not by the question, but by how quickly the answer came to my mind. Judy Trentadue. An old friend who had died, way too young, from cancer. She was a good wife to Bart. A great mother to Linda, Laura, and Rob. A first-class hairdresser. A tremendous friend to me and many others. Her wisdom was uncanny. I shared with the gathering how much I still missed Judy and her wisdom.

> "The fairest thing we can experience is the mysterious. It is the fundamental emotion which stands at the cradle of true art and true science. He who knows it not and can no longer wonder, no longer feel amazement, is as good as dead, a snuffed out candle. It was the experience of mystery—even if mixed with fear—that engendered religion "
> —ALBERT EINSTEIN, THE WORLD AS I SEE IT

I sought to explain how she would say just the right thing at just the right time. How she seemed to know me better than I knew myself. How understanding she was. How her wisdom was never cruel. It was always coated with encouragement and respect. Her words inspired me to do, and be, better.

Judy's funeral was the largest I have ever conducted. I recall that at the close of the service, I went outside for some air (and to fall apart). A little boy came up to me on his tricycle. He was puzzled by my alb, my minister's vestment. He asked me why I was wearing a dress. My response probably scarred him for life. A hopelessly religious mishmash of words that made no sense, even to me. He then said, "Did a famous person die?" I told him, not really. "But there are so many cars. They must be famous." I said to him, "Not famous, just very wise." He winced, even more puzzled. He rode off, and yelled back, "I think your dress looks dumb!" I have never forgotten that kid. I have also never forgotten that, when it came to Judy, I had told him the gospel truth.

11

BEING AT HOME IN
YOUR HEART AND SOUL

"Blessed are the pure in heart: for they shall
see God."

MATTHEW 5:8 KJV

"Your heart will always be where your treasure is."

MATTHEW 6:21 CEV

"Above all else, guard your heart, for it is the
wellspring of life."

PROVERBS 4:23 NIV

I do a good deal of counseling for adults on Shelter
Island, and on the East End of Long Island. A wide range of
folks with a wide range of needs. Mainly, what draws people
in for an appointment with me is their desire to feel better.
To get unstuck. To free themselves from a habit or an
emotion that's creating havoc. To be happier or healthier or

more hope-filled. To locate a purpose for their lives. To find some meaning, some value, some worth.

I want to share with you something I find profoundly sad. Something both annoying and disturbing. Something that speaks volumes about our culture and our lifestyles. That something is this: Most adults who come to see me take months before they can speak, with any candor, about why they came. They have no real idea of what they are feeling, or why. They have a terrible time trying to explain what they are thinking, often claiming it's nothing at all. If you try to move to particulars, like the cause of their sadness or rage or hurt or disappointment, I'm frequently met with the blankest of stares. If I go spiritual on them, and try to draw out a statement of their values or beliefs, I create a level of anxiety that threatens to explode.

My most basic questions are met with befuddlement. Tell me what makes you happy? When was the last time you experienced joy? What triggers your anger? What are you most proud of accomplishing? Tell me some of your goals and dreams. What was your childhood like? Tell me about your adolescence. It isn't that people have nothing to say. It is just that I get perfunctory answers. Slivers of truth. A little dab of history or experience. Told with zero enthusiasm. As if one were reading from a weather report. I find it mind-boggling and, yes, even tragic to hear people speak of their lives in such bored tones.

Isn't this the reason why they sought help? Well, yes and no. Yes, they knew they were not feeling right. They knew they were off or stuck or depressed. They knew they needed to talk. What is sad is that they have so little to say. They are truly *unaware* of what is happening to them. They are frequently oblivious to their own lives. They can tell you the basics of what they have been *doing*, but are clueless when it comes to what they have been *being*. Improving a life is seldom about *doing* something different. It is almost always about *being* something different. Being on a new job. Being in a new hometown. Being the owner of a new car or the occupant of a room on a cruise ship. No doubt about it, these things can help. But the impact is short-lived. It is only when we inwardly change our Self that we find the long-term help we desire. A change in attitude, an act of forgiveness, a relationship with fresh intimacy. A closer connection to God. This is where Life is transformed. It is on the inside that the true emotional and spiritual healing begins. Newness begins within. It is not a purchase, or even an accomplishment. It is a perspective or state of mind. A new way of looking at Life. A new strategy for finding happiness—even joy.

I think Jesus was often perplexed by His own disciples' lack of awareness. They, too, failed to understand much about their lives. They were often out of touch with the point or purpose of Jesus' ministry. They were followers, but Jesus expected them to be fully engaged in delivering the message. His frustration with them often stemmed from the spiritual fog they chose to live in. At times, Jesus tired of having to lift the fog to be heard. In fact, I believe He grew enraged by how often He needed to repeat the same message over and over again. Though He was patient, Jesus was also wonderfully human. I am thrilled that He lost His patience. I mean, really, how many times can you say, "forgive"? Or say, "love your neighbor as yourself"? Or preach good news to the poor?

What Jesus wanted for His disciples is exactly what He would want for you and me. He wants us to know our own hearts. To be aware of what's going on within our souls. He wants us to feel at home with who we are. Our heart and soul are our essence. The core of what we feel, think, and believe. It is our essence that declares to us what is essential. What should concern us ultimately. Form our top priorities. Be our focus, our vision. It is our heart and soul that free us to live the questions. To live out our longings, to follow our bliss, to write the Fifth Gospel with our lives. Jesus wants us to be true to our Selves. Jesus understood that if we were true to our Selves, we would also be true to Him. Even if we do not declare Him Lord. Or consider him to be the long-awaited Messiah. Or find any reason to worship Him. To be our Selves is what best serves Jesus.

self-esteem

The heart and soul—or either, or both—are our essence. They are the seat upon which the soul sits. The Self is sacred. As sweet as it may sound, the Self is like the famous snowflake—no two alike. Consider this for just a moment: That you are truly one of a kind. Unique. You are of such value. You are a wonder to behold. You are a beloved child of God. There truly is no one exactly like you in all the world, nor has there been in all of history.

In truth, self-esteem is both a work and a grace. The grace is obvious. You yourself are held in high esteem by the One who created you. Everything about you speaks of God's pride—your body, your mind, your spirit. Flaws and all. You are an amazing piece of work. A truly remarkable creation. Imagine how life would change if only you believed this to be true. If you were to get up each day, then pause and consider this spiritual fact. How different you would be, and would behave. How much more loving and forgiving. Centered and grounded. Aware and awake and available. Just the act of noting your status as a beloved creation might free you to unleash all the talents and gifts that make you *you*. Self-esteem is built upon a foundation of such belief. To be grounded in the Grace of God. A structure that supports you with strong crossbeams of respect and understanding. All self-esteem begins with recognition. The realization that we are a magnificent work of art. The artist was, and is, God—however we understand God. Even with our chips and cracks, we are one fine work of art.

> "To be nobody but yourself—in a world which is doing its best, night and day, to make you everybody else—means to fight the hardest battle which any human being can fight and never stop fighting."
> —e. e. cummings

Self-esteem must also be a work, an effort, a daily decision and choice. It is not enough to simply know that you matter, or even to claim to believe it. It is crucial that you conduct your life in such a way that the world will know it, too. This means to be true to your calling. What is your calling? What do you believe you were meant to *do?* To *be?* What comes naturally to you? What do you lose track of time doing or being? When are you in a state of joy—enjoying the moment? When and where and how do you feel most alive? What makes your blood boil? What gives you a lump in the throat? Goose bumps? Moves you to tears? Sends shivers up and down your spine? When were you left speechless, blown away, transformed? The answers to these questions, and more like them, are clues to your calling. We are all called. We all have a genuine reason for being on this Earth. Something to add. A way to make a difference. A gift that we can offer on bended knee.

Self-esteem will grow in direct proportion to your actually living out your longings. The truer you are to using the gifts you have been given, the happier you will be. The more often you are doing work that consumes your whole being, the more you will know joy. The more able you are to find relationships that expect your best, demand excellence, and encourage creativity, the more likely you will be to achieve a full and fulfilling life. Self-esteem is the result of taking a dream and making it actual. It is built by practicing the art of life. It is shaped and formed by solid

> "It is difficult to make a man miserable while he feels worthy of himself and claims kindred to the great God who made him." —ABRAHAM LINCOLN

bricks of discipline. Concentrated effort to show the world the stuff you're made of.

But self-esteem is never the result of owning more and more "stuff." It is not about buying

> "Never bend your head. Always hold it high. Look the world straight in the eye." —HELEN KELLER

things. It is not connected to power or prestige or position. It is certainly not about popularity. We have all known our fair share of popular people who are real jerks. True self-esteem is not arrogance or conceit. It is not having a big head or a bloated ego. It is simply the result of deep inner satisfaction. Knowing that the way you're living your life is the right way to live it. Knowing that now is the right time. Knowing how to do it. Doing it, being it, living out the dream. Making it yours. Becoming the dream itself. True self-esteem is hard work. An art. It is demanding your Self to be itself. Honest. Congruent. And real. It is trusting that you have something to offer, and then offering it. Without hesitation or excuse. Putting it out there for all to see.

self-discipline

Self-discipline can be tricky. Too often it takes the form of self-punishment. It is linked to guilt or shame, or both. Neither of these feelings is self-discipline. Both are simply beating up on yourself. Self-punishment may make you feel better, somehow. If you need to feel bad about being bad, I guess it might serve as some strange form of repentance. But it does nothing to improve your character. Self-discipline is all about improvement. Think of it not in terms of restraint or constraint, but of working toward a goal. The kind of self-discipline that enables progress to be made. Facilitates movement. Eases a step forward. Each small step marking an increment in a much longer path of growth.

> "Now, discipline always seems painful rather than pleasant at the time, but later it yields the peaceful fruit of righteousness to those who have been trained by it." —HEBREWS 12:11

In high school I played football. My coach was Jerry Fishbain. Though I never liked the sport, and played mostly to read my name in the papers, I knew he was an excellent coach because he taught us the fundamentals. He was big on getting back to basics. How to tackle, how to block, how to run low and tuck the ball in tight. He was fierce when it came to being in shape. We ran drill after drill during hot, sticky August two-a-day practices. Result: We got in good shape as a team. We knew our plays. We worked effectively as a unit.

We won our first game. The newspaper commented that we were a well-coached and well-disciplined team. We were also a small, slow, not all that athletically talented team. We were, however, mentally and physically tough. Our self-discipline led to a strong belief in ourselves. The results were dramatic. We won a conference championship. We played way beyond our abilities. We were a bunch of guys who rarely tired, and made few penalties. We ran our plays with precision. We seldom gave our opponents a turnover.

Our endless practicing of the basics made us function like a well-oiled machine. Individually, we weren't all that much, but as a team we were damn good.

I learned the same lesson in art. My college art teacher was Dorothy Divers. For 10 weeks we drew bricks. Big bricks, small bricks. Stacks of them. A solitary brick under a light. Bricks in shadows and in bright sun. By the tenth week, I was so sick of bricks I could spit. She told us to go outside and draw any building on campus, using all we had learned about perspective and shading. I drew Old Main. It was, far and away, the finest drawing I had ever executed. I thanked her for 10 weeks of bricks. I knew that her lesson in self-discipline had resulted in my first true piece of art.

Jesus knew the importance of self-discipline. He understood how discipline creates freedom. The freedom to be your Self is the greatest freedom of all. It is truly the acid test of life. A life well lived must be a life that is true to your own callings. A full life cannot be spent fulfilling the wishes of others. It must adhere to the dictates of your very own soul. Jesus' disciples were expected to be well-disciplined. In mercy and justice, in love and forgiveness, in generosity

> "A man's conquest of himself dwarfs the ascent of Everest." —ELI J. SCHIEFFER

and graciousness. Jesus expected His followers to have well-disciplined hearts. Hearts strong enough to forgive and forget. Hearts strong enough to fight on behalf of the unpopular cause, or for the outcast in society. Hearts ready, willing, and able to take a stand, and then walk the walk.

Not a heart with callouses. Instead, a bleeding heart. A heart cut open by a deep compassion for others, and a passion for Life itself.

Have you ever seen a ballet? It is remarkable. The skill and strength and stamina involved is mind-boggling. What is most extraordinary is how the dancers make it look so effortless. So easy. The leaps and turns and lifts and spins. The whole dance, every step choreographed in precise detail, is made to appear as if it were a walk in the park. So it was with Jesus' disciples. He wanted them to be so good at the art of loving that it became second nature to them. The second nature, of course, was Christ Himself. It was He they followed. He they sought to become. As for forgiveness, He admonished them to practice it over and over again. Seventy times seven, He said. Again—until it just flowed.

> "The fruit of the Spirit is love...." —GALATIANS 5:22

To be at home with your heart and soul is to feel as though you have mastered the craft of being *you*. You have confidence. You believe in your Self. You trust your talents. You know your gifts. You are disciplined in actualizing your dreams. When you are at home with your heart and soul, you feel at one with your calling. You rule the empire of your Self, but you do so with respect and tolerance and an abundant forgiveness. This is as Jesus would want and hope. This is how He lived. It is how His ministry was able to transform the contours of the human heart, as well as the shape of the world itself.

the way of the heart

When you are at home in the heart, it becomes a way of life. The heart takes the lead. The soul goes center stage. It becomes the catalyst for your actions, and may even determine your feelings. Think of the heart and soul as your spiritual compass. Informing you of where you are going, and, spiritually speaking, telling you why you are going there. Only the heart and soul can see deep inside. Only the heart and soul can cultivate a true vision. Only the heart and soul can reflect the will of God. To try to be like Christ is not to physically imitate Him. That would be impossible. The goal is to *become* Him in spirit. To place His heart in your chest. To allow His soul to guide you.

Think of the heart and soul as light. Initially, maybe being no stronger than a candle or a flashlight's beam. In the darkness of our world, we may barely be able to see our own feet. So we need to walk slowly but surely, carefully and cautiously. As we become more at home with our heart and soul, the flame begins to burn brighter. Think of a flaming torch. More ground is illuminated. We can see a good deal farther on. As our heart and soul continue to mature, their light will increase. It will become a beacon, a new dawn. We can now see the gift of a day stretched before us. Like a laser beam. We can even see

> "There is only one corner of the universe you can be certain of improving, and that's your own self."
> —ALDOUS HUXLEY

inside ourselves and others, and locate a wound for healing. The more at ease we are in heart and soul, the more comfortable and at home we are. We will be truly enlightened. We will become one with the light.

The way of the heart is not the easy way. It is not a sweet path of innocence. The way of the heart requires boldness, courage, discipline, and a deep faith. The way of the heart is a route that requires great love, mercy, peace, and hope. It is a path strewn with obstacles and roadblocks and dead ends. Since it does not lead to big money, it is the road less traveled. Since it is not a way around pain but through it, it is often avoided. There is, indeed, a purity to the way of the heart. No, it is not a direct route. Its purity lies in its destination. The focus is always on getting there. Getting where? Not to some mythic Heaven, but to life. Real life, fully and honestly lived. A real life that can yield a deep intimacy and satisfaction. A real life that can transform the world.

> "This is the message we have heard from him and proclaim to you, that God is light and in him there is no darkness at all." —1 JOHN 1:5

I think of the way of the heart as consisting of ten steps:

Step #1—Be awake and aware of your Self and your world

Step #2—Accept your humanity with great humility

Step #3—Know that you are a beloved child of God, and act that way

Step #4—Work on being merciful and compassionate

Step #5—Be passionate and bold; be creative and take risks

Step #6—Be honest

Step #7—Love your Self, others, the outcast, the enemy, God

Step #8—Keep maturing (changing and growing)

Step #9—Create a world of peacemakers and hope-builders

Step #10—Let Jesus be your guide to a new vision for a new world

Ten steps that can turn your life around. Ten steps that can cut a path to a genuinely good life. Ten steps we could take all the way to Heaven, but we won't have to—because we will have brought Heaven to Earth.

12

B^EING ^AT H^OM^E W^ITH F^AM^ILY

The home of my adolescence was at 1312 Yout Street, in Racine, Wisconsin. It was a modest lower flat. Coal heat. No running hot water. My bedroom also contained the kitchen sink. It cost our family $50 per month. Francis and Betty Zahalka lived upstairs. I knew each and every neighbor on my block. My friends were over constantly. My parents were easygoing and super popular with my peers. Kids have keen radar for being liked and welcome.

My father went to school until age 13. Left England, came to America at 17. The year was 1928. The Great Depression left him without a home. He lived for a time at a police station in Evanston, Illinois. He became a motorcycle cop. He would next learn the trade of typewriter repairman. He stayed in that job until he retired with a small pension, which vanished upon his death. He was kind and generous and had an explosive temper. He loved kids. He lived in fear. His later years were spent mostly listening to a police radio. He developed Alzheimer's disease in his early 70s. He went into a second childhood, though in many ways it was still the first childhood, which he had never really left. He died in the year 2000. I never knew what he believed. To this day, I have no idea whether the thought of Jesus ever crossed his mind.

My mother was brilliant. Still is. She never went to college, as that was a privilege reserved for wealthier people. She was a bastion of compassion and care. Her children were her life. This, at times, left scars. Children are not to be worshiped. An unintentional, but damaging, message. She married a man she liked but did not love. She was, however, committed to him and our family. She enjoyed life best when we kids were home, and when the house was loaded with noise and need. Most of her life has been riddled with disappointment.

> "Home is a place where you grow up wanting to leave, and grow old wanting to get back to."
> —JOHN ED PEARCE, LOUISVILLE COURIER-JOURNAL MAGAZINE

Places she wished she had seen. Things she wished she had accomplished. I suspect that her biggest regret was never finding her true soul mate.

She is alive and well today in Racine. Her eyesight is almost gone. Hearing reduced. A shrinking, curling spine that's painful. A mind that can tell you more about our health-care system than you care to know. A passion for all things Democratic. Her greatest pleasures are a good cup of coffee, a tasty bowl of soup, a luscious dessert, a long drive, and an even longer talk, plus any time at all spent with her children or grandson. A simple, bittersweet life. I do know that Jesus has crossed her mind, but only in terms of trying to live like Him. Her mercy is legendary in our family. She is the soul of her family. The caregiver of my own family. Yet, despite all, the idea that Jesus might have something to offer her is not up for consideration.

My sister, Jackie, recently retired and lives near my mother in Racine. She is a good woman who never married. She was meant to be a mother. It is sad that she never had children, and yet she offered care to so many kids over the years that it's is hard to imagine how she could have done so if she'd had her own family, as well. She has my mother's heart and my father's temper. She has worked her butt off her entire life, and has little to show for it. She is presently living on less than ten grand a year. I adore her. She takes good, good care of Mom. She has never taken herself seriously, or recognized her ample gifts. Her weight—being heavy is so different for females—has kept her from realizing many of her dreams. Her faith consists simply of being good to others. She rarely expects anything in return. She asks nothing of God. I do not know why.

This is a simple portrait of my family. Just a few brushstrokes of the pen, some taps on the computer keyboard. I paint this portrait because they are me. I am my family. Not all of me, of course, but a pretty good chunk. The same is true for you. Yes, we can move beyond our respective families. We can choose totally different goals than those they would have chosen for us. We can live out dramatically different values. Our lifestyles can be unrecognizable from theirs. Nevertheless, blood is thick, and roots go deep. It is impossible to erase the emotional and spiritual impact of our family. Those tracings remain indelibly imprinted on our soul.

So it is for Bill Grimbol. I am kind, compassionate, and a first-class caregiver. If my temper goes, look out. I am generous to a fault. I have always battled a host of worries and fears. I have spent seven years in therapy trying to get free of them. I no longer wait for the bomb to drop, but I do scan the sky now and then. I have married two soul mates. I have never worshiped my son Justin, but I have spoiled him—just not rotten. I have accomplished more than my family ever dreamed I would. I am ambitious and driven. At times, I have felt as if I have tried to live for all four of us. I still love a long drive and talk, and I cannot complete a day without coffee. I live modestly, but well.

I have a deep and abiding faith. On this note I truly part company with my family. I do not know why. Maybe finding a faith was my only means of rebellion.

> "Parents need to fill a child's bucket of esteem so high that the rest of the world can't poke enough holes in it to drain it dry."—ALVIN PRICE

Choosing another way. Not being so frightened or anxious. Not feeling cheated or betrayed. My faith became my core. I will admit to being convinced that Jesus was a Democrat (though He might have laughed at their frequent ineptitude). Other than that, my faith was a complete departure from my family's way of life. I think it saved me. Not from sin, but from deadening fear and frustration. From expecting the worst, and looking for it. From longing for something different, but never creating it.

I am not sure how this little vignette sounds. I have a lovely family. I adore them. I miss Dad. I want to be honest, really honest. To show my family in all its humanity. To let you know we all come from humble beginnings. We all come from stock that may be good, or good for nothing, or both, depending on the day. My family was, above all else, loving. It woefully lacked confidence. It was haunted by fear, riddled with worry. There was little room in it for God. We Grimbols needed to be in control. To make the boogeyman go away. We were in charge. No wonder we were so afraid!

I believe Jesus wants you to be *you*. To be your truest Self. I believe Jesus wants you to be true to your calling, and to live your longings. If any of this is to come to pass, you will have to know your family. Inside and out. You are a walking family portrait, like it or not. You will need to know the histories of your family members. Their hopes and dreams, their flaws and foibles. Most of all, their impact on you. How have they shaped and formed you? What has been the impact of their commentary on our own life? We write the story. But family writes the critique. What is it about them that you hope to keep? What are you desperate to change? Do you want a marriage like your folks'? Will you parent the way they did? Are they, or were they, happy? How has their happiness, or sadness, affected you? Are you living out your dreams, or theirs? Are you becoming a clone of them, or your own person?

Home means family. Family means roots, deep and tangled—a web. Pull on one part of that web, and the whole web trembles. We need to know our roots, intimately. We need to practice rigorous honesty when it comes to assessing the impact of our home lives. We need to face the Truth about the good, the bad, and the ugly of our upbringing. We can forgive most anything, but what we do not name and claim we simply cannot change. The spiritual life is dependent on awareness. Knowing our roots is vital to knowing our Selves.

when we all have to just get along

There are no perfect families. None. Not a one. *All* families squabble and struggle. All families deal with communication breakdowns. All families fail to compromise. All families could improve upon their listening skills and their compassion and their caring for one another. I know of no family that gets straight A's on the family report card. Every family gets a few red N's. All families flunk a subject or two along the way. All families have members who are absent for key quizzes and tests. I think many families should have been held back a year for more training. Maybe two years, even three.

The work of being a family is daily. It is required and often rigorous. If the work is done well, the family creates a home that is safe and creative. Home becomes a think tank, a studio, a lab, a sanctuary, and a respite. What is the work of which I speak? The basics—good communication, effective listening, choosing compromise. Creating a context that's conducive to honest and open exchange. The capacity to disagree, and yet forge ahead. Maintaining a positive attitude. Keeping problems in perspective. Being willing to work at forgiveness. Striving for the kind of love that is unconditional.

When individuals are seeking to live well under one roof, they need to consider the realities. The clashing of wills, the competing of dreams, the challenge of sharing, the ongoing demands of caring. Trying to meet everyone's needs, to some degree. It takes no effort to be a family. After all, a roof over a collection of heads can qualify as "family living." Rather, I mean becoming a *real* family. A gathering of souls who are bound by history and heritage and love. A constellation of folks who are consistently supportive of one another.

> "Before most people start boasting about their family tree, they usually do a good pruning job."
> —O. A. BATISSTA

Such families create true homes. Their homes are built on Grace. They are forged out of the unconditional love of God.

Have you ever thought about why Jesus chose to have disciples? Why He elected not to go it alone? Why He brought 12 tag-a-longs with Him? I think the need was for family. Community. The support of a group that shared His own vision. Jesus and His disciples experienced all the joys and problems of being a family. They fought, they disappointed each other, they denied and betrayed and doubted one another. They also were there for each other. They offered comfort and concern to all the family members. They loved one another. They were an unusual family, but a family nevertheless.

when we have to say goodbye

Raising an adolescent is never easy. Raising the parent of an adolescent is no piece of cake, either. No question but that the teenage years can be a turbulent time in a family and home. Why? Well, this one is obvious. You have the teenager readying himself or herself to leave the nest, and the parents getting ready to push them out for their fledgling flight. Both parties will be swept often by anxiety and grief. No matter how frequently an adolescent protests that he or she cannot wait to get out of the house, the actual departure is like pulling a bandage off an open sore. No matter how proud the parents claim to be of their teenager spreading their wings, the loss looms huge on the horizon.

Let me share my own experience as a parent. I have only one son. So I have gone through this only once. I am no expert, but I can tell you I have never experienced anything that so graphically informed me that I was growing old. As Justin moved out of his childhood, and endured the battles of adolescence, I was too busy to bother with aging. But . . . when I witnessed his graduation from Buxton, where he attended his high school years, I felt overwhelmed by the passage of time. Eighteen years had come and gone. Had put up camp like a gypsy, and was now tearing it down and scooting off. His graduation was a true point of demarcation. Not only had Justin grown up into a young man, but I could feel the beginnings of my own descent into old age. I was 50 years old when Justin graduated. So I knew I was no youngster. Still, preparing to see him off to college was a blatant visual aid of my own aging.

I ask you to be kind to your parents. I mean it. They, too, are going through a life passage. It creates a lot of loss— a shock of age, a stunning onslaught of grief. As an adolescent, you will find this a difficult time. Saying good-bye sounds simple. It is not. It is a huge emotional and spiritual leap. It requires a genuine capacity to grieve, to admit the pain of leaving, to embrace the loss. To recognize the enormous changes that are occurring. Home will always be home, but will never be lived in the same way again. Your parents will always be your parents, but neither seen nor understood in the same manner afterward. Roles alter and reverse. Rules shift and disappear. The rituals are transformed. Holidays and birthdays and anniversaries—all will be experienced in new and different ways.

> "Adolescence is perhaps nature's way of preparing parents to welcome the empty nest." —KAREN SAVAGE AND PATRICIA ADAMS, *THE GOOD STEPMOTHER*

Grief is a tough emotion. It is an uprooting. The ground sways beneath our feet. We feel insecure and sad. We have our doubts raised. Our anxiety level increases. We know there may be a "hello" around the corner, but the "good-bye" is still terribly difficult. It is a rite of passage, a measure of maturity. For both parent and adolescent, it remains one of the toughest of life's spiritual assignments. Think of it this way. It is a 17- or 18-year project. All kinds of work and effort and love have gone into carving out your relationship with your family. Suddenly, it's over. On many levels it's finished. Nearly a fourth of your life has been swallowed whole. It's not easy to digest all the implications.

Jesus knew how tough this parting would be. He knew it would be difficult for His disciples to uproot themselves from their own families and follow His lead. He recognized the agony of turning your back on family to set out on your own adventure. He knew it was required by life, especially the spiritual life. "Those who love their father or mother more than me are not fit to be my disciples; those who love their son or daughter more than me are not fit to be my disciples" (Matthew 10:37 GNB). Jesus' words are neither callous nor cruel. They reflect His honest awareness of the difficulty inherent in departure. Especially a spiritual one.

when a house is not a home

Not all houses become homes. Not all families function as a true family. This is most often the case in homes where the secret of abuse is taking place. The abuse of alcohol and drugs. Or physical abuse. Verbal or emotional abuse. Sexual abuse. I would also include spiritual abuse. The latter occurs when someone tries to force another to believe as they do. Forcing their faith down a child's throat. Making someone sell their soul in exchange for a faith they neither found, nor necessarily believe in. Mental illness can also create a strain that qualifies as abuse. It actually can contaminate the spirit of the entire house.

When abuse occurs in a home, it is as if a large animal came into the middle of your living room and took an enormous dump. Nobody admits it is there, so nobody cleans it up. The smell is, well, outrageous. The family begins to take routes around the steaming pile. They try air fresheners of all kinds, but they all smell sickeningly sweet. The stench remains rank. Someone places a few potted plants around the mess, in hopes that nobody will see it. The fact is, most people notice something. They may not know what it is, but they do know it is there and that it smells bad.

As time passes, the family begins to spend less and less time at home. It is easier to be out of the house. When they are in the house, they go to their room, and shut the doors. They keep the windows open for a quick exit. "It" (whatever the abuse is) is seldom mentioned. Once in a while there will be a bad joke told about it, or a vicious sarcastic remark made. At times people stare at it and weep. In a few years, most of the family will have moved on and out. But the pile is still there. It sits like a monument. The family will have few memories that are not dominated by the dump in the living room. It is as if that pile of crap were the single cloud that can block out the whole sun for the entire family.

It is impossible to feel at home in an abusive home. There is no calm or contentment there. Self-esteem cannot be found, or made. Communication remains taut and tense. Intimacy cannot spring up. Forgiveness feels fake. Until someone takes the risk of cleaning up. Then the shit can be removed, efforts made to scrub away the stain. The whole home has to be aired out, as does the family. It all takes time. Still, on certain hot humid days, the stench momentarily wafts across the room. It is never gone forever.

I think you know what Jesus' take on abuse would be. It's an abomination. All of it. The idea of raising a hand, whether physical or emotional, to a member of your own family. Whittling away at someone's self-esteem by a barrage of verbal taunts. The sexual molestation of a child's body, soul, and innocence. A parent who is a drunk. The youth who is an addict. Jesus would respond with a fierce Grace. Yes, you are still loved, He might say, but get help. Get it now. Do not continue behavior that is harming the lives of others. You have no right to do so. You know how to get well. You know how to get help. Have the maturity and faith to get help.

 ## ask not what your family can do for you

You are probably a member of a family. You most likely eat and sleep and live in a home you share with other members.

You may have parents, or a parent, under the same roof. Siblings or pets, or both. Your home may include a grandparent or an aunt or uncle, or even a family friend. Your parents may be gay or divorced or separated. Your parents may embarrass you by acting as if they still are on their honeymoon. You may have a sister you adore. You may have a brother you would like to take an ax to. There are a myriad number of family types. Different configurations and styles. If it calls itself a family, it is.

Many adolescents are quite passive when it comes to home. You may expect a lot, assume a lot—which is not all bad. Home should be a place of rest and ease. It should be a context of safety and security. However, home and family should also be a place where you *want* to offer to others some of the best of who you are. Don't give your peers all the good stuff, and the people at home the scraps. Don't forget what a brief time you get to be part of your home, your family. Savor it, know it to be sacred, cherish as many days as you can. I know that adolescence takes up most of your time and energy. The teen years demand an incredible effort. Being on stage and in the spotlight for a decade or more is enough to drive anyone nuts. The identity crisis, the quest for love, the popularity contests—it all makes for a bumpy ride. Still, you have to give a little.

> "Honor thy father and thy mother: that thy days may be long upon the land which the Lord thy God giveth thee"
> —EXODUS 20:12 KJV

Here are some questions you need to ask yourself. They will help you clarify whether you are, in fact, offering the best of who you are. Even if that is so only part-time:

1. Do I spend all my time in my room?

2. Do I ask my family members about themselves, their day, their lives?

3. Am I a good listener?

4. Do I show my affection?

5. Have I ever given a spontaneous gift of affection?

6. Will I let my family in? Do they know me at all?

7. Do I have to win every argument?

8. Do I offer help of any kind?

9. What might make my parents' lives easier?

10. Do I use my family as a scapegoat? When? Why? How?

11. Do I show any interest in other family members? Especially in their talents?

12. Do I apologize?

13. Do I forgive? Forget?

14. Do I allow members of my family to change?

15. Does my family know anything about my faith? What I believe in?

16. Have I ever shared my dreams with them?

17. Have I ever asked my parents or grandparents to tell their story?

18. Have I ever written them a letter expressing strong feelings—good or bad?

19. Have I ever admitted telling them a lie?

20. Have I asked myself what it would be like if they were gone?

Surprisingly, these are all spiritual questions. Jesus would advocate the deepening of your spirit. Asking these questions, and giving them honest answers, will give you insight into how to be a loving participant in your own family. Jesus expected children to show honor to parents. These questions will help you do just that.

13

BEING AT HOME
FOR A FRIEND

"A faithful friend is the medicine of life ..."

ECCLESIASTICUS 6:16A KJB

"This is my commandment, that you love one
another as I have loved you. No one has greater
love than this, to lay down one's life for one's
friends."

JOHN 15:12–13

Now is an excellent time to recap some of my understandings of Jesus, and to restate my take on *His* take on your life
as an adolescent:

1. Jesus wants human beings to be human—fully human,
honestly human.

2. Jesus wants you to be you, and nobody else.

3. Jesus considers you to be God's beloved child.

4. Jesus wants you to be at home being you.

5. Being at home means to feel comfortable and at ease.

6. Being at home means to feel centered and grounded.

7. Being at home means to be confident and courageous.

8. Jesus wants this experience of being at home to permeate your life.

9. Jesus wants you to have a full life.

10. Jesus wants you to enjoy your life.

It is this perspective that I seek to apply to all aspects of an adolescent's life. It is a strategy for living for young people. A spirituality. A way of being and doing. It is my belief that it will help you to become honestly and genuinely your Self. To help you make a difference. To feel as though you belong. To give you a large sense of purpose. If you are at home with your Self, you will be exactly who God created you to be. You will do what God expects and hopes.

> "True friendship is like phosphorescence— it glows best when the world around you goes dark." —DENISE MARTIN

Now is a good time to turn to friendship, an area that dominates every teen's life. I know of no adolescent who does not want or need a friend or who does not spend a good deal of time worrying and wondering about his or her relationships. Peers are *everything* in the teen years. I have watched teens spend a whole day together. Nonstop activity and togetherness. Then they go home, and immediately call the same friends to see how they are doing. This is as true for boys as it is for girls. The social networking is amazing. The introduction of personal computers, the cell phone, and text messaging has made connectedness easy, and often overwhelming. To say the least, the status of friendships is a natural preoccupation for most youth.

if you want a friend, be one

Once, for weeks before a youth activity, I had listened to several members of my youth group complain about their friends. It was nothing major. Just catty banter back and forth. But it bothered me how they casually ripped on their friends. Until the friend arrived, of course, at which point he or she would be greeted with warmth and enthusiasm. I decided to try something, a gimmick. I read them Paul's letter to the church in Corinth, the entire 13th chapter. It is a chapter that speaks of the qualities of love. They are also easily applied to friendship. Paul addresses the need for patience and kindness. Issues a call *not* to be jealous, or boastful, or rude. Paul reminds us *not* to insist on always having *our* own way. He asks us *not* to be irritable or resentful; *not* to look for faults; and instead to celebrate the good stuff. He admonishes us to believe in our relationships. I broke the chapter down into 17 expectations of love and friendship. I next asked my youth group to rank themselves on all 17. What kind of friend are you?

"If I speak in the tongues of mortals and of angels, but do not have love, I am a noisy gong or a clanging cymbal. And if I have prophetic powers, and understand all mysteries and all knowledge, and if I have all faith, so as to remove mountains, but do not have love, I am nothing. If I give away all my possessions, and if I hand over my body so that I may boast, but do not have love, I gain nothing.

"Love is patient; love is kind; love is not envious or boastful or arrogant or rude. It does not insist on its own way; it is not irritable or resentful, it does not rejoice in wrongdoing, but rejoices in the truth. It bears all things, believes all things, hopes all things, endures all things.

"Love never ends. But as for prophecies, they will come to an end; as for tongues, they will cease; as for knowledge, it will come to an end. For we know only in part, and we prophesy only in part, but when the complete comes, the partial will come to an end. When I was a child, I spoke like a child, I thought like a child, I reasoned like a child; when I became an adult, I put an end to childish ways. For now we see in a mirror, dimly, but then we will see face to face. Now I know only in part; then I will know fully, even as I have been fully known. And now faith, hope, and love abide, these three; and the greatest of these is love."

I CORINTHIANS 13

As we reviewed the results, it was that obvious that the exercise had an impact. Maybe it is simply that we don't evaluate our friendships often. Or, at least, not often enough. We don't take sufficient stock of ourselves. Are we aware of how we function as a friend? Do we work at our friendships? Do we try hard to be there for our friends? Are we loyal? Trustworthy? Do we offer encouragement and support? Are we an advocate for our friends? A champion? Do we treat them with respect? Are we careful about their feelings? Are we willing to apologize when we are wrong, or have made a mistake? Do we accept an apology? Are we committed?

This particular discussion wound up taking three consecutive Sunday nights. We explored and examined our roles as friends. We shared both our failures and our successes. We gave ourselves a report card. We wrote ourselves a letter about how to improve. I think we all learned a great deal. I also think it was one of the first times the Bible managed to speak directly to their lives. The goals set forth in 1 Corinthians, chapter 13, are concrete. Easy to understand,

> "In my friend, I find a second self." —ISABEL NORTON

even easier to evaluate. As our youth learned, Jesus asks a lot from a friend. He also gave a lot, in the spirit of not receiving much in return. What impressed the youth most was Jesus' ability to forgive. To move on past a mistake. To keep on loving, when a disciple had given Him every reason to drop the friendship.

I was also struck by one more thing, on those three Sunday nights. What the youth hated most were the mind games that friends can play with one another. The silent treatment. Pouting. Ignoring you. Not admitting when you are hurt or angry. Pretending things are fine when they are not. Saying one thing to one friend, and something altogether different to another. Believing gossip, rather than going directly to the source. Failing to honor commitments, and offering silly excuses for doing so. And, the biggest game of all, just plain lying. Good friends need to have game-free relationships. Good friends don't lie, pretend, wear masks, back stab. They are up front and always on the up-and-up.

> "A friend is someone who makes me feel totally acceptable." —ENE RIISNA

being the presence of home

Have you ever asked yourself what happens to people when you enter a room? What your presence is like? What your spirit is all about? How you impact a room or a group? So ask yourself: Do you lift up spirits? Or are you a downer? Are you a force of negativity? Or do you find the good in others? Do you radiate interest or disinterest in their lives? Do you make life easier or harder? Do you sit back and critique, or do you get directly involved? Do you make things lighter? Do you have a sense of humor? Are you the life of the party, or a portable death knell?

Each of has a presence. It is our spirit. Our spiritual perspective. The way we see and hear. It is an attitude—a point of view, an approach, a lifestyle, a faith in action. Your presence is how others experience you. The energy you give off; your life force, if you will. I am always amazed how someone can seem to light up a room, while others are like a walking eclipse of the sun *and* the moon. I wonder if they are aware. Are you aware? Have you taken a good, long look at your own presence around others? It is important that you do so. It is especially important to your spiritual life.

Your friends need you to be a positive presence. Your friends, like you yourself, need to experience the presence of home. A friend who is such a presence is one who makes us feel we matter and belong. They offer us loyalty and uncon- ditional love. They overlook our flaws, and encourage our efforts. They celebrate our suc- cesses. They give us confidence. They become our confidants. They are a sanctuary, a place of rest, a space of Grace. With a friend who makes us feel at home, we do not

> "A friend is someone who can see through you and still enjoys the show."
> —FARMERS ALMANAC

feel alone. We feel as though we have someone at our side, and behind us. Someone we can lean on, depend upon, trust totally. It is the feeling of being held securely in an embrace. It squeezes out all the worries and fears.

Jesus was such a presence. He offered people a spirit of concern and compassion. His care was palpable. Jesus was a presence, in the physical sense. He was there for his friends.

He was there when they were in crisis. There to address their needs. There to share their sorrows, and to rejoice in their happiness. Jesus shared His life with His friends. He was aware. He was available. His affection was real and plentiful. His touch was strong and deep. He listened with His heart. He had uncanny insight. He was simply a heart unleashed. A man who took burdens upon Himself. A man who was willing to put others first, and Himself second. A man willing to literally die for his friends, and for all humankind.

> "A friend is a lot of things, but a critic he isn't." —BERN WILLIAMS

being jesus

It is Christmastime as I write this, and I'm listening to one of my most beloved carols, "O Little Town of Bethlehem." In my favorite verse, we sing for Jesus to be "born in us this day." I have always thought that my friends deserve my very best. For me, that best would be to actually *be Jesus*. Not to mimic Him, but to *be* Him. I have no idea what this would mean. I mean, to attempt to see my friends as Jesus would see them. Hear them as He would hear them. Experience them as He might. Know them as He does. Enjoy them and cherish them as I know He would. Find the grace in them. Bring out their best. Love them fully and honestly. Forgive them. And forget anything in our relationship that needs to be discarded.

A tall order? Of course. Impossible? Yes and no. No, we cannot hope to *be Jesus* in thought, word, and deed. Yes, it is well worth the try. Even the attempt is transforming. Merely trying is a substantial spiritual shift. A faith leap. To see our friends as if they were God's beloved children would bring out a whole new dimension of intimacy between us. Our friends would feel deeply appreciated and respected. They would know the touch of Grace. A touch so tender that it would remove all anger and fear and hurt. A touch that would wipe all tears from the eye.

As an experiment, try it. Try seeing a friend through Jesus' eyes. As you understand Jesus. You don't have to worship Him to have some kind of understanding of His presence. You probably have some kind of take on Him already. An attitude or perspective. If not, simply ask yourself how Jesus might see your friend. How a friend would appear in Jesus' vision. What He might have to say to your friend. How Jesus might enable you to experience your friend in a whole new light.

14

B^EING ^AT H^OME ^AT SCH^{OO}L

"I have never let my schooling interfere with
my education."

MARK TWAIN

"We learn to walk by stumbling."

BULGARIAN PROVERB

The importance of school cannot be underestimated. Just for
the amount of time you will spend there, it needs to be a
place where you can at least feel comfortable. School is a
vital context for learning. It is also critical to your maturation and socialization. It will help determine major chunks of
your future. Like it or not, it is a community that will have a
lot to say about how your entire life turns out. It only makes
sense to make the best of it. Turning it into enemy territory is
just plain dumb.

I can't imagine Jesus having a lot to say about school, in terms of learning. Except to take the opportunity seriously. Do your best. Make an effort to be a solid student. I think most of His input would be about the kind of community member you choose to be. School should not be something that happens to you. It should be a place that you help create. What would be essential to Jesus is not what you *do* at school, but rather who you *are*, what you are while *being* there. What kind of presence you take to the classroom. What kind of impact you make—on your peers, the teachers and staff, the school as a spirit.

> "Be yourself. No one can ever tell you you're doing it wrong." —JAMES LEO HERLIHY

Doing your schoolwork is a given. Doing your homework is also a given. Helping everyone to feel at home at school is a choice you have to make every day until you graduate.

If you are to bring your spiritual Self to school, in order to be at home there, here are some of the things you will very much need *to be*. Let's just call them our "Be-Attitudes."

be real

Again, think of how much time you actually spend in school. It would be dangerous to be a phony there. If you sell your soul to be popular, or the reverse (acting like a first-class cynic about everything in school), you are wasting a tremendous opportunity, let alone time. Unfortunately, school can be a place that encourages the selling of your soul. The popularity contests can be all-consuming. Sports can take on a ridiculous level of importance. Grades can become an unhealthy obsession. Then there are those of you who do nothing but socialize, who waste the chance to learn, who are afraid to admit that you just might be intellectual. Who cannot let anyone see that in fact they might care about being a good student.

Be honest with your Self. Bring the real you to school. Don't try to be someone you are not. Do not make fitting in something that requires you to forfeit your talents or gifts. Don't let the peer-pressure cooker leave you like a limp, overcooked vegetable, with no energy to learn and no nutrients to challenge your brain. Teachers need to know the real you, so that they can help you achieve. That's why they're there. Coaches and administrators also need to know the real you. I admit it, some of them may not like the real you. But, as long as you are not being mean or nasty, you have a much better chance of overall academic and social success by being true to your Self.

Being true to your Self means to admit who you are. Admit your interests. Admit your intellect. Admit where you struggle to learn. Admit to being up or down, or in between. Admit when you know. Admit when you don't. If you are going to be there, open your mouth. Let people in on who you are, even if at times this may provoke a negative reaction. On the whole, people respond best to folks who remain true to themselves. Real people win out in the end. At least, they never lose what is most valuable—themselves.

be involved

Why not be involved? Why be a part of a community and not care about it? I am not saying you have to be someone who runs around joining every committee and club, trying to please everyone. I mean, figure out where and how you can plug in, and then do so. Make an investment. Show some interest. Be present. Be a good listener. Ask good questions. Be available. Raise your hand once in a while. Contribute.

be in balance

I find that many adolescents feel burned out. This means they feel that Life's tasks and duties keep increasing, even as the rewards and satisfactions keep decreasing. Like a fire in the hearth, eventually the fire goes out. It is not easy for young folks to rekindle it.

So make sure you get enough rest. Make sure you at least attempt to eat decently. Most of all, make sure you have time to play. Recreation time. Also, re-creation time, where you rebuild yourself.

> "In order to maintain a well-balanced perspective, the person who has a dog to worship him should also have a cat to ignore him." —*PETERBOROUGH (ONTARIO) EXAMINER*

Happy youth get better grades. Happy and healthy youth do better in sports. I can't prove this, but it is my own observation, over some 30 years of working with youth. You need to take a break. If all you do is take a break, though, then you need to do some hard work. The key here is to be in balance.

This past Sunday I met with my 10th and 11th grade Spiritual Growth Group. I asked the kids if they wanted to do anything over their winter break in February. Brian Hausman said, "Can we just go? No plans. No agenda. Just go?!" The rest of the group immediately chimed in their agreement. I asked them to be a bit more specific. They said they just needed to be together and have a good time. Their lives were so routine and predictable, they felt an acute need to shake things up a bit. I understood. And I agreed. Wish us luck. We are going. I truly do not know where. Pray that I will be able to convince some parents to trust me on this one.

> "Ask any decent person what he thinks matters most in human conduct: five to one his answer will be 'kindness.'"
> —KENNETH CLARK

I am taking them because my youth are right. Their lives *are* in a rut. I can see it in them. I can feel it. The only difference between a rut and a grave is the depth. This will be a chance to regain balance. A week of doing nothing. Going nowhere. Just letting Life happen. Going with the flow, rather than pushing the river. Should be good for us all.

Keep your life in good balance. It will enable you to be at your best. It will allow you to be a far more positive presence. It will keep your attitude healthy, and your perspective clear. It will remove a lot of the anxiety and stress and worry that can kill a day, a week, a lifetime, a soul. If you are still struggling with the tensions and troubles in your life, or have gone through some kind of major trauma, for God's sake get some help. Literally, for God's sake. Be woman enough. Be man enough. Be adult enough to ask for help. Why not? You deserve to feel good about your Self and your Life. You deserve to get unstuck. You deserve to be able to move on, in a positive direction.

be kind

These days, school can be ruthless. Mean girls somehow got fashionable. Cliques got to be notoriously brutal. Jocks got to act like total jerks. Druggies got to be, well, druggies—sarcastic and out of it. I know of no high school that could not do with a good dose of human kindness.

Remember, it is not all about you. Be sensitive. Be aware of what others are going through. Including the adults. You are right, the lousy grade may just be the result of one teacher's having had a lousy day. It isn't too much to ask of you to care. Be considerate. Be gracious. No, I am not asking you to be Mary Poppins or Saint Francis of Assisi. I just think you can be a presence of decency. Treating others

> "Kind words can be short and easy to speak, but their echos are truly endless." —MOTHER TERESA OF CALCUTTA

as you would like to be treated. Jesus asks you to be loving. To even love your enemies. I won't go that far. I will only ask you to be kind to everyone. A little kindness can make a huge difference in someone's day. In the way a school feels and functions. Ask yourself when was the last time a teacher got a compliment. Then give one. Observe the reaction.

Do I want you to be Goody Two-shoes? No. I didn't say to offer fake kindness. I didn't ask you to walk around with a smile wrapped around your head like a halo. I am not encouraging you to function as if you are a candidate for homecoming king or queen. I am asking you to care. Then to show it. To be kind, to make a difference, to be a good person. Why? Because being a bad person is contagious. Because being a bad person can become a really bad habit. Because it is truly *not* who you, down deep, wish or want to be. Because Jesus said so. So there!

be open

This "Be-Attitude" is basic, but crucial. Far too many adolescents arrive at school closed minded, shut up, shut off, and shut down. How sad. What a complete waste of time and talent and teachers and money. What a complete waste of your gifts. No matter how you try to defend it, it will remain indefensible.

> "The beautiful souls are they that are universal, open, and ready for all things." —MONTAIGNE, "OF PRESUMPTION," ESSAYS (1580–1588), TR. CHARLES COTTON AND W. C. HAZLITT

The least you can do is go to school and be open. Have an open mind. Have an open heart. Open your mouth, your eyes and ears.

Open your Self to learn and challenge and change and grow and experience and experiment and argue and defend and prove. Open up to the possibilities. Be willing and ready to receive.

> "Where there is an open mind, there will always be a frontier." —CHARLES F. KETTERING, QUOTED IN *PROFILE OF AMERICA*

I can't count the times I have seen teens slouched in a school desk chair. Eyes half shut and downcast. Arms folded in front like a locked fortress. Feet forming a crossed barrier. It is almost as if they have come ready to defy anyone to reach them. It is as if they have a sign in their eyes that reads CLOSED. Not open for business. Nobody home. This property is abandoned.

That is tragic. Truly. It saddens Jesus, too, I am sure.

What a difference you can make in your school day by simply arriving in class with an open spirit. Open to ideas, to new experiences, to caring. Open to taking your place in the community. Open to being invested and involved. The difference would, and could, be staggering.

being at home away from home

This one is risky. School seldom truly feels like home. It can have its moments, but I must admit that it can still have a pretty viciously competitive atmosphere. Nevertheless, on a spiritual basis, I think it is worth a try to make it your home by day. If you function at school as if it were your home away from home, it will allow you to be real. To be honest, to be present, to care. To be an active force for compassion within the school community. To help the community to think and feel and function like a family.

I regularly conduct workshops in various school districts. This work has taken me all over Long Island, as well as into neighboring Connecticut and Massachusetts. I speak most often on recognizing and responding to teen suicide and depression, as well as how to grieve as a community. Thus, the topics I address automatically invite a high degree of intimacy. I have come to observe those schools that clearly do function as a family, as well as those that are much more a factory. The school as family is where the communication is open and honest and the affirmation consistent. Family schools are quick to compliment (both students and teachers), careful to critique, and cautious about people's feelings. Though they have a high degree of honesty, they also demonstrate precious little negativity.

"The only means of strengthening one's intellect is to make up one's mind about nothing—to let the mind be a thoroughfare for all thoughts." —JOHN KEATS, LETTER TO GEORGE AND GEORGIANA KEATS, SEPT. 17–27, 1819

By contrast, schools that are like factories have minimal communication. As always, it starts at the top. If the teachers and staff do not trust the administrators, or if they work in an atmosphere of suspicion and mistrust, you and your schoolmates can feel it immediately. That kind of school will focus on test scores and discipline, and nothing else. It may get the job done, but fail to help raise the adolescents in its charge to adulthood. It may achieve high marks on the standardized tests, but low marks in being a community that cares about its own members. I have listened to more than one or two administrators brag about how many of their kids went on to Ivy League colleges, but seemed oblivious to how miserable a majority of their staff and students were every day.

> "Kindness is a language which the deaf can hear and the blind can read."
> —MARK TWAIN

It is truly sad. Such factory schools are sad places. Teachers cannot get out of there fast enough. Students cannot get home soon enough. They are like a busy industrial building, and the parts on the conveyor belts (the students) are getting all their needed bits and pieces. Except for the one that matters most. Such factory places forget the heart. They offer their adolescents almost nothing in terms of self-esteem, compassion, care, or any encouragement to be true to themselves or their dreams. I have an acid test: I ask an administrator to introduce me to some of the students, at least some of those who will be graduating. Do they know any, by name, by talent, by personality? Do they really know? Do the students know them? This will tell you whether you are at a family school or a factory school.

15

BEING AT HOME IN THE WORLD

When my son, Justin, was an infant, I often found it tough to sleep at night. I was a first-time dad, and I worried incessantly about his safety. I felt a compulsive need to check on his breathing. So, there I would be, about three o'clock in the morning, standing next to his crib, lowering my head until I could sense his breathing. Once I had found that magic breath, I was able to sleep a couple of hours. I was usually back in there by 5 or 6 a.m.

On one such long night of breathing patrol, I left his crib, having performed my duty, and decided to go to a nearby 7-Eleven for coffee. It was nearly dawn, and I doubted I could fall back to sleep. I grabbed a large java and a copy of *USA Today*, then headed back home. I seated myself at the kitchen table and began to read the newspaper. The front page featured a large photo of a child in Africa who was starving to death. To be honest, I forget which country the child was from. I only recall the look of pure anguish on his father's face. His father, who held him in his arms, was waiting for his son literally to die.

At that precise moment, I had a revelation—an epiphany, an insight. I could care less what you call it. I could hear Jesus in my head. Not the voice, so much as the message. I could hear Jesus asking me to care about each and every child in the world, exactly as I cared for my own dear son. I was being asked, or called, or commissioned, to listen for the breathing of the children of the world. I felt overwhelmed by the scope of the task. I was moved to tears by the meaning behind the message. All children are God's children. As that African father felt, so feels God. When a child is wounded, abused, hungry, homeless, maimed, or murdered, God feels the pain. Whatever tragedies befall a child, anywhere in this world, they are God's personal tragedies.

I recall that moment with clarity. It was a point of recognition, as if from a laser beam. I became fully aware of my role as a global citizen. It would not be enough for me merely to care about the safety and well-being of my own child. If I was to be a true follower of the man named Jesus, I knew I could not ignore *any* of the children of the world. I had a responsibility to care deeply about each and every soul on the planet. To pray for them. To offer love and respect when I could. To be a presence of compassion and concern. That was my spiritual job.

You, too, share this task. Whether you choose to believe in Jesus Christ or not, the duties are prescribed by Life. It is the enforcement that is done by faith. You, too, need to see yourself as a global citizen. But what does that mean?

being color blind

America is a racist nation. Face it: We are a racist people. If I preach a sermon about the poor treatment of people of color in this country, I can be guaranteed to get several letters and e-mails and calls in response. Racism is a raw nerve ending in America. We like to think of ourselves as quite civilized, and tolerant, but I think in our heart of hearts we know different. If Jesus sets the standard, which is to be color blind, then I suspect we know we all fall pretty short of the mark most of the time.

Now, don't get all defensive. I know you do not think you are a racist. (If you do, you have real problems.) I don't like to think of myself as racist, either. But I am. I am, by the color of my skin. White. I am, by being part of a long history of racism. I have been raised in it and by it. I am, because so many institutions that I love are quietly, even secretly, racist. Is there any institution more segregated than the church? I know, in my soul, that if Jesus came to apply for the job to replace me as pastor, and He were a black candidate, He would never, ever get the job. A million reasons would be given. The real reason would never be admitted. If Jesus were black, He could not serve as the Presbyterian minister on Shelter Island.

Recently Michael Richards, who played Kramer on the wildly popular *Seinfeld* TV show, was being heckled during a comedy performance in Los Angeles. The hecklers were black. For whatever reason, the heckling really got to Richards. He exploded in a racist rant that was embarrassing and terribly harmful to his career. Afterward, you could feel his deep remorse. He could not believe he had done something so stupid. So blatantly racist. He kept trying to prove he was not a racist. But he was, and is. He is not a bad man. He is just like so many of us. Underneath the surface, deep under our skin, is a lifetime of prejudice and racial oppression. We cannot completely remove its stain. We will all need to apologize at some point. Some far more vociferously than others.

> "Forgive us for not wanting to recognize our relatives in Your family who are black or red or yellow or white, whose children's children may be our grandchildren; for accepting people we like, but rejecting those we do not like because they are not of our class or color."
> —UNITED PRESBYTERIAN CHURCH, *LITANY FOR HOLY COMMUNION* (1968)

I think that a good first step in becoming color-blind is to try to look at another person through Jesus' eyes. It will help you and me, both, see the person as just a person. It will free us from some of the built-in stereotypes and fears that haunt our racial relationships. It will help us rid ourselves of some of the unconscious attitudes that we grew up with. My grandmother always told me she loved black people, but hoped I would never marry one. I know she thought she was not a racist. What a confused, crazy message that was. To say that I love them, but don't marry one. "One"—ay, there's the rub. Racism is built upon seeing a whole race as if it were one person. The whole race as having that one person's attributes. Look through Jesus' eyes. It will take some work. Our image is fairly distorted. Take your time. Look hard, look long, look deep.

A global citizen cannot adhere to racist notions. He or she cannot stereotype or scapegoat other human beings on the basis of color. He or she cannot be filled with prejudice or, worse yet, hate. A true global citizen is color-blind. Seeing people as people. Seeking all folks as God's folks.

not all-american

In my introduction, I wrote that Jesus is not American. He is not. He is not on our side. We are not His chosen people. This is not the promised land. Jesus belongs to the planet, to humanity, to every race and religion. It is this kind of fanatic patriotism that is so dangerous in our world. Yes, I do see this same fanaticism in other parts of the globe. Yes, it is equally disturbing. I target America here, only because this book will be read primarily by Americans. Plus, I *am* an American. I want to change the nation in which I live, the community where I have the best chance to exert good influence.

Becoming a global citizen means getting smart about the rest of the world. Remember the old joke: If you know how to speak three languages, you are trilingual. If you know how to speak two languages, you are bilingual. If you know how to speak one language, you are American. This does not say good things about America. It says we have a superiority complex. We believe that we are the best and the brightest. That our lives are of greater value. Can you imagine how appalled Jesus would be by the notion of a First World and a Third World? Imagine trying to defend that concept. We—you and I and all of us—need to become far more aware of what is happening in our world, the larger world that is Planet Earth.

I have had the rare privilege of sharing communion with Archbishop Desmond Tutu. For the past several years, I have done so about a half-dozen times. Each communion was memorable. I once brought my son. After the sacrament and a laugh-riot of a breakfast, I drove my son back to school. He commented, "Dad, we prayed for people all over the place. A lot of the places I have never even heard of. I didn't even know what was happening there, or why we were praying for them. I really want to know." To be honest, I was impressed by the same simple reality. The Archbishop is vitally aware of what is happening around the globe. His prayers of mercy stretch to every corner of the planet.

After one such communion, the Archbishop commented directly on the need for American youth to become smarter about the issues of the world. He gently and graciously spoke of how he, while teaching in our country, was forced to alter his curriculum, simply because of the ignorance that American students showed for the world around them. Obviously, as a devout man of God, the truest follower of Jesus I have met, he was trying to say something critical to us as Americans. He wanted us to know that it is not so important whether America is the wealthiest and most powerful nation on earth. What truly matters is the size of our collective heart. Will we be a people who are a true force of moral goodness? Will we feed our hungry and clothe our naked? Will we make sure our people have homes and health care and opportunity based on ability?

compassion

Last year I went home for Christmas. For me it was the first Christmas I had celebrated in Racine in 20 years. The first time, in all those years, to be with my family. It was a real nostalgia fest. My father passed away in 2000, and he was the one missing link in the picture. In his honor, I took a walk. It was the same route I has taken with him hundreds of times as a kid. He liked a long walk after dinner, and I enjoyed keeping him company. We didn't talk much. We just walked. We might chat about a local sports teams, or the Green Bay Packers or the then Milwaukee Braves, but that was about it. Dad was never much of a talker. One night, though, he talked the whole time about England. He told me story after story from his childhood and adolescence. Forgetting that I had heard these stories a million times before. I was bored. He was delighted. So it goes.

As I walked alone last Christmas, I was quick to notice the enormous change in our old neighborhood. The neighbors were now mostly black, or brown. Several Mexican restaurants had opened. I could hear Spanish being spoken as people gathered in front of stores and shops. There was even an Iranian supermarket, whose smells were strange and acrid. I was getting irritated. "This is my neighborhood," I thought. "You are stealing my memories." And yes, I probably thought, "And you just a bunch of foreigners."

When I got home I told my mother about the changes I had experienced. I must have sounded disgusted. She told me that was not like me. I asked her what she was talking about. She said I needed some compassion. She told me these families were filling my old neighborhood with the sights and sound of their cultures, just as they had done when they first came here (and just as my own ancestors had come here). My mother is a very wise woman. She told me she was tired of hearing people complain about people not speaking English. She said when she came from Denmark, two teachers spent hours with her after school to teach her English. She said she was sure they did it for free. They did it because they had

> "Resolve to be tender with the young, compassionate with the aged, sympathetic with the striving, and tolerant of the weak and wrong. Sometime in life you will have been all of these."
> —BOB GODDARD

compassion for her. She asked me where this compassion was in my own generation.

Well, shut my mouth. Mom had taught me a lesson. Bittersweet. She was so right. No matter how compassionate I believed I was, I could also be selfish and elitist. I could see a whole neighborhood as mine, and the new inhabitants as foreign invaders. My mother's questions were stinging. Why don't we have folks lining up willing to teach English for free? Why *aren't* our churches holding potluck suppers to welcome our new neighbors? The East End of Long Island is loaded with immigrants who have come here looking for work. The efforts to welcome these folks are few and far between. This is not a matter of immigration policy, it is a matter of caring about our fellow human beings. Again, imagine explaining our rigid immigration policy to Jesus.

> "Greed is a bottomless pit which exhausts the person in an endless effort to satisfy the need without ever reaching satisfaction." —ERICH FROMM, *ESCAPE FROM FREEDOM*

The night before I left to go home, I took the same walk, by myself. This time I greeted people. I took my time. I got rid of my fear and awkwardness. I went into a few shops. I ate a burrito at a cute little place with fabulous food. Yes, it was a whole new Racine for me. An entirely new neighborhood. But it was still God's. Only, this time, I was the one who had to fit in.

Compassion is crucial in our world today. Walking a mile in our neighbor's shoes. Knowing our neighbors. Caring

about them. Think about it. Jesus asks us to love our neighbors as we love ourselves. How are we doing? Pretty poor? I
think so. How can we improve? Compassion is the discipline
we need to put into practice. It is compassion that will teach
us how to understand and respect our differences. How to
just get along.

This is our world. We must become global citizens.
Our problems are often the very problems of our global
neighbors, whether just across the border or on the other
side of the world. And vice versa. Terrorism is worldwide. It
is everyone's issue. Global warming could change the course
of our planet, indeed could alter the history of humanity.
The population explosion remains the single greatest threat
to our world. Resource depletion. The breakdown of the
personal and global immune system. Pollution and the presence of nuclear arms. Cancer and
AIDS. Obesity and starvation.
While some folks scavenge the
dumps for garbage to eat, others
are getting liposuction to remove
unwanted fat. The issues of our

> "Greed's worst point is
> its ingratitude." —SENECA,
> *LETTERS TO LUCILUS* (1ST
> CENTURY A.D.), 73.3

world are huge and complex, and will require an all-out
effort to resolve. That, plus a good bit of care, compassion,
concern, and just plain love.

There is one final issue that I must address with you. If
you wish to consider becoming a true global citizen. Jesus
was clear on this point. I need to be, also. The issue is
money. Greed. Stuff. We live in a culture that is addicted to

accumulation. We buy what we don't need. Need what we don't want. The world cannot survive with Americans consuming so many of the world's resources. I don't know about you, but I don't want to live in an America where I reside in some gated community to keep the riffraff out, then from the comfort of my recliner watch the starving

> "Want is a growing giant whom the coat of Have was never large enough to cover." —RALPH WALDO EMERSON, *THE CONDUCT OF LIFE* (1860)

children of the world on my huge flat-screen TV. I do not want to have a closet full of clothes I do not wear, two or three gas-guzzling vehicles, and a lifestyle of mostly luxury, while a majority of the world strives simply to survive until the next tiny meal. This is the message offered by the Jesus I know. It is firm and fierce. The message is that greed is unacceptable. Donald Trump is not a role model. It is not OK to transform Christmas into a commercial extravaganza.

Think about the role of money in our lives. You cannot have Jesus in your backpack, and not address this fundamental issue.

PART THREE

LEAVING FOR HOME (LIVING THE CHRISTIAN LIFE)

The parable of the sower and the seeds is sweet and simple. It is easy to understand. The metaphors are direct and quickly revealing. We are being told that faith is like seeds.

Seemingly small and insignificant. Tiny glimpses of grace. Moments of extreme clarity. Experiences which take our breath away. Epiphanies which leave us with a lump in the throat. Falling in love. Being in love. Choosing to love or forgive or both. These are the seeds of faith.

> "That same day Jesus went out of the house and sat beside the sea. Such great crowds gathered around him that he got into a boat and sat there, while the whole crowd stood on the beach. And he told them many things in parables, saying: 'Listen! A sower went out to sow. And as he sowed, some seeds fell on the path, and the birds came and ate them up. Other seeds fell on rocky ground, where they did not have much soil, and they sprang up quickly, since they had no depth of soil. But when the sun rose, they were scorched; and since they had no root, they withered away. Other seeds fell among thorns, and the thorns grew up and choked them. Other seeds fell on good soil and brought forth grain, some a hundredfold, some sixty, some thirty.'"
>
> MATTHEW 13:1–8

The parable is focused on the soil. Is the soil receptive to these seeds, or is it not? We hear of four different soils. The first is a well worn footpath. It is as hard as rock. Baked by the sun. Worn down by thousands of passing feet. The seed can only sit on the surface. The birds come and eat it. Feet continue to trample it down. This soil is like a hardened heart or a closed mind. Not one thing can get in. If people want nothing to do with faith. If they slam the door shut on their soul. There is little a seed can accomplish.

The second soil is shallow and rocky. There is no room for roots. This is like a soul which has no real room for faith. What little faith there is, it is nothing but talk. Without roots, this faith will wither and rot in a crisis. It is akin to having a shallow friend. You can count on the friend when things are smooth and good, but when there is a problem of any kind, this is a friend who will disappear. We live in a culture which encourages shallow. Even a shallow faith. Jesus has little use for a faith without any depth to it.

The third soil is thorny. The thorns can represent worries and fears. Anxiety and stress. The pursuit of money and fame. Anything which can become all consuming. Anything which can be so addictive, we will sell our soul to have it. Thorny soil is totally non-productive. It has nothing to offer except pain. Trying to till this soil is bound to cause a puncture wound or two. Thorny soil, in the long run, is useless.

Fourth and finally, there is fertile soil. Soil which is receptive to the seed. Soil rich in questions and longing and spiritual seeking. Soil which is open to the growth of a strong faith.

A faith which will bud, blossom, and bloom. A
faith which will grow and mature. A faith which will
become a life lived. A living faith. Fertile soil is not auto-
matic. It requires good care. Rigorous maintenance. There
is hard work involved in creating the fertile soil which is
conducive to faith growth.

First and foremost, the soil needs light. Plenty of it. If
we are to follow Jesus, we need to be fully awake and aware.
In the light. Enlightened. I think of being in the light as being
honest. Wide open. True to our Selves. Telling the truth.
Living the truth. Living in the light is the elimination of
denial, lying, and phoniness. It is to be genuine.

The soil also needs water. It needs to be properly
nurtured and fed. Jesus would want his followers to have
time to pray and study. Time for worship. Time to serve.
Priorities known and ordered. Most of all, Jesus would
water the soil of faith with love. The followers of Jesus
cannot simply study loving, they must do it. They must live
their love. They must love their life.

The soil needs to be weeded. Get rid of the bad habits
and the bad attitude. Recognize the waste of time and energy
that is hatred and revenge. Know the great loss which is the

result of finding fault, and blaming others for what we our selves must do or change. The followers of Jesus cannot be cynics. Knowing the value of nothing, and the price tag of everything. They must have a spiritual perspective. Knowing what counts. What matters. What lasts.

The soil may need some fertilizing. Jesus expects his followers to face their crises. Pick up their crosses. Jesus asks us to be unafraid of sacrifice. Willing to know suffering. Understanding the vital importance of grieving. Jesus asks us to love the tough to love. The outcast. The enemy. The person who drives you nuts on a daily basis. The one you are sure Jesus would hate. Even him or her—the call remains love.

Fencing may be required. A scarecrow. The tilling of the soil. Turning it over on a regular basis. We must do whatever it takes to keep the soil rich and ready to receive. We tend to spend no time on the care of our spiritual soil. It is usually the last consideration. We just assume the soil will always be rich, and will eventually grow something. This is not the case. It needs our work. Our effort. Our desire to keep it in the best possible shape.

The goal of good soil is growing. Growing good crops. In the spiritual sense, this means growing up a good person.

A person who is a good neighbor and friend. A soul who knows how to preach good news to the poor and lost. An individual who does good things. Kind things. Considerate and generous thing. A good person is a gracious person.

Jesus wants us to grow up. To become a whole person. To be a person who creates. Creates a truly good life. A life of love and laughter. Mercy and justice. Making peace and celebrating diversity. Being tolerant and remaining open to all. A life full of faith and fun. Hope and joy. Point and purpose.

Good soil brings forth good life. Living and growing things. Jesus would want us to be abundantly alive. Living our faith. Making our faith a daily testament. Actualizing what we claim to believe. This whole section will be about living the Christian life. Whether you do so or not is solely up to you.

Good soil yields a good harvest. A harvest of holiness. The holiness being maturity. A mature faith yielding an abundant supply of love and forgiveness. Maturity asks you to leave home. To break away from the security of your home and family. You are called to claim your own individual identity. To be a person capable of deep and lasting intimacy. To declare your independence.

True maturity is a spiritual growth which will show
you how to leave home to then head for home. Becoming
whole = heading home to God. Spiritual maturation is
leaving for home. Only this time the home is the breast of
God. It is to become his child. To live as his heir. To be confident in your calling, true to your longings, and busy with the
business of building the Kingdom. Leaving one home for
another. Not a better home. A different home. A deeper and
fuller home. A home where faith abides. A home where
peace does pass all understanding

The chapters in Part III, "Leaving for Home," are
about the mature life of the Christian. I will do be my best
to describe what this life and lifestyle might look like. Again,
this is my perspective. My take on the Christian life. This is
definitely not an easy path. The choices are often painful.
The way harsh. If you are to choose it, I want you to consider what it truly is all about.

The mature Christian life is homeward bound.
Determined to find a faith that you can actually and honestly
live. A faith that makes sense. A faith that is content in the
midst of mystery. A faith that can witness miracles. A faith
that knows when, where, and how to serve. A faith that
animates a life with meaning. Creates hope and happiness.

Knows joy. A faith so full of love, it literally flows over. Sound over the top? It is. A bit. I want to set the bar high. You are capable of great things. In this I share Jesus' perspective 100 percent.

Weeding and watering. Fertilizing. At times some pruning, or fencing, or the inclusion of a scarecrow. Whatever it take to keep the soil ready to receive. Ripe to grow good things.

The Christian faith requires fertile soil.

16

WALKING HOME

Following Jesus means movement. It means maturing, growing, learning. It is the expansion of the soul. The broadening of our horizons. The enlargement of our heart and mind. It is, simply, increasing our capacity to love and to forgive. Faith in Jesus is never idle. It cannot just sit there and do nothing. It must do the will of God. And the will of God is to be true to your Self. To be true to your true Self is to become the loving, forgiving, and creative soul you were meant to be.

Many of you think of spirituality and faith as being quiet. A little Bible study, a whispered prayer life, a calm retreat in the country. Contemplating the will of God. Well, it is all of that, but there is so much more. Christians recognize the need for solitude. The yearning for peace and quiet. The longing to be away from it all. However, this is always as a means of renewal. Of relocating one's energy and enthusiasm. Reigniting the fires of discipleship. Jesus knew when to get away. He did so Himself, often retreating to the desert for time alone with God. This time was always followed by immersion. By diving back into the world and the work of doing, and being, Grace.

The Christian life is not about making life easier. It is about making you stronger. Following in Jesus' footsteps requires courage and commitment as well as overwhelming compassion. It is not a means of playing it safe, though you may indeed feel more secure. It does not simplify things, though it may afford focus. It is not a lifestyle that offers easy answers, but it is a way of life that offers delightfully haunting questions.

walking the walk

Christian faith is a walk. Not a walk in the park, nor a casual stroll. It is more like a rigorous hike. You need to be well exercised, well trained, well prepared. Jesus will often ask you to go where you have never gone before. To travel to places that appear dangerous. To climb high and rappel low. To ford streams and run rapids. Christian faith is a true journey.

Because Jesus calls upon us to be fully honest, filled with compassion, we are not allowed the luxury of denial or indifference. Yes, I have walked right by a homeless person. I have neglected to look into the eyes of a soul I knew was mentally ill or hungry. I have never *not* known I was shirking my duty. Discipleship does not let you off the hook. It is not that I spend hours wallowing in guilt. It is just that I am aware. I cannot deny who I am, or what I am called to do and be. Either I do it or be it, or I don't. I never try to crawl up on the cross with Jesus, but I do know my responsibilities. I know whether they are fulfilled or neglected.

The Christian walk asks us to do some crazy things, believe some crazy things, follow Jesus to some crazy places. When I use the word "crazy," I am speaking of how the world would see it. Let me describe the Christian walk as it is described in a couple of parables from scripture. You will quickly see how being a disciple takes you on a pretty wild ride, in some most-unexpected directions, and to some strange places.

> "Then He said to him, 'A certain man gave a great supper and invited many, and sent his servant at supper time to say to those who were invited, "Come, for all things are now ready."
>
> But they all with one accord began to make excuses. The first said to him, "I have bought a piece of ground, and I must go and see it. I ask you to have me excused." And another said, "I have bought five yoke of oxen, and I am going to test them. I ask you to have me excused." Still another said, "I have married a wife, and therefore I cannot come." So that servant came and reported these things to his master. Then the master of the house, being angry, said to his servant, "Go out quickly into the streets and lanes of the city, and bring in here the poor and

the maimed and the lame and the blind." And the
servant said, "Master, it is done as you commanded,
and still there is room." Then the master said to the
servant, "Go out into the highways and hedges, and
compel them to come in, that my house may be
filled. For I say to you that none of those men who
were invited shall taste my supper." ' "

LUKE 14:16–24

In this parable, Jesus has planned a great banquet. He
has sent out all the invitations. Each of the invited guests has
things to do and places to go, so each makes excuses not to
attend. Jesus next tells His followers to go out into the streets
and invite the misfits and the outcasts, as well as the losers of
the world. They all welcome the invitation. They arrive, and
the banquet is held.

Following Jesus entails being with people whom the
world despises. The world does not want you to touch or be
in touch with those who are homeless, or addicted, or mentally ill, or in prison. The world wants your life to be neat
and tidy, clean as a whistle. Jesus asks you to get down and
dirty. To embrace the lowest on the ladder. To offer love and
respect even to those who may not have earned it, and who
certainly have never known it.

When I was a young kid, a mentally challenged man
named Dave lived in our neighborhood. After his mother
died, he often walked around and around and around our
block. This was especially true on holidays. David was on a
quest. His goal: an invitation to a hot meal and a conversa-

tion with a neighbor. My mother was the one who issued the invitation. We had him to our table more times than I could count. She did his wash. She made his favorite things— chocolate cake, mashed potatoes, orange Jell-O with mandarin oranges. I never wanted her to invite him. Never. I got ticked off at Mom for doing so. It was so irritating.

Mom walked the walk.

"For the kingdom of heaven is like a landowner who went out early in the morning to hire laborers for his vineyard. Now when he had agreed with the laborers for a denarius a day, he sent them into his vineyard. And he went out about the third hour and saw others standing idle in the marketplace, and said to them, 'You go also into the vineyard, and whatever is right I will give you.' So they went. Again he went out about the sixth and ninth hour, and did likewise. And about the eleventh hour he went out and found others standing idle, and said to them, 'Why have you been standing here idle all day?' They said to him, 'Because no one has hired us.' He said to them, 'You also go into the vineyard, and whatever is right you will receive.'

"So when evening had come, the owner of the vineyard said to his steward, 'Call the laborers and give them their wages, beginning with the last to the first.' And when those came who were hired about the eleventh hour, they each received a denarius. But

when the first came, they supposed that they would
receive more; and they likewise received each a
denarius. And when they had received it, they
complained against the landowner, saying, 'These last
men have worked only one hour, and you made
them equal to us who have borne the burden and
the heat of the day.' But he answered one of them
and said, 'Friend, I am doing you no wrong. Did you
not agree with me for a denarius? Take what is yours
and go your way. I wish to give to this last man the
same as to you. Is it not lawful for me to do what I
wish with my own things? Or is your eye evil
because I am good?' So the last will be first, and the
first last. For many are called, but few chosen."

MATTHEW 20:1–16

To most Americans, this parable makes no sense. The
owner of the vineyard pays wages to his workers at the end
of the day. He pays the same wages to the man who was
there for one hour as he does to the man who toiled all day
long. In the world's eyes, this is crazy in the extreme. What is
the point?

The point is that God does not measure as the world
does. The point is that nobody has earned the Grace of God.
The point is that everyone is worthy of that Grace. The point
is that God is an equal opportunity employer. The point is to
see the payment in the work, not in the wages. This is what
it means to walk the walk. It means to do the work of love,
without waiting for the wages to be paid. Not looking for

the rewards. Trusting that the rewards will come—rewards such as satisfaction, joy, meaning. Lovely gifts await those who expect no wages.

When I do a good deed, I have to admit that most of the time I want it recognized. I wish for everyone to know. I try not to want this, but, man, is it hard not to. So I casually drop my good deed into the middle of a conversation. I might bring it up in a sermon or a class. Somehow I always manage to let somebody know, someone who will tell others. So that my reputation as a good guy will grow. This is not walking the walk.

A few years ago, I mentioned in a class that I had a young man who needed to be in treatment for his chemical dependency. He had no medical insurance, no source of income, no benefactors. I spoke with sadness about having someone who wanted help desperately, but could not get it. Later that day, I found an envelope on my desk with $10,000 in cash in it. No note, no expressed wishes or desires, nothing but the cash. To this day I do not know who sent this young man to treatment. It was either one of the 24 people in the class, or someone they contacted. I will never know.

That anonymous donor truly walked the walk.

walking humbly with god

Humans love to boast. I am not sure whether that is our nature, but it is definitely our inclination. Humility does not come easy to us mortals. Humility is a choice, a discipline. It means living our faith as a quiet witness. I am a strong believer in the usefulness of being a quiet witness. I have grown weary of hearing people talk

> "He has told you, O mortal, what is good; and what does the Lord require of you but to do justice, and to love kindness, and to walk humbly with your God?"
> —MICAH 6:8

about Jesus. Dropping His name every other sentence. Feeling the need to quote scripture all the time. Praying out loud before dinner at Denny's. Always calling attention to their faith. Showing off how devout they are. Trying to prove they are a fine example of Christian faith. They should learn that Christian faith without a good dose of humility becomes ungracious, even obnoxious. Faith must never show off. That is unbecoming of a Christian.

A few years back, I officiated at a funeral for a woman I hardly knew. She was a quiet widow who lived in one of the few remaining small cottages on the island. In the week before her funeral, at least three dozen folks stopped by my office to tell me what she had done for them. Paid their medical and fuel bills. Had a new stove delivered on Christmas Eve. Gave a whole family tickets for a trip to Disney World. No, she wasn't all that wealthy, she simply loved to give away what she had. Her happiness in life came from surprising folks with an act of pure generosity.

This same woman also created handmade cards, and wrote intimate notes to folks who needed a spot of good cheer or simply a reminder of a special occasion. One man had gotten 42 handmade birthday cards. He brought in the whole stack. The significance lay not in the number, but in the fact that she was the only person to remember his birthday. Admittedly, he had been a big old crab, but he still had a heart. She knew this. She was also the one who baked birthday cakes and delivered them to any man or woman recently widowed. She also made a pie a month for each...for the entire first year of their loss.

I knew that this was her quiet witness, her faith in action, her way of following Jesus. So I had the 42 cards matted and framed as a collage. I gave it to the old grouch and got a huge smile, and a moist eye. I realized then who she was, and who he was, and how much she had done in service to Jesus Christ. It isn't all that hard or complex. It is just quietly going about the business of letting folks know you really care.

 ## footprints

"One night I had a dream. I was walking along the beach with the Lord, and across the skies flashed scenes from my life. In each scene I noticed two sets of footprints in the sand. One was mine, and one was the Lord's.

"When the last scene of my life appeared before me, I looked back at the footprints in the sand, and to my surprise I noticed that many times

along the path of my life there was only one set of
footprints. And I noticed that it was at the lowest
and saddest times in my life.

"I asked the Lord about it. 'Lord, you said that
once I decided to follow you, you would walk with
me all the way. But I noticed that during the most
troublesome times in my life there is only one set of
footprints. I don't understand why you left my side
when I needed you most.'

"The Lord replied, 'My precious child, I love
you and would never leave you. During your times of
trial and suffering, where you see only one set of
footprints, I was carrying you.' "

FROM A MEMORIAL CARD
LEFT AT A FUNERAL HOME ON MIDDLE ISLAND

The above quotation has been used so often, I feared
using it once again. I wondered if it had lost its clout. Then I
reread it out loud, and decided it was still worth repeating.
Its message is airtight and right on the money.

The greatest benefit to following Jesus, *I believe*, is the
amount of time you get carried by Him. Jesus is the event of
Grace. For me, His love knows no bounds. I am His child.
And I am beloved of Him, cherished by Him. I repeat this
often, because it is so vital to being a Christian. We need so
badly to get away from the old theology. The one that taught
us to think of ourselves as terrible, rotten sinners in the
hands of an angry God. I know Jesus has carried me—often.
I am no small load, in any respect. He has gotten me

through, even when I did not know it or claim it. He has brought me home to rest when I was tired, or burned out, or burned up, or overwhelmed.

the dash home

I read of a man who stood to speak
At the funeral of a friend.
He referred to the dates on his tombstone
From the beginning . . . to the end.

He noted that first came his date of birth
And spoke the following date with tears,
But he said what mattered most of all
Was the dash between those years.

For that dash represents all the time
That he spent alive on Earth . . .
And now only those who loved him
Know what that little line is worth.

For it matters not how much we own—
The cars . . . the house...the cash;
What matters most is how we live and love
And how we spend our dash.

So think about this long and hard . . .
Are there things you'd like to change?
For you never know how much time is left
That can still be rearranged.

If we could just slow down enough
To consider what's true and real,
And always try to understand
The way other people feel.

And be less quick to anger,
And show appreciation more,
And love the people in our lives
like we've never loved before.

If we treat each other with respect,
And more often wear a smile . . .
Remembering that this special dash
Might only last a little while.

So, when your eulogy's being read
With your life's actions to rehash . . .
Would you be proud of the things they say
About how you spent your dash?

ANONYMOUS

Life is short. It's incredibly brief. We need to savor it, cherish it, enjoy it. Make a difference in it. This lovely passage speaks of its brevity—a mere dash to the finish line called death. We each may run only a lap or two. Our lives are sometimes like a wind sprint, a 50-yard dash. What makes the dash worthwhile is what's on the other side of the finish line. Coming home to a God who embraces us. Who runs to meet us. Who will carry us for good chunks of the race, even across the finish line.

A walk, or a hike, or a journey. A sprint, a dash. No matter how you look at it, life is movement. Just as the Earth is always in motion, so are we. This motion is called maturation. If that maturation becomes focused in faith, in a life lived in the spirit, then our spirituality will deepen in the process. It will grow richer and fuller. The Christian life is a movement, heading toward home. Home is God. Home is a place of Grace, an open door, an embrace of unconditional love, a banquet meal, a warm bed. It's a family of faces who adore you. The Christian life is one that *leaves* home to *find* home. A life that is building homes all along the way. These homes are our residences for the Kingdom.

baby steps

Being a Christian moves us in a direction, and at a pace, that often seems at odds with the world. Being a Christian is indeed following the road less traveled. It is a way that is not concerned with material things or external appearances. It is not about climbing up the social ladder. Instead, it is more about coming down to Earth. Following Christ will take you into our cities and their slums and ghettos and back alleys. It will ask you to be there for the farmer being foreclosed, or the coal miner who is losing his livelihood, or the immigrant who can't get work to feed her family. Jesus asks us to visit people—the prisoner, the sick and the shut-in, the brokenhearted, the war-wounded as well as the war veteran who may have been forgotten. Jesus asks us to walk in and walk up to those who need our attention most.

So much of America seems to be about getting away. About finding the perfect vacation spot, going on a luxury cruise, being pampered at a spa. Even the ads for wilderness experiences carry huge price tags, and promise gourmet meals and chocolates on your pillow. By contrast, following Jesus is about getting back into it all. Finding your way into the midst of the world's pain and suffering, and seeking to be a presence of healing grace. It is not at all that Jesus resists fun. It is not that Jesus doesn't know how and when and even where to relax. Rather, it's that Jesus is still mainly about getting busy with the building of the Kingdom. Jesus' expectations are high. He works hard, and He asks us to do the same. Really, it amounts to this: You need to be mature to make the choice. Much of what our American culture is about invites us to pretend that we can be forever young. But Jesus asks us to become true disciples—forever good, instead.

I am being honest with you here. I know this may be a real turnoff for you. But I have confidence in your integrity. You will know if what I'm saying makes sense, rings true. If the way outlined by Jesus is a map you believe will lead you to satisfaction. If it is, you will follow that map. If it is not, you will not. If you feel it worth considering, you will do your best to explore the option.

The walk following Jesus consists of baby steps. Not big, huge strides. Acquiring faith is done in increments. Small ones, like the seeds you planted earlier that were its beginnings. Little things, but ones that make a big difference. A little kindness, a little love. A little laughter, a little patience, a little respect. A little compassion, a little perseverance. All these little things—and many, many more—can transform your life, your family, your community, your church, even your world.

17

CREATING A SPIRITUAL HOME LIFE

"Without the ability to imagine, even just for a few moments, what life looks like seen through another's eyes, without the capacity to empathize with the pain or delight of another, to know that *there have I been, and there I am*, without the courage to go beyond the boundaries of our own self-interest, prejudices, cares, needs, and meet others without defenses, how can we affirm, with Paul, that 'if one part of the body suffers, all the other parts suffer with it; if one part is praised, all the others share its happiness' (I Corinthians 12:26)? It is not just that we *have* bodies, we are a body, in which the divisions are the illusion and the barriers and the disease. Of all the divisions, the most damaging is that of one part of ourself from another part of ourself. As long as we are strangers to ourselves, then we will be deeply strangers to others. Sometimes it may be our experience of being deeply loved by another that will bring us home.

"Life is kinder than we let it be, for there are so many occasions for love, if we don't let fear overpower us. So many opportunities for healing, for wholeness, and all of them signs of the grace of God that desires to go on loving us and healing us and calling us home to ourselves and to each other. But without the facing of fear, even stumbling, even trembling, even sick to the pit of our stomachs, without these abandonments of jumping off the cliff into the arms of God, then we can only armor, repeat, retrench, self-protect, and whine at anyone who is different from us. And face lives without passion, without sap, without grace."

KATHY GALLOWAY,
GETTING PERSONAL: SERMONS AND MEDITATIONS

Coming home to Jesus is a spiritual journey. For those of us who feel we have arrived at our destination, reaching home with Christ, we have begun to set up spiritual house. A spiritual house has a firm faith-foundation. A strong prayer life. Ample time for devotions and contemplative reflection. This means thinking, deeply and seriously. Not in a morbid or depressed way. Just reflecting on your life and how it is actually going. Some study of scripture is required. A daily reading of a newspaper will help. Faith goes hand in hand with an awareness of the world and its issues. The basement of our spiritual house is built out of simple materials. It will hold the burdens you may ask it to carry. Worship is the mortar used to give its bricks strength.

Our spiritual home will have a sturdy framework of service and sacrifice, of play and recreation, of bearing silent witness. The home that is built to the specifications of Jesus Christ must follow a clear blueprint. Serving others shapes most of the living space. Nooks of sacrifice are warm places to linger. Our house always has a playroom or a den, just for family fun. Our entire home is encased in walls of quiet witness, simple actions of compassion and care, generous acts of sharing. A genuinely kind remembrance. A celebration of fighting for a cause. While the spiritual home has nothing lavish about it, it is indeed built to last.

The roof is all about protection, keeping out the natural forces, wind and hail, falling branches and electric wires. The roof is putting God first. It is the wisdom and willingness to keep God as our top priority. The roof need not be pretty. But it does need to be made of weatherproofed materials. Faith cannot always expect fair weather.

You will encounter one surprise as you begin construction of your spiritual home. You'll find no windows or doors, only the openings. In spirituality, every effort is made to let the spirit flow. To allow new ideas and beliefs to freely enter. A spiritual life feels safe, even with easy access. No locks are needed, no keys. The spiritual home is a structure that offers comfort and security to the traveler passing through.

What is the spiritual home life all about? How do you make a spiritual house into a home? Well, here again, it is not about *doing*. It is all about *being*. I can't tell you what Christians do to make a house a home. It's not that I don't know. It's that, for every Christian, the blueprint is different. After all, these are not suburban dwellings, but instead are like those old Victorian homes that ramble all over the place. Where all the rooms have different shapes, the closets are of differing sizes, and the stairways branch off in all directions. I can tell you something about what Christians will *be* in their spiritual home—that's a more manageable topic. I can tell you how I believe Christians feel about being at home, and what they experience within their spiritual dwellings.

living the questions

A spiritual home is loaded with questions. Good questions, questions that make you think and feel, that poke and prod you to make necessary changes. Questions that look deep, that form visions inside you, that listen, and hear what we are thinking, that make us more mature, invite spiritual growth, and enable God to be present. Good questions are like the fertile soil of which I spoke earlier. They provide a ground that is most conducive to growing a healthy spiritual life.

Good questions are not about answers. We actually live our answers. Good questions point us in the direction we need to move. They inspire us to become. If, one day, you ask the question "What does God want from me today?" and then you let your Self ponder your own inquiry, I will guarantee that you'll see your answer in the choices you make that day. By simply choosing to be aware, which is the role of the question, you will gain a focus on living your answer. I am not sure how or why this works, but I know it does. What does not work is when someone *tells* you how you should spend your day. That is like nailing the coffin lid closed. The question swings the door of the day wide open.

living your longings

A longing is a yearning. It is a deep, profound emotion. It is not, however, emotional. It is a wish in the raw, a wanting with your whole heart. It is the spirit hooking up with a passionate need. It is when the spirit says, "*Yes!*" When we know something is right for us. This is the way Life is meant to be. I am being who God wants. Somehow, in some way, we all are in synch with our longings. Our bodies tell us it is so. We feel energized, yet calm. We feel centered, grounded, but ready to fly. We have confidence without conceit. We have conviction without judging anyone. We are ready for Life. We are ready to dive in, for we know how to swim, so we can hardly wait to get in the water.

We all have longings. Some of these longings are basic to the human condition. Common to our spiritual home are the following:

1. **The longing for calm**—when the worries and anxieties disappear

2. **The longing for balance**—when we feel up to the task of juggling Life's multiple tasks and responsibilities

3. **The longing to be known**—the deep desire to have someone love us enough to know us inside and out

4. **The longing for meaning**—when we feel we have a grasp of what truly matters in Life

5. **The longing to fall in love**—a passionate wish to be "naked" on all levels with another human being

6. **The longing to belong**—we all want to be a part of something larger than ourselves

7. **The longing to make a difference**—we all want to make our mark on Life's hide

8. **The longing to create**—we all wish to contribute our vision or voice to the mix; we not only want to make a difference, we want to make something that is our personal offering

9. **The longing for courage**—we all want to overcome our fears on behalf of our beliefs

10. **The longing for faith**—we all want to have faith in something, a belief system that enables us to have a good life

We human beings have many more kinds of longings. These are just a sampling. They are as diverse and unique as we ourselves are.

The spiritual home pays attention to longings. It looks for them, listens for them, seeks them out. It notices when the soul aches, or the heart desires. The spiritual home allows you not to get caught up in being busy. Being preoccupied with trivial pursuits, or doing everything to keep everyone else happy, though never keeping your Self or God happy. Having a list of things to do that's a mile long. Being oblivious of what you need to be. A spiritual life needs to be surrounded with the sound, the sweet and amazing sound, of Grace. Grace expresses itself in a calling. Calling us back to Life. Calling us to be our real Selves. Calling us to be aware of our talents and gifts. Calling us to live out those divinely implanted abilities. Calling us to come home to the God within us and all around us.

living the fifth gospel

May I repeat one of my favorite phrases: *I love the Bible*. But I do not worship it. The Bible, for me, is a starting point, not the finishing line. It is not a manual to follow, but rather a collection of inspiration. I think it's not a bad idea to memorize some verses from it, though memorization of scripture has little to do with discipleship. I think a spiritual life is, instead, about living the Fifth Gospel with your life. It is about creating a spiritual home modeled after the one first constructed by Jesus Christ. His gospel contained certain essential elements. These component parts would need to become a part of your spiritual life.

Writing the Fifth Gospel with your life would include the following:

1. **The sermon on the mount**—If you had just one sermon to give, what would you say?

2. **The parables**—What are the little stories of your life that have taught you some big-time lessons?

3. **The miracles**—When have you been left dumbstruck by Life's beauty, or by the healing power of prayer, or when has something happened that writes God's signature across your heart and mind?

4. **The epiphanies**—When has God turned your world upside down, and offered you a glimpse of Grace? A moment of such clarity that you were almost blinded by its light?

5. **The wisdom sayings**—What are those bits of unforgettable insight, prophetic vision, and the voice of pure common sense that make all the sense in the world?

6. **The declaration of passionate priorities**—When were you most true to your calling? When did you pick up your cross and carry it? What was the spiritual cost to you?

7. **The letters**—How have you intimately communicated your beliefs to your closest friends and loved ones?

8.The acts—How have you witnessed to your faith in thought, word, and deed?

9.The revelation—What is your vision and hope for the future?

10.The resurrection—How do you understand life beyond the grave?

These are merely the puzzle pieces. Put them together, though, and you have a full-color, panoramic gospel—of a kind. Your very own. You have borne own testimony, your witness, an expression of how you understand God. Writing a Fifth Gospel is performance art. It is strange and powerful, funny and profound. It is superbly worth seeing. Only a few will stop to watch. They like the safety of an audience in an arena. Performance art can make the viewer uncomfortable. It may actually include the audience in the performance itself. What you are watching is a life that reveals a deep relationship to a higher power. For the Christian, it offers a peek at the face of Jesus Christ.

 ## choosing joy

"Joy is what makes life worth living, but for many joy seems hard to find. They complain that their lives are sorrowful and depressing. What then brings the joy we so much desire? Are some people

just lucky, while others have run out of luck?
Strange as it may sound, we can choose joy. Two
people can be part of the same event, but one may
choose to live quite differently from the other.
One may choose to trust that what happened,
painful as it may be, holds a promise. The other
may choose despair and be destroyed by it.

"What makes us human is precisely this
freedom of choice."

HENRI J. M. NOUWEN, *BREAD FOR THE JOURNEY*

He was just 14 years old. Ben. Tall and thin, handsome, with a wide grin and very black eyes. He wore
fashionable clothes, but they were wrinkled beyond label
recognition. He was bright, sensitive, insightful. He had been
referred to me by a family friend who had heard me speak.

I asked him what brought him to see me today. He
rattled off a tragic litany of events. His father was in prison
for grand larceny. His mother had a nervous breakdown
during the trial, and was home, but in fragile shape. His
older brother was active with cocaine, and had major issues
with his temper. My visitor was often the punching bag. The
family had recently moved, and was nearly broke. Christmas
was coming and his family seemed in shambles. He felt as if
he were ready to faint. Every day, at some point, he would
break out in a cold sweat and his head would kind of
swoon. He would lie down wherever he was and try to get
the world to stop spinning.

We had a good discussion of the issues he faced. He was able to see that he could not be responsible for his dad, his mom, or his brother. He was, without question, the adult in the family. The one everyone turned to, as well as ganged up on. He had become the family's heart, its soul. In that family, this was like being declared the winner at a demolition derby. Together we set some concrete goals for our counseling. We also came up with an emergency plan of action if his brother became violent again. We also decided to work toward getting the mother to be more active in pursuing her own emotional healing.

At the end of the session, Ben asked me, "Well, do I still get to have Christmas?" I asked what he meant. He told me they would be staying at a small motel near the prison for the holiday, and his mom did not seem interested in having a tree, or presents, or even a nice dinner. She complained bitterly about their financial status. I asked if he had any money at all. He told me he had 20 bucks. I asked him if he would let me add another 20 to the pot. We then came up with a simple game plan for Christmas day. He would get a small tree at the supermarket, and he would decorate it with some popcorn and berries—something he had done with his dad when he was quite young. He would get a Starbucks gift certificate for Mom and Brother. He also decided on KFC for Christmas dinner, which everyone secretly loved; the store was near the motel.

The week after Christmas, we had our next appointment. He excitedly told me he had a great Christmas.

Everyone loved his game plan. He said his mom said it was the most joyful day she had had in ... well, forever. Just 40 bucks and a very young man with a big heart. He made a choice: He chose to make a little joy. It's not all that hard, really. It is mostly about finding unacceptable the *lack* of joy. About refusing to be down, and instead being damn determined to be up. The minute you start moving up, with joy as the mountain you are climbing, the peak seems to come down to meet you. Ben had given the gift of joy that Christmas. He had become joy's messenger to his family. In the giving, by the tone of his telling of the story, he had found his own chunk of joy.

A spiritual home is often filled with joy. By choice, by making it happen, by putting the needs of others before your own. By refusing to let others' spirits sag. By eliminating their cynicism and negativity. By being positive and rejecting the downward path. Joy comes to those who know God hovers close, and can always be reeled in. God may even be as close as a KFC.

> "Claude has the most illogical mind that I have ever encountered so this may be the first and last time that he is ever quoted in a book. He may ask such questions as 'What time is orange?' or 'How was tomorrow?' But still he does have a wisdom all his own....Well, one day Claude was at the beach with Jean-Pierre and several others of the community. The ocean was at low tide so there was an immense stretch of flat, sandy

beach. They began making designs in the sand. Claude drew a big circle with a couple of marks inside that could have been facial features. 'What's that?' asked Jean-Pierre. With a big smile Claude replied: 'It's Madame Sun.' 'That's good,' Jean-Pierre said. 'Now let's see you draw joy.' Claude took a look around him at the wide beach that stretched out in both directions as far as the eye could see, then turned to Jean-Pierre and said with a huge smile in all seriousness: 'There's not enough room!'"

—BILL CLARKE, S. J., ENOUGH ROOM FOR JOY: JEAN VANIER'S L'ARCHE—*A MESSAGE FOR OUR TIME**

a good home

A spiritual home is a good home. It celebrates the truly good life. A lifestyle that is focused on goodness. On good conversation with good friends, good music, good books. On good movies and good times. We all know what the "good" stands for. It represents that which brings out the best of who we are. A good conversation illuminates. A good book inspires. A good friend offers us insight. A good home expects the best, gives the best, calls upon the best.

A spiritual home is a good host. It welcomes Life. The *all* of it. A spiritual home has no secrets. There is no denial, no negativity, no need to keep things quiet. A conspiracy of

---

* Jean Vanier, a Canadian, founded the international L'Arche communities, where people who have developmental disabilities and the friends who assist them create homes and share life together.

silence never reigns there. A spiritual home is alive with conversation, chatter, laughter, and sharing of all kinds. A good host in such a home makes everyone feel welcome. The good host in a spiritual home welcomes every visitor's thought, feeling, and belief. A good spiritual home greets the dawn with a smile of hope, the dusk with a sigh of satisfaction.

A Christian strives to build a strong and beautiful spiritual home. For that is where the soul dwells. Such a home is inhabited by your spirit, your essence, the very best of your Self. It is here that you know you are good enough. It is here where you can lay claim to your calling. It is within this sanctuary that you find the energy and strength to follow Jesus in the world. It is within this domain that you come alive, alert, awake, and aware. Ready to face the world and transform it. Filled with the love you will now choose to share. Capable of a mercy that is deeper than you dreamed you could go.

The Christian lifestyle is the *really good life*. Genuine goodness—doing good, and being good. Having good friends and family. Spreading the good news. Having good times. Relishing the sweet Grace of being good enough. Having God inform you on a daily basis, that you are his beloved child. The Christian home perpetually has a feast laid out on the table. Like the line delivered by Auntie Mame in the Broadway musical, "Life is a banquet, but most poor suckers are starving to death." A Christian comes to your banquet table. Will have a second, and maybe a third,

helping. Never misses dessert. A Christian is too wise to be a
sucker for anything. Not worldly wise—spiritually wise.

> "Sometimes at dusk we see the loveliness of a
> doe and her fawn walking across the field, but
> they have stayed away from the garden, chewing
> instead the bark of tender new trees.
>
> "Broccoli, Brussels sprouts, carrots, don't
> mind the cold. We'll be picking them long after the
> ground is rimed with frost. We have discovered a
> new vegetable this summer, spaghetti squash, which
> we scrape out with a fork, after cooking, in long,
> spaghetti like strands. Leeks are a delight, creamed,
> or in soup, and spinach salad. We glory in the
> goodness of creation every day. All that weed-pulling
> was worth it, though weeds have their own beauty,
> and like mosquitos and flies, are an inevitable part of
> the summer.
>
> "At night now the sky is clear, with no heat
> haze. One night we eat supper out on the little
> terrace which we have made with flagstones and lots
> of honest sweat. We linger at the picnic table
> through sunset and star rise, and suddenly someone
> says, 'How light it is on the northern horizon!' We
> blow out the lamps and there is the staggering
> beauty of the northern lights. There is something
> primal about those lights pulsing, in pale green and
> rose, upwards from the horizon. They give me the
> same surge of joy as the unpolluted horizon near

the Strait of Magellan, showing the curve of the
home planet; the same lifting of the heart as the
exuberance of the dolphins sporting about the ship
after we had crossed the equator.

"I sit at the table as we all watch the awesome
display of beauty, and there again is the promise of
the rainbow covenant of Easter, radiant, affirming.

"And it is good."

—MADELEINE L'ENGLE,
AND IT WAS GOOD: REFLECTIONS ON BEGINNINGS

And it is good. These are the words of God upon
seeing His creation. These are also the words of Christians as
they see their lives in a new light. Through Christ's eyes.
From a whole new perspective. Those who truly choose to
follow in Christ's footsteps see the whole of Life as a miracle,
as a wondrous opportunity to experience the presence of
God. To bring heaven to earth. And to witness to the transforming power of God's love.

18

THE HOUSE OF
FORGIVENESS

The Christian life is a residence. It may be a mansion, or a hovel. It is always a home, a way of life, a perspective. It's both an attitude and a discipline. A Christian today is called to many things—the building of the Kingdom, a faith in miracles, a comfort with mysteries. Called to gain a passionate belief in justice, to develop a willingness to make peace and love one's enemies and locate the lost and mend a broken heart. But one thing is most central to the Christian life. One thing that lies at the heart of following Jesus Christ. One thing that undergirds the entire enterprise of Christian faith: *forgiveness.*

I have been a pastor for 30 years. I have taught and preached the Christian way virtually every day, in one form or another. I have discussed following Christ with literally thousands of youth, and an equal number of adults. I have come to believe that the greatest spiritual struggle of us Christians is the demand that discipleship makes of us to forgive. We humans have a hard time giving up our anger, letting go of our grudges. We love to cling to our rage. We point out people's flaws or failings with an incessantly wagging finger. When we have been wronged, we want the world to know. We want others to hear our side, and we want justice. We want, most of all, to get even.

Yet Christianity is not about getting even. Christianity is about Jesus, who was the event of Grace. It is Grace that declares that it will not abide by the rules of fair play. Grace is free. It is unfair. It takes no sides, and declares no winners. It refuses to hear calls for retribution. It is even uncomfortable with human demands for remorse. Grace offers forgiveness to those who do not deserve it. *Those are us.* Grace erases wrongs and makes right. Grace enables us to be free of guilt—free to be the person we were created to be.

Christians are human. Grace is divine. We humans struggle with receiving and giving Grace. We do not believe we deserve it. We want to have paid our dues. We are also not ready to grant Grace to others. We have carefully counted and categorized the wrongs committed against us. If only in our own mind, we have made a good case for our anger, revenge, or rage. We know why we have removed our love from others' lives. We are clear about why we have given up. And we are not inclined either to forgive or to forget. God's expectation of us is too high. We have not attained this level of spiritual maturity. Plus, the choice to forgive is only to be followed with another choice that begs for the same.

Over and over, I find forgiveness to be the great stumbling block in the Christian life. Christians who are married or in committed relationships, but are unable to forgive their mate or partner. Who count up hurts and disappointments. Who keep track of every incident of neglect. Who discard treasured friendships over one tragic mistake, such as a criticism, a broken confidence, a betrayal. A friend may walk away from years of caring, solely on the basis of a brief incident of selfishness. Jealousy and envy can keep us from forgiving. We seem to have a need to punish someone, or anyone—a desire to humiliate or embarrass others. Especially within the family unit, issues of forgiveness abound.

> "One of the most lasting pleasures you can experience is the feeling that comes over you when you genuinely forgive an enemy—whether he knows it or not." —O. A. BATTISTA

As a Christian minister, I officiate at a lot of weddings. Often, what I experience at a rehearsal for the ceremony is truly tragic. The bride or groom will pull me aside just before we start the rehearsal. I am then told where I should seat certain people. Who in the family does not speak to someone else in the family. Where first or second or third Mom should be seated, or where to put Dads #1, #2, and #3. How to handle sisters who have not spoken to each other in years. Or brothers who claim to hate each other. Or whole families who cannot get along even for the hour of a wedding service. The irony is, *I am conducting a Christian wedding*. Uniting for life two Christians who want me to orchestrate the wreckage that results from a failure to forgive. It is not a pleasant task.

Forgiveness is paramount. There can be no claiming one's faith in Jesus without first acquiring a deep understanding of the importance of being forgiven, and being forgiving. No faith can be maintained without forgiveness. Lacking that attitude and that act, our faith becomes no more than a caricature—a comic-book type of Christianity. It is forgiveness that keeps us rooted in being human, and keeps us on our knees long enough to know that we are not God. It is forgiveness that builds the strong fortress of genuine Christian faith. Forgiveness will defend us against attacks of self-righteousness, pride, and arrogance. Forgiveness will keep away the swarming armies of our culture, which call upon us to keep score in our human relationships, as well as in every aspect of life. Our culture wants winners. But forgiveness cannot be won—it can only be received, and given back.

forgiveness is a grace and a work

It was a hot and sticky August afternoon. We had gathered for a family reunion in upstate New York. The family's country house was large, with rooms of every size and shape. Nothing seemed to fit, except that everything actually did. The house had a huge yard with a stone fire-place. The sound of the running water of the nearby creek, and of the splashing swimmers screaming with delight, enticed us with the promise of soon being cool.

I was seated at a table in the yard with my wife, Chris, and my son, Justin, enjoying fresh tomatoes and corn on the cob. The corn was dripping in butter, and delicious. The tomatoes so ruby red that your mouth watered before you got to them. Chris and I had white wine, and Justin, who was then 5 years old, had his juicy-box. A car pulled up. It was a member of Chris's family—the individual who had molested her for several years. I had never met him. He arrived alone, without his family. He warmly but shyly greeted the family, while avoiding our table.

Chris stood up, walked over to him, gave him a kiss on the cheek, and welcomed him to the reunion. She then casually returned to our table, bringing with her more corn and butter and salt. I had wanted to kill him. Now I wanted to kill her. How could my wife offer that monster a welcom-ing kiss? How could she be so gracious? Why was she offering him a blanket of forgiveness? Why not at least give him an evil eye? A stare that could wound him? Why not at the minimum toss a sarcastic comment or two his way, make him know she knew? This was the worst-case scenario. He now could be believing that he was off the hook, totally.

By the time the party wound down, I was fuming. I left, not speaking to Chris—a particularly ineffective tech-nique used by some men to express anger. It is called the silent treatment. I know, it's stupid. Still, I was giving her that treatment, with both barrels. On the way back to our motel, Chris asked me what was wrong. I said nothing. Justin asked me why I wasn't talking. I told him I had nothing to say. Once we were back in the room, and Justin was glued to a *Pooh* video on the TV, I unleashed my displeasure on Chris. How could she kiss him? How could she act as if nothing had happened between them? Why did she let him off the hook like that?

This is what my wife said to me, or—at least, to the best of my ability, how I remember it:

"I needed this reunion. I really needed to see the whole family. I needed it to be happy. I was not about to let those memories ruin another thing in my life. So—I did it for me. *For me!* I have control of those memories now. I will do with them as I please. I wanted him to know he had no power over me. Certainly, no power over my happiness. I wanted him to know I have a good husband, a beautiful son, and a good life. I wanted him to know that I was in charge. I wanted a happy reunion, and I was going to have it.

> "When a deep injury is done us, we never recover until we forgive."
> —ALAN PATON

"I also wanted him to feel my faith," she continued. "That I am forgiven, by the Grace of God. I feel that in my bones. I can't prove it, I just claim it. I offered him some of my Grace. I let him know that my faith has freed me from the past."

"But you *aren't* freed," I protested. "You aren't over it! It's with us every single day. I'm the one who hears you cry at night. I know the nightmares that leave you dripping in sweat. I have seen you faint at the drop of a hat—over a memory return. You are *not* free." I spoke with some anger and more authority than I was entitled to.

"I know that," said my wife, "and you know that. But…he doesn't need to know it. But I *am* freer. I am getting there, Bill. I am steadily undoing these chains. I know I will never forget. I know I'll always be scarred. But I also know that I can feel better, be better. I have to move on. I do. I will. I have to pick up this cross and carry it. I wanted him to know he couldn't have my happiness. It was mine, and I have it now—not often, but sometimes. You and Justin are my happiness, my ministry. I love my work. I even like *me* these days. That's the result of Grace. My happiness. That is a pure gift. I shared it with him, Bill, that's all.

> "The more a man knows, the more he forgives."
> —CATHERINE THE GREAT, EMPRESS OF RUSSIA (1762–96)

"I did what Jesus would want. I wore Him like a cloak. I put Him on. It was Jesus doing the kissing. Not me. But—I approved." Chris then sighed, and wept copious tears.

That day, my beloved wife revealed to me the nature of true forgiveness. Forgiveness is, first, Grace before it is anything else. We receive the forgiveness that is Grace, we claim it, we know it and are known by it. We are embraced by its unconditional love. It squeezes out our guilt. It wipes away our tears. It restores our soul. It re-creates a sense of hope. Grace shatters our sin, puts it into manageable human pieces, offers itself as the glue to grant us wholeness again.

Forgiveness is a Grace first, and then work later. Chris was allowing Grace to work within her and out of her. She was allowing it access to her memories—healing them with hope, binding deep wounds with happiness, freeing her from the constraints of her grief. The grief of having lost her innocence and childhood to incest. She was coming back to life, slowly but surely, bit by bit. She was doing the work of forgiveness. Claiming her pain, naming her guilt, giving herself over to the transformation of this furnace we call Grace. She was allowing Grace to be reflected in her Self. She had become a mirror for Jesus. Allowing the image of Christ to shine off her.

Forgiveness is also work—the work of letting go, letting up, letting in. Primarily, it is allowing God access to your soul. Being ready to be healed. Willing to have your wounds mended once and for all. Feeling comfortable when letting go. None of this is easy. It asks you to get rid of the anger, to not listen to the voices calling for revenge, to not respond to the desire for things to be made fair or to get even. The work is mostly internal. It is spiritual in nature—tilling your spiritual soil. Making things ready for the seeds to be planted. It may not look much like work, but ask any good gardener. Growing a healthy plant takes a lot of sweat-labor, patience, and perseverance.

forgiveness is bits and pieces, and unbroken

My wife taught me something else about forgiveness that has truly stuck with me. Forgiveness is not a one-time event. We seldom have that capacity within us. It is never as simple as saying to someone, "I forgive you." It requires saying, "I forgive you," over and over and over again. It is done in increments—a bit here, a bit there. The pieces of forgiveness begin to take shape. The puzzle is slowly put together. It's not so puzzling, after all. The pieces are good-sized, the fit is obvious. It just means taking the time and effort to get it done.

When my grandmother cooked, she never used a recipe. She would always tell me that it took a little of this, and a little of that. She intuitively knew how much. They always came out perfect, her recipes—for the taste would be exquisite. I think of forgiveness the same way. We know how to do it. When to think it, feel it, choose it, give it, and finally reflect on it. We know there is no recipe for forgiveness. It consists of a little remorse. A dash of compassion. A few spoonfuls of humility. A lot of gratitude. And a bunch of Grace. We put it together until it tastes just right.

forgiveness is not and forever

Forgiveness is not something we can experience in the past. We cannot go back to retrieve it. Nor can we locate it in the future. There are no maps that plot where it can be found in the world of tomorrow. It is only available now. Here, in the present. It can only be offered now. It only matters at this very moment. It is a choice—a choice made within a day, a choice we make and live. A choice that makes us, changes us, alters our being. That improves our mood and brings out our best. Once experienced, forgiveness is forever. It cannot be removed or erased. It is a permanent stain. It is eternal. Oh, yes, we can reject it when offered by others. We can refuse it, walk away from it, deny it access. *But*, once issued, it is always present. It will haunt us forever—knocking on the door of our heart, infesting our spirit, orbiting our soul until it sees an opening where it can land. And it *will* land.

> "The day the child realizes that all adults are imperfect he becomes an adolescent; the day he forgives them, he becomes an adult; the day he forgives himself he becomes wise."
> —ALDEN NOWLAN, *BETWEEN TEARS AND LAUGHTER*

unforgivable

But what about Hitler? (I can hear you asking.) What about Charles Manson? What about John Wayne Gacy? What about dozens of other horrific serial killers or mass murderers or despots? What about the Holocaust? What about genocide in Rwanda? What about slavery and slave owners? Are there crimes or sins that are simply unforgivable? Will God turn His back on some of His children?

Does hell await these lost souls? Will they burn in an unquenchable fire?

I can only tell you my own truth. I believe that Jesus will find a way. He will somehow bring all His children home, every single one of them. It may not be before the grave. Or it may be long past it. But somehow Jesus will bring each and every child of His into the tender mercies of His loving arms. I know, it sounds too schmaltzy, too sweet. Grace is schmaltzy. It *is* sweet. It makes absolutely no sense to the wise of the world. I believe there may be a hell. I also believe there is nobody there. The Jesus I believe in would never condemn one of His children to eternal damnation. After all, we are His—His creation, His offspring. There is simply no way that the Jesus who is the event of Grace would turn His back and slam the door on one of His own.

So how will He do it? How can He forgive that which appears unforgivable? I have no idea. I just know that the love of God is unconditional, that the forgiveness offered is complete. I know that the incessant Grace of Christ will track down every soul—every last one!—and will bring them back home to the God who adores them. The God who will never lose an opportunity to restore them to eternal life. A life of timeless joy.

This is the Jesus *I* know. The Jesus *I* see. The Lord *I* hear and touch, who touches my life and opens me up. Who offers me glances and glimpses of Heaven. Who opens a window to the beyond, then points the way. This is the Jesus

I have chosen to believe in. I am not always crazy about where we have gone together, He and I, but I do know I would be crazy not to follow.

Other Ulysses Press Titles

BUDDHA IN YOUR BACKPACK:
Everyday Buddhism for Teens
Franz Metcalf, $12.95
Especially written for teenagers, *Buddha in Your Backpack* explains Buddhism and shows how Buddha's teachings can add a little wisdom and sanity to their high-velocity lives.

A CHORUS OF WISDOM
Edited by Sorah Dubitsky, Ph.D., $14.95
Essays from over 25 visionary thinkers that offer insight and revelation in a manner that is sure to bring positive change.

JESUS AND BUDDHA: The Parallel Sayings
Marcus Borg, Editor   Introduction by Jack Kornfield,
$14.00
Traces the life stories and beliefs of Jesus and Buddha, then presents a comprehensive collection of their remarkably similar teachings on facing pages.

JESUS AND MUHAMMAD: The Parallel Sayings
Joey Green, Editor   Foreword by Dr. Sayyid M. Syeed
Introduction by Dr. Kenneth Atkinson, $14.00
Presents for the first time parables of Jesus and the parallel ethical teachings of Muhammad.

JOURNEY TO TIBET'S LOST LAMA
Gaby Naher, $14.95
A personal, spiritual, and historical journey to the exiled 17th Karmapa and into the fascinating culture of Tibet and its Lama heritage.

SOLOMON'S BUILDERS: Freemasons, Founding Fathers and the Secrets of Washington, D.C.
Christopher Hodapp, $14.95
Solomon's Builders guides readers on a Freemason's tour of Washington, D.C. as it separates fact from myth and reveals the background of the sequel to *The Da Vinci Code*.

WHAT WOULD BUDDHA DO?: 101 Answers to Life's Daily Dilemmas
Franz Metcalf, $10.00
Much as the "WWJD?" books help Christians live better lives by drawing on the wisdom of Jesus, this "WWBD?" book provides advice on improving your life by following the wisdom of another great teacher—Buddha.

YOU DON'T HAVE TO SIT ON THE FLOOR: Making Buddhism Part of Your Everyday Life
Jim Pym, $12.95
Explains how to make Buddhism part of daily life while being true to one's customs and beliefs. Pym draws on his experiences being raised as a Christian to show how opening the way for East to meet West can enrich our lives.

To order these titles or other Ulysses Press books call 800-377-2542 or 510-601-8301, e-mail ulysses@ulyssespress.com or write to Ulysses Press, P.O. Box 3440, Berkeley, CA 94703. There is no charge for shipping on retail orders. California residents must include sales tax. Allow two to three weeks for delivery.

about the author

The Rev. William R. Grimbol is a popular and down-to-earth keynote speaker and pastor of the Shelter Island (New York) Presbyterian Church. For two decades he has directed the church's "Make Hope Happen" ministry program for children and youth in the area. He frequently leads conferences, workshops, and retreats, and also speaks in schools. He has worked with young people and families for almost 30 years and is well known for his work on preventing and treating youth suicide and depression.

He is highly regarded as a spiritual mentor and inspiring speaker, challenging audiences to make a difference and to celebrate diversity as they build their personal faith.

Pastor Grimbol is the author of many books on Christianity and the Bible. His titles include *The Complete Idiot's Guide to Spirituality for Teens* and *Befriending Your Teenager*. He is also an avid watercolorist and photographer.

about the illustrator

Bridget Halberstadt is a professional graphic designer, illustrator, and fine artist. She graduated from the California College of Arts and Crafts with a BFA in 1993. She and her husband, Michael, founded and operate HalfCity Design and Photography in the San Francisco Bay Area. To see more of her work, visit halfcitydesign.com.